WINNING
THE
TAX
GAME

Canadian Cataloguing in Publication Data
Cestnick, Timothy J., 1966–
    Winning the tax game: a year-round tax and investment guide for
Canadians
Includes index.
ISBN 0-13-976929-3

1. Tax planning – Canada – Popular works. 2. Income tax – Canada –
Popular works. I. Title.

KE5682.C47 1998   343.7105'2   C98-932071-5
KF6297.ZA2C47 1998

            Prentice Hall Canada Inc.
            Scarborough, Ontario
            Pearson Education

Prentice-Hall, Inc., Upper Saddle River, New Jersey
Prentice-Hall International (UK) Limited, London
Prentice-Hall of Australia, Pty. Limited, Sydney
Prentice-Hall Hispanoamericana, S.A., Mexico City
Prentice-Hall of India Private Limited, New Delhi
Prentice-Hall of Japan, Inc., Tokyo
Simon & Schuster Southeast Asia Private Limited, Singapore
Editora Prentice-Hall do Brasil, Ltda., Rio de Janeiro

ISBN 0-13-976929-3

Director, Trade Group: Robert Harris
Editor: Joanne Wise-Gillap
Assistant Editor: Joan Whitman
Production Coordinator: Shannon Potts
Art Direction: Mary Opper
Cover and Interior Design: Gary Beelik
Cover Image: Kirk McGregor
Interior Illustrations: Jason Schneider
Page Layout: Monica Kompter/Silver Birch Graphics

  2 3 4 5 FP 02 01 00 99

Printed and bound in Canada

Visit the Prentice Hall Canada Web site! Send us your comments, browse our
catalogues, and more. **www.phcanada.com**

For tax updates, visit **www.waterstreet.ca**

This book is intended to provide information of a general nature and is not a
substitute for legal, accounting, or taxation advice which, by its nature, must
be tailored to each individual's circumstances. Readers should consult a
competent professional for advice applying to their particular circumstances.

Dedication

To the most important person in my life—my wife Carolyn—whose
love, support and patience never end. And to our son Winston,
whose birth has brought new meaning to our lives.

Acknowledgments

I must admit, I'm extremely proud of what this book has turned out to be. And without question, it was a team effort. Special thanks to Chris Saunders, CA, for his hours of research and contributions to Chapters 7 and 8. Thanks also to the enthusiastic staff at The WaterStreet Group, particularly James Lefebvre whose research was invaluable, and to Karen Cestnick whose administrative abilities constantly keep me on track. I extend my heartfelt thanks to my editor Joanne Wise-Gillap, whose common sense, patience, and hard work made her a joy to work with, and made this book so much better. I'd like to acknowledge the contributions of my production editor Karen Alliston, and the various designers and artists who worked on this project. Thanks to Robert Harris at Prentice Hall for his confidence in me and in this project from the very start. Finally, a very special thank you is reserved for my wife Carolyn, who has supported me through the challenging but exciting changes that have taken place over the last year—all husbands should be so fortunate.

Table of Contents

Tax Planning Tip Sheet

This Tax Planning Tip Sheet has been designed to make you a winner in the tax game. It lists all the tax-saving tips that I discuss throughout the book. Start by reading a chapter, then come back here to review the tips for that chapter. For each tip, simply answer the question: Does this apply to me? Once you're done, take a closer look at the *Yes* and *Not Sure* answers. These strategies will form the foundation of your tax plan.

Don't worry about putting all the ideas into practice in a single year. It's not likely to happen. Choose up to four to implement this year. Keep the other ideas on file and think about setting them in motion next year or the year after. And by the way, I highly recommend that you visit a tax pro with your Tax Planning Tip Sheet just to make sure you're on the right track. A tax professional will help you to do things right. Now, go hit that grand slam!

Tim's Tips	Strategy	Does This Apply to Me?		
		Yes	No	Not Sure
Chapter 1.	Pre-Game Warm-Up: The Basics of Tax Planning			
1.	Avoid taxes like the plague, but don't evade them.	○	○	○
2.	Understand this thing called your Marginal Tax Rate.	○	○	○
3.	Know the difference between a deduction and a credit.	○	○	○
4.	Always wait to trigger a tax hit.	○	○	○
5.	Pay your taxes on time, but not ahead of time.	○	○	○
6.	Think of taxes when big things happen in life.	○	○	○
7.	Dispute your assessment when you think you're right.	○	○	○

Tim's Tips	Strategy	Does This Apply to Me?		
		Yes	**No**	**Not Sure**
21.	Deduct legal costs incurred to collect support payments.	○	○	○
22.	Consider preserving pre-May 1997 support agreements.	○	○	○
Chapter 3.	Signing With the Team: Strategies for Employees			
23.	Take non-taxable benefits as part of your compensation.	○	○	○
24.	Calculate whether a taxable benefit works to your advantage.	○	○	○
25.	Negotiate a loan from your employer instead of from a bank.	○	○	○
26.	Opt for stock options or similar tax-efficient compensation.	○	○	○
27.	Claim all the employment deductions you're entitled to.	○	○	○
28.	Say "thanks, but no thanks" when offered a company car.	○	○	○
29.	Claim automobile expenses that exceed your allowance or reimbursements.	○	○	○
30.	Defer tax with a registered pension plan (RPP), RRSP, or deferred profit sharing plan (DPSP).	○	○	○
31.	Push the tax on your bonuses to a future year.	○	○	○
32.	Consider a leave of absence or sabbatical plan to defer tax.	○	○	○

Tim's Tips	Strategy	Does This Apply to Me?		
		Yes	No	Not Sure
33.	Roll as much as possible of your retiring allowance to your RRSP or RPP.	○	○	○
34.	Consider a non-competition payment for potential tax savings when leaving your job.	○	○	○
Chapter 4.	Becoming a Free Agent: Strategies for Self-Employment			
35.	Count the costs before leaping into self-employment.	○	○	○
36.	Structure your work so that you're self-employed, not an employee.	○	○	○
37.	Make sure you have a reasonable expectation of profit.	○	○	○
38.	Consider incorporation once your business has grown, but not before.	○	○	○
39.	Choose the right year end for your business.	○	○	○
40.	Maximize your deductions for home office expenses.	○	○	○
41.	Maximize deductions related to business use of your automobile.	○	○	○
42.	Categorize your meals and entertainment expenses to maximize tax savings.	○	○	○
43.	Maximize your eligibility to claim capital cost allowance.	○	○	○
44.	Pay salaries to family members for a number of tax benefits.	○	○	○

Tim's Tips	Strategy	Does This Apply to Me?		
		Yes	No	Not Sure
45.	Understand the various "taxes" affecting your business.	○	○	○

Chapter 5. Bulls, Bears, and Baseball: Strategies for Investors

Tim's Tips	Strategy	Yes	No	Not Sure
46.	Deduct as much of your interest cost as possible.	○	○	○
47.	Call your profits *capital gains* and your losses *business losses*.	○	○	○
48.	Claim a capital gains reserve to spread your tax bill over time.	○	○	○
49.	Consider an investment holding company in certain situations.	○	○	○
50.	Consider buying shares in a Canadian-controlled private corporation (CCPC) for a capital gains exemption—and more.	○	○	○
51.	Use real estate properly to generate wealth and minimize taxes.	○	○	○
52.	Participate in real estate investment trusts (REITs) or royalty trusts for tax-efficient cash flow.	○	○	○
53.	Think twice before you buy into a mutual fund at the end of the year.	○	○	○
54.	Avoid index-linked guaranteed investment certificates (GICs) outside your RRSP or registered retirement income fund (RRIF).	○	○	○
55.	Invest in labour-sponsored funds for tax efficiency and good growth potential.	○	○	○

Tim's Tips	Strategy	Does This Apply to Me?		
		Yes	No	Not Sure
68.	Boost the value of your RRSP with tax-free rollovers.	○	○	○
69.	Ensure that your child files a tax return to maximize RRSP contribution room.	○	○	○
70.	Claim your RRSP deduction in the right year.	○	○	○
71.	Contribute to your RRSP instead of paying down your mortgage.	○	○	○
72.	Contribute to a spousal RRSP to equalize incomes in retirement.	○	○	○
73.	Make RRSP withdrawals during periods of no or low income.	○	○	○
74.	Consider the impact of using RRSP assets to buy a home.	○	○	○
75.	Consider the impact of using RRSP money for full-time education for you or your spouse.	○	○	○
76.	Take three steps to minimize the tax hit on RRSP withdrawals if you're planning to leave the country.	○	○	○
77.	Roll your RRSP to a RRIF or annuity to defer tax well beyond age 69.	○	○	○
78.	Defer tax on your RRIF withdrawals as long as possible.	○	○	○
79.	Consider opting out of your company pension plan if you have the choice.	○	○	○
80.	Look into an individual pension plan (IPP) to avoid a big tax hit when leaving your company pension plan.	○	○	○

Tim's Tips	Strategy	Does This Apply to Me?		
		Yes	No	Not Sure
92.	Consider an estate freeze to minimize your tax bill on death.	○	○	○
93.	Leave it to your spouse to defer the tax hit longer.	○	○	○
94.	Minimize the tax on your RRSP or RRIF assets upon death by naming the right beneficiaries.	○	○	○
95.	Instruct your executor to make a final contribution to your RRSP after your death.	○	○	○
96.	Save your heirs tax by setting up a testamentary trust in your will.	○	○	○
97.	Give to charity and save a bundle. But do it properly!	○	○	○
98.	Suggest an offshore inheritance trust to non-resident family members.	○	○	○
99.	Negotiate a $10,000 death benefit with your employer.	○	○	○
100.	Use life insurance to soften the blow of a tax bill at the time of your death.	○	○	○
101.	Forecast your U.S. estate tax and apply eight strategies to minimize the tax bill.	○	○	○

FOREWORD: STEPPING UP TO THE PLATE

If you want to win the game, you've got to step up to the plate.

L et me tell you about Renee. She visited my office for the first time not long ago. And from the moment she sat in the chair across from me, even before she said a word, I assumed two things. First, I assumed that she was feeling the weight of a tax burden that only Canadians can truly understand. Second, I assumed that she was in my office to learn what she could do to fix the problem. I was only half right.

While it was true that Renee was discouraged about the level of taxes she had come to expect as a Canadian taxpayer, she wasn't in my office to learn how to lighten the load. The fact is, Renee and her husband Gerrald had already decided to leave Canada, and they were looking for me to explain the tax implications of making the move.

I couldn't resist asking the question: "Renee, before we talk about leaving the country, what is it that you and your husband have done in the last couple of years to save income taxes?" Her response didn't surprise me.

"Tim, there's really nothing we can do. We're claiming the $1,000 pension credit and a deduction for our safety deposit box fees. But big deal: these things save us next to nothing each year."

You see, this couple had come to the conclusion that their only hope for a prosperous retirement was to get up and leave Canada. Given their net worth, level of income, and our Canadian tax burden, Renee and Gerrald were convinced that they were bound to run out of retirement savings before running out of retirement.

Here was a woman who was truly discouraged. You could see it in her eyes. It was as though someone had left her a hundred kilometres from shore in a canoe without a paddle. If you had checked the dictionary on that day under the word "discouragement," you might have found the family's name with a picture of Renee and Gerrald.

Discouraged? Why Be Discouraged?

It was the day after my meeting with Renee that I learned a lesson about discouragement—and from an unlikely source, I might add. I was driving down Lakeshore Road in Oakville, Ontario, where I grew up, and I saw some kids playing baseball at Bronte Park. I grew up playing baseball at that same park, and I was reminiscing a little, so I got out of my car and walked over to the baseball diamond.

The kids were having a great time. They were laughing and cheering. They were even shouting the same insults that we used to shout as kids. You know, things like: "Batter needs a beach ball" and "Pitcher has a rubber nose, wiggles every time he throws." The point is, you couldn't find a glum face at that park.

I leaned over and asked one of the kids what the score was. A little boy smiled up at me and said, "Fourteen nothing!" Impressed, I replied, "Fourteen nothing, that's great, you're killing them!" "Nope," the boy corrected me. "We're losing fourteen nothing!" Surprised me for sure. From the way the kids were laughing, you'd never know they were down for the count. I had to ask the question: "If you're losing fourteen nothing, how come you're so happy? Why aren't you discouraged?"

I'll never forget what that little boy said next: "Discouraged? Why should we be discouraged? We haven't even been up to bat yet."

Good point. There's no use being discouraged if you haven't been up to bat.

Renee and Gerrald are like many Canadians: They had not yet stepped up to the plate.

If you want to win the tax game, you've got to step up to the plate.

Get in the Game

It's frightening to think of how many Canadians have done little or nothing to reduce their income taxes. Here's what I mean: According to Revenue Canada, taxpayers under age 45 in 1995 used, on average, just 11 percent of the registered retirement savings plan (RRSP) contribution room available to them. And those 45 and over didn't fair much better, contributing just 18.6 percent of what they were entitled to contribute to an RRSP. These stats don't faze you? Try this on for size: a full 67 percent of all Canadians who were eligible to contribute to an RRSP in 1996 chose not to make a contribution at all! Yikes. Frightening is the only way to describe it. The truth is, any financial planner, broker, or tax professional will tell you that contributing to an RRSP is every Canadian's first line of defence against the tax collector.

Do you think that Canadians who are not even putting money into their RRSPs are likely to implement other, more intricate, tax planning strategies? Don't count on it.

You should realize that the odds are against you. Seventy percent of you will read this book cover to cover and then simply file the information in a drawer at the back of your mind labelled "interesting tax stuff." Thirty percent will actually use the information to create tax savings. If you've read this far, then you've shown up at the ball park. The question is, will you choose to be part of that 30 percent who actually get into the game?

Making It Easy

I've got some good news for you. I've made it very easy to get into this game we call tax planning. Throughout this book, you're going to find tip after tip of good tax ideas. Not all strategies are going to apply to your situation, but many will. And I've made it very easy to keep track of those tactics that are bound to save you many tax dollars.

You see, at the front of the book you'll find your own Tax Planning Tip Sheet, listing all the tax-saving tips from each chapter. As soon as you've read a chapter, flip to the front of the book and review the tips for that chapter. Ask yourself, "Does this tip apply to me?" Then check ○ *Yes*, ○ *No*, or ○ *Not Sure* for each tip. Follow me? When you've finished this book, all those *Yes* and *Not Sure* answers on your Tip Sheet will form a complete list of tax-saving measures, ready for your use or further research.

By the way, you'll do yourself a favour by paying a quick visit to a tax professional, armed with your Tax Planning Tip Sheet. Your advisor will confirm whether the strategies will work for you, will answer any questions you may have, and will be able to help you implement the ideas, if necessary. Trust me, the tax savings you'll enjoy will almost certainly far outweigh the cost of a one-hour visit to the tax pro.

There's one more thing to keep in mind: Tax rules are always changing. The advice I offer here is current as of June 30, 1998. A good tax pro will be able to bring you up to date on late-breaking developments from the Department of Finance or Revenue Canada.

Calling All Hitters

Have you heard of Charlie Grimm? Charlie was a baseball manager—he used to manage the Chicago Cubs. There's a story about a scout who called up Charlie Grimm one day. The scout was so excited he could hardly utter the words. "Charlie! I've just discovered the greatest young pitcher I have ever seen! I watched him pitch a perfect game. He struck out every man who came to bat. Twenty-seven stepped up to the plate, and twenty-seven struck out! Nobody even hit a foul ball until the ninth inning. I've got the kid right here with me. Do you want me to sign him?"

"No," replied Charlie. "Find the kid who hit the foul ball and sign *him*. I'm looking for hitters."

Charlie Grimm was looking for hitters. And so am I. With these pages I'm going to get you off the bench and put a bat in your hands.

But remember: If you want to win the tax game, you've got to step up to the plate.

CHANGES MAKING THE HEADLINES

In the world of tax, change is the only constant.

If you're looking for a quick summary of what's changed in Canadian tax rules in the last year, you've come to the right place. Here's a summary of key changes and proposed changes up to June 30, 1998. Most of these were introduced in the 1998 federal budget. Keep in mind that proposed budget measures are generally enforced by Revenue Canada even before they're passed into law.

xxii WINNING THE TAX GAME

Topic	What's New?
Tax Calculations	
Supplementary personal tax credit	The 1998 federal budget introduced a new personal tax credit. It adds $500 to the existing basic personal amount of $6,456. The supplementary credit is clawed back by 4 percent of income over $6,956 ($6,707 in 1998) and disappears by the time income reaches $19,456.
Surtax reduction	Beginning in 1999, the 3-percent surtax levied on all individuals will be eliminated for those earning $46,515 or less. For 1998, the surtax is simply reduced by 50 percent for those taxpayers. Once income is over $46,515, the surtax reduction is clawed back, and by the time income reaches $62,193, the full 3-percent surtax applies again.
Alternative minimum tax	Beginning in 1998, any deductions claimed for amounts contributed to a registered pension plan (RPP) or RRSP will be ignored when calculating the alternative minimum tax (AMT). A refund for unused AMT credits arising in 1994 or later years will be issued to the extent those AMT credits arose as a result of RPP or RRSP deductions.
Education	
Canada Education Savings Grant	Beginning in 1998, the federal government will help you use a Registered Education Savings Plan (RESP) to save for a child's education. This help will come in the form of a grant —called a Canada Education Savings Grant (CESG). The grant is paid directly into the RESP, and equals 20 percent of RESP contributions, to a maximum of $400 for each year the child is 17 or under in the year.

Registered Education Savings Plans Beginning in 1999, the amount that may be transferred from an RESP to the RRSP of a subscriber has been increased from $40,000 to $50,000. On the downside, RESPs registered after 1998 cannot be used to pay for a course of study that is less than 3 months in duration (certain shorter programs may qualify). As well, RESPs registered after 1998 cannot have beneficiaries who are over age 20 if the plan allows for more than one beneficiary.

RRSP withdrawals for education Beginning in 1999, individuals may withdraw up to $10,000 per year tax-free from an RRSP, to a maximum of $20,000 over four years, in order to obtain full-time training or education. Amounts withdrawn must eventually be paid back to the RRSP over a 10-year period.

Student loans For 1998 and beyond, students will be entitled to claim a tax credit equal to 17 percent of interest paid on most student loans for post-secondary education. The credit can be carried forward for up to five years if it's not needed to bring taxes to nil in the current year.

Part-time students Beginning in 1998, part-time students will be entitled to claim an education amount of $60 per month for part-time attendance at a qualifying post-secondary school. In addition, part-time students will be entitled to claim a deduction for child care expenses.

Family Care

Canada Child Tax Benefit In 1998, the new Canada Child Tax Benefit system will be introduced. It's not significantly different from what we've had since 1993. The plan will provide annual benefits up to $1,020 for the first child under age 18, plus a National Child Benefit Supplement of $605 for the first child if your income is under $20,921. The amounts are increased for additional children.

Child care	Effective in 1998, the limits for deductible child care expenses have been increased to $7,000 (from $5,000) for children under age 7, and to $4,000 (from $3,000) for children aged 7 to 16.
Care-giver tax credit	Beginning in 1998, you can claim a tax credit of up to $400 if you live with an adult who is dependent on you because of a physical or mental infirmity, or because of age (65 or over). The credit will be clawed back when the dependent's income exceeds $11,500 and will completely disappear when the dependent's income reaches $13,853.
Disability credit	After February 24, 1998, occupational therapists and psychologists are included in the list of professionals who can certify the existence of a severe and prolonged impairment for the purpose of claiming the disability tax credit.

Relocation

Moving expenses	The definition of moving expenses has been broadened to include costs associated with maintaining a former residence for up to three months or $5,000, whichever is less. In addition, costs for revising the address on legal documents (such as a driver's licence or automobile permit) will be deductible, as will costs for connecting and disconnecting utilities.
Relocation payments	Beginning with relocations after September 1998, any payments received by an employee from an employer as reimbursement or compensation related to the financing of a new residence will be taxable. In addition, any reimbursements for a decrease in value of a home or proceeds for the impairment of the selling price of a former residence will be taxable over $15,000.

Business Deductions

Private health services plan

In any fiscal year that begins in 1998 or later years, premiums paid by a proprietorship or partnership to a private health services plan will be deductible, provided certain conditions are met.

Income Splitting

Dividend sprinkling

A Supreme Court decision that was handed down on May 21, 1998 brings good news for taxpayers. The case of *Neuman v. The Queen* has re-established that dividends may be paid to family members who are not actively involved in the business. Mr. Neuman had been taxed on dividends paid by the family management company to his wife under the notion that she was not involved in the business on a day-to-day basis. The decision was overturned at the Supreme Court. *Dividend sprinkling* to family members is valid once again—for the time being.

PRE-GAME WARM-UP: THE BASICS OF TAX PLANNING

Only fools come to bat without first tying their shoes.

1

To this day, I can still remember my first season—in fact, my first game—in the Oakville Minor Baseball Association. I was six years old, a pretty good hitter for a rookie, and knew next to nothing about running the bases. My first time at bat, I belted a line drive into left field then proceeded to run as fast as I could directly to third base. I can still remember the umpire showing me which way to run after hitting the ball.

Eventually, I became a pretty good base stealer—but only after I learned the basics. Once I had the basics down, my playing improved to a whole new level. And so will yours.

In this chapter, we're going to look at the basics of the tax game.

Playing by the Rules

Tim's Tip 1: Avoid taxes like the plague, but don't evade them.

There's a big difference between avoiding taxes and evading them: One's okay; the other's a definite no-no.

Tax avoidance simply involves structuring your affairs legally so that you're paying less tax than you might otherwise pay. You do, after all, have the right to pay the least amount of tax the law will allow. Avoiding tax could involve using loopholes, which are inadvertent errors in the Income Tax Act, but more commonly will involve using provisions of the law to your advantage.

Tax evasion, on the other hand, is an attempt to reduce your taxes owing or increase refundable credits by illegal means, such as making false statements about your income or deductions, or destroying records. Trust me, if Revenue Canada's Special Investigations Unit catches you in the act of evasion, you're in for a rough ride. Here's what happens: You'll not only have to make good on the taxes you've evaded, but you'll face penalties equal to 50 percent of those taxes. In addition, you'll face interest charges from the year of the crime until the day you pay those taxes and penalties owing. To top it off, you could face criminal charges filed by Revenue Canada which may result in additional criminal penalties of 50 to 200 percent of the taxes evaded, and up to five years in prison. Yikes!

If you've been evading taxes and haven't yet been caught in the act, there's some good news for you. The tax collector has said, in

Information Circular 85-1R2, that if you come forward and correct deficiencies in your past tax affairs—through what's called a *voluntary disclosure*—you'll be given a break. No penalties will be levied, and no prosecution will be undertaken. Folks, this is not such a bad deal. And by the way, once Revenue Canada has begun an audit or enforcement procedure, you can forget about making a voluntary disclosure: it's too late at that stage.

TO MAKE A LONG STORY SHORT:

- Tax avoidance involves legally structuring your affairs to take advantage of provisions or loopholes in our tax law.

- Tax evasion is a no-no. It can bring civil and criminal penalties, and can mean up to five years in prison.

- A voluntary disclosure may be your best option to come clean if you've been evading taxes.

A voluntary disclosure (VD) will allow you to come clean if you haven't exactly been honest, but it may open a can of worms, too. You see, a VD could lead Revenue Canada to take a hard look at your financial affairs, including bank and brokerage account transactions. Sure, a VD may be your best bet if you're talking about significant tax dollars, but a simple adjustment request to your prior years' tax returns may be a better option if the dollars are minimal. Talk to a tax pro before deciding which way to go!

Caution!

Knowing the Numbers Game

Tim's Tip 2: **Understand this thing called your marginal tax rate.**

You're going to hear a lot about marginal tax rates as you browse the pages of this book—and for good reason. Your marginal tax rate is

Did You Know?

Like most industrialized countries, Canada has a progressive tax system. This simply means that the more money you earn, the higher the percentage of your income you'll likely hand over to the tax collector. The theory is that taxpayers with higher incomes are able to bear a larger tax burden than the rest.

used to calculate all kinds of things. In particular, if you want to know how much tax a deduction is going to save you, or what the after-tax rate of return on your investments happens to be, you'll need to know your marginal tax rate.

Quite simply, your marginal tax rate is the amount of tax that you'll pay on your last dollar of income. Suppose, for example, you're living in Ontario and you earned $65,000 in 1998. How much more tax do you suppose you'd pay if you earned one more dollar of income? The answer is 50.3 cents. You'd keep just 49.7 cents for yourself. In other words, your marginal tax rate is 50.3 percent. Similarly, if your marginal tax rate happens to be 27 percent, then 27 percent of the last dollar you earn will disappear in taxes. For a list of marginal tax rates by province, check out the tables starting on page 272.

You're going to discover that marginal tax rates really depend on three things: Your province of residence, your level of income, and the type of income earned. Basically, the higher your level of income, the higher the percentage of that income the tax collector is going to take. Further, dividends and capital gains are taxed at lower marginal rates than interest, salaries, and other types of income.

Judi and Ned are shareholders in a small business, Money Inc., located in Manitoba. In 1998, Judi received a salary of $70,000, while Ned earned $35,000. In addition, each received dividends of $5,000 from the company. Who do you think had the higher marginal tax rate on the salary? Good guess. Judi did.

In fact, Judi's marginal tax rate on her salary in 1998 is 50.1 percent in Manitoba, while Ned's marginal rate is just 43.7 percent. As for the dividend income, Judi will face a marginal tax rate of 36.1 percent, and Ned will pay 29.2 percent.

TO MAKE A LONG STORY SHORT:

- Your marginal tax rate is likely the most important tax figure for you to know.

- Simply put, it's the amount of tax you'll pay on your last dollar of income.

- Your marginal tax rate depends on three things: Your province of residence, your level of income, and the type of income earned. To determine your marginal tax rate for 1998, see the tables starting on page 272.

Tim's Tip 3: Know the difference between a deduction and a credit.

No doubt about it, you've heard of them before. Deductions and credits are the friends of every taxpayer. The question is, do you know the difference between the two? Most Canadians don't. Let me explain.

A *deduction* is claimed to reduce your taxable income. Once you've calculated your taxable income, it is multiplied by current federal tax rates to arrive at your federal tax. Make sense? But we're not done yet. Once your federal tax is determined, that amount is reduced dollar for dollar by any *credits* that you claim, to arrive at your basic federal tax. Finally, you'll have to add federal surtaxes and provincial taxes to arrive at your total tax bill.

DEDUCTIONS AND CREDITS: WHAT'S THE DIFFERENCE?

	Net Income
Subtract	**Deductions**
	Taxable Income
Multiply	Federal Tax Rate
	Federal Tax
Subtract	**Credits**
	Basic Federal Tax
Add	Federal Surtax
Add	Provincial Surtax
	Total Tax Payable

What's the bottom line? A deduction will reduce your total tax bill by an amount equal to your marginal tax rate. Consider Roshaan's story.

R oshaan had income of $40,000 in 1998 which puts her *marginal tax rate at about 41 percent. She claimed a deduction of $10,000 for child care expenses in 1998, which brought her taxable income down to $30,000. How much tax do you think Roshaan saved in 1998 because of her $10,000 deduction? The answer is $4,100 (41 percent of $10,000).*

Since a deduction saves you tax at your marginal tax rate, you can expect to save about 27 percent if your income is under $29,590, 41 percent between $29,590 and $59,180, and about 50 percent if your income is over $59,180. These figures are Canada-wide averages.

A tax credit, on the other hand, will save you federal tax, dollar for dollar. That is, a $100 tax credit will actually save you $100 in federal taxes. And there's more. Those credits will also save you federal surtaxes and provincial taxes, since these are calculated as a percentage of basic federal tax. The general rule of thumb is this: A $100 credit will save you between $150 and $175 in total taxes after you factor in the surtax and provincial tax savings.

Here's one last word on credits. There are two types: *Non-refundable* credits can be used to bring your total tax bill down to zero, but don't offer any relief beyond that point; *refundable* credits, as the name implies, can result in a cash refund once your total tax bill reaches zero.

TO MAKE A LONG STORY SHORT:

- A deduction reduces your taxable income and offers tax savings equal to your marginal tax rate.

- A credit reduces your basic federal tax bill, dollar for dollar, and results in savings on surtaxes and provincial taxes.

- There are two types of credits: non-refundable and refundable.

Timing Your Taxes

Tim's Tip 4: **Always wait to trigger a tax hit.**

You know, there are a lot of events in life that can lead to a tax bill. And most of the time, there are things that you can do to delay the tax collector's knock at your door. Here's an example: Every time you switch from one mutual fund to the next outside an RRSP or registered retirement income fund (RRIF), you're triggering a taxable event and could have some tax to pay. If you're intent on switching those funds, why not wait until January of the next year to make that switch? This will push the tax bill one year into the future.

Want another very common example? Kathie has a story to tell.

Kathie: Last year I wanted to help my daughter Laurie who has been struggling to save the down payment for a home. Since I had some stocks that I had inherited a few years ago, I decided to give them to Laurie.

Tim: You were in for a nasty surprise, weren't you?

Kathie: That's for sure. I didn't realize that simply giving something to my daughter could lead to a tax bill.

Tim: Yup. Any time you give an asset away, you are deemed to have sold it at fair market value. So if the property has gone up in value since you acquired it, you could have a tax bill to pay. The only exception is when you give the property to your spouse. In this case, your spouse acquires it at your original cost so that there won't be a tax bill to face until your spouse disposes of the property.

Kathie: I wish I'd known that earlier.

After speaking with Kathie, it became obvious to me that, despite the tax bill, Kathie is still glad she gave the stocks to Laurie. It was the only way she could help her daughter. The question is this: Could Kathie have waited to trigger the tax hit? Sure, she could have waited to give Laurie those stocks until Laurie was ready to buy the home that she is still saving for today. This way, Kathie's tax hit could have been put off for a year or two.

I can understand that there might be good reasons for switching your mutual funds, giving assets away, or involving yourself in other taxable events, but my point here is simple: Be sure to understand what kind of events can lead to a tax hit, and then wait to trigger that tax bill if you can.

TO MAKE A LONG STORY SHORT:

- Educate yourself on what kind of events can lead to a tax bill.

- There may be good reasons for involving yourself in some of these taxable events, but wait until a future year to trigger the tax hit if you can.

Action Step

Tim's Tip 5: **Pay your taxes on time, but not ahead of time.**

Wouldn't it be nice if you could simply wait until April 30 each year to pay your entire tax bill for the previous year? Sure it would. But forget it—the tax collector has other ideas. You see, the government figures that if you're earning income in a particular year you should make your tax payments throughout that year. I'm referring, of course, to source withholdings and installments.

For guaranteed tax savings, do all that you can to push a tax bill to a future year. The amount you save will depend on your rate of return on the money between now and the time you have to pay your tax bill. If you owe $100 in taxes but can push the tax bill off for 5 years and can earn 15 percent on your money between now and then, you'll cut the real cost of your tax bill in half! Consider the numbers below:

TRUE COST OF $100 TAX BILL			
Rate of Return	**True Cost of $100 Tax Bill Paid in the Future**		
	1 Year	**5 Years**	**10 Years**
5%	$95	$78	$61
10%	91	62	39
15%	87	50	25
20%	83	40	16

Source Withholdings

I can still remember the feeling of receiving my first real pay cheque after graduating from university. I was broke, so any amount of money seemed like an oasis in the desert. But still, my reaction was mixed. I was thrilled to have some cash to waste away and shocked that the tax collector would have the nerve to take such a hefty portion for the government to waste away. That year, I claimed a number of deductions that saved me $3,000 in taxes, which came back to me as a refund when I filed my tax return. I was not amused: The last thing I wanted was a refund!

You see, most Canadians are of the opinion that, next to being shot at and escaping by the skin of your teeth, there's nothing more satisfying than a big tax refund each year. The problem with a refund is that it means just one thing: You have effectively made an interest-free loan to the tax collector during the year. Rather than allowing this to happen, why not request permission from Revenue Canada to reduce the taxes that are deducted at source? Your employer will gladly go along with the idea as long as Revenue Canada has given the green light. All that's necessary is to provide Revenue Canada with proof that you're expecting a refund due to any number of deductions, such as RRSP contributions, charitable donations, medical expenses, alimony and maintenance payments, and so on.

Your aim should actually be to pay a small balance each year when you file your tax return; then you know you haven't made your tax payments ahead of time.

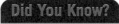

Income taxes were first introduced in Canada in 1917. The Income War Tax Act levied a 4-percent tax on Canadians to help finance World War I. It is commonly believed, based on comments made by Sir Thomas White, the Finance Minister of the day, that income taxes were to be a temporary measure.

Installments

If you happen to be self-employed or you receive a decent income from your investments each year, you're an obvious candidate for making quarterly installments, since folks in these situations are not often subject to source withholdings. This leaves installments as the only other option to ensure the tax collector gets paid throughout the year. Installments are due on the 15th of the month in March, June, September, and December.

In a nutshell, you'll be required to make installments if the difference between your total tax payable (federal and provincial) and any amounts withheld at source is more than $2,000 in the current year and either of the two preceding years. If you live in Quebec, the threshold is $1,200 of federal tax, since provincial tax is not collected by Revenue Canada in Quebec.

You've got three options for calculating your installments:

Second Prior Year Method. For your March and June installments, calculate one-quarter of your total tax liability from two years ago. For your September and December installments, calculate one-quarter of your total tax liability from last year. This means that in 1999, your March and June installments would each be one-quarter of your total 1997 tax. The September and December installments would each be one-quarter of your total 1998 tax.

Prior Year Method. Calculate each quarterly installment as one-quarter of your total tax liability from last year.

Current Year Method. Estimate your tax liability for the current year and pay one-quarter of that amount each quarter. If you estimate wrong here, you could face interest and penalties, so revise your estimate quarterly.

You may want to choose the option that provides the lowest quarterly payments. Don't worry about interest charges: As long as your payments are made on time and in accordance with either of the first two methods, you'll escape interest. If, however, you choose the current year method, a wrong estimate could lead to interest and penalties.

TO MAKE A LONG STORY SHORT:

- Don't hope for a refund when you file your return. Aim for a small balance owing instead.

- Request to have source withholdings reduced where you expect a refund due to certain deductions.

- You may have to make quarterly installments where your income is not subject to source withholdings.

- Consider the installment method that results in the lowest quarterly payments.

Tim's Tip 6: **Think of taxes when big things happen in life.**

Matthew paid me a visit not long ago. He wasn't sure if there were any tax issues to worry about in his situation, so he thought he'd play it safe and visit me to find out. When I asked him to tell me what's been happening, he replied in a single breath:

"Tim, my wife and I aren't getting along so well so we decided to separate earlier this year and my son is away at school for the first time and has been withdrawing funds from the registered education savings plan we set up for him ten years ago and my California condominium was sold in the year because we haven't been using it very much and my wife and I are going to split the money from that sale then I became concerned about my personal liability in my business so I set up a corporation but only after I gave my brother some money to help him in his own business. Is any of this going to affect my taxes?"

"Yes, Matthew, I would say so," I said.

Folks, any time a big event happens in life, ask yourself the question, "Will this affect my taxes?" While I couldn't possibly list every event to watch for, here are some of the most common that cross my desk:

- getting a separation or divorce
- negotiating salary or other compensation
- moving to another province or country
- setting up a business in another country
- investing offshore
- buying or selling a vacation or rental property
- starting or incorporating a business
- investing in someone else's small business
- inheriting assets
- creating or revising a will
- giving assets away during your lifetime.

If these or other big events appear on your horizon, visit a tax professional— sooner rather than later. You'd hate to find out after-the-fact that the tax collector wants more than you bargained for.

Who should you visit when it's time to see a tax pro? Many people out there call themselves tax experts. Some are really just tax preparers. If in doubt, your best bet is to visit a tax professional who has completed the Canadian Institute of Chartered Accountants' in-depth tax course. This is a two-year comprehensive course that only those specializing in tax full-time are permitted to take. Most students of the course are chartered accountants, but you'll also find lawyers, certified general accountants, certified management accountants, and a few others as well.

TO MAKE A LONG STORY SHORT:

- Think of taxes any time big events happen in life.

- Visit a tax professional before the events take place, if possible.

Fighting When You're Right

Tim's Tip 7: **Dispute your assessment when you think you're right.**

If one thing can be said about Canadian taxpayers, it's that we're a passive bunch. By this I mean that many Canadians are content to accept any assessment issued by Revenue Canada, under the assumption that Revenue Canada must be right. I admit, when the government receives your tax return, takes a look at it, and then issues you an assessment notice making changes to the return you've filed, it's easy to assume that you—or your tax preparer—probably made a mistake when filling out the forms. Bad assumption. The folks at Revenue Canada are prone to making mistakes as often as anyone else.

Notice of Objection

After filing your tax return, you can expect to receive a Notice of Assessment from Revenue Canada within 8 to 12 weeks. If you disagree with Revenue Canada's assessment of your tax return, don't let it go. Your first line of attack is to call your local Revenue Canada taxation office to talk over your concerns. You might just resolve the whole issue at that time. If that call doesn't resolve the problem to your satisfaction, then you should consider filing a Notice of Objection.

A Notice of Objection can be filed on Form T400A, but doesn't have to be. You can also file an objection by detailing the facts and your reasons for objecting in a letter addressed to the Chief of Appeals at your local tax services office or taxation centre. Remember, you've got to file your objection on time; otherwise Revenue Canada is not obligated to hear you out. For individuals and testamentary trusts, the deadline for any Notice of Objection is 90 days after the mailing date noted on your assessment, or one year after the due date of the tax return you're fighting, whichever is later. If, for example, your 1997 assessment notice is dated May 30, 1998, you'd have until April 30, 1999 (one year after the due date of your 1997 return) to file an objection.

Take 'em to Court

What happens if you file a Notice of Objection and the tax collector still refuses to assess your return as you think it should be assessed? Your next option is to take Revenue Canada to court—to the Tax Court of Canada (or the Court of Quebec for Quebec tax issues).

At the Tax Court of Canada you've got two options: the *informal* or the *general* procedure. With the informal procedure, you can represent yourself, or have anyone else (your accountant, lawyer, another advisor, or a friend, for example) lend a hand in the appeal, and you can expect to have a judgment on your case in 6 to 12 months. To be eligible for the informal procedure, the amount of tax in dispute has to be less than $12,000 for each year in question, or less than

Try to resolve your beef with Revenue Canada without filing a Notice of Objection. But keep an eye on the filing deadline, and be sure to file your objection on time to preserve your right to appeal if the discussions don't go your way. When a Notice of Objection is your best bet, visit a tax pro to have it prepared properly.

Why wait to file? If you jump right to the Notice of Objection first, there's always a chance that your objection could be denied, leaving you with no alternative other than to take the tax collector to court. Keep your options open.

Caution!

$24,000 in disputed losses where disallowed losses are the issue. If you don't qualify for the informal procedure, the Court's general procedure is your other option.

The general procedure is going to mean a visit to a lawyer who will represent you in court. Don't get me wrong: You can represent yourself in court under the general procedure as well, but I wouldn't recommend it. Formal rules of evidence and other legal procedures will apply, and unless you're completely familiar with these, you won't stand a chance on your own.

If the Tax Court of Canada judgment doesn't work out in your favour, you can usually appeal to the Federal Court of Appeal. The final step is to request an appeal to the Supreme Court of Canada, although very few cases (three or four each year) make it that far.

TO MAKE A LONG STORY SHORT:

- If you disagree with your Notice of Assessment, call Revenue Canada to straighten things out.

- If a phone call doesn't help, consider filing a Notice of Objection within the required time limits.

- Your last line of attack is to take Revenue Canada to court, starting with the Tax Court of Canada's informal or general procedure, and potentially ending at the Supreme Court of Canada.

Getting into the Game

Okay, you've taken the first step: You know the tax basics. It's time to turn to the Tax Planning Tip Sheet at the front of the book and review the strategies introduced in Chapter 1. Ask yourself, "Does this tip apply to me?" Each *Yes* or *Not Sure* could bring you one step closer to the winner's circle.

HOME TEAM
ADVANTAGE:
TAX PLANNING
FOR THE FAMILY

The thing that a parent will never understand is why all bachelors aren't rich.

2

It seems like only yesterday that Carolyn and I got married. In fact, we tied the knot on August 3, 1997. I have to admit, one of Carolyn's virtues—and she has many—is that she can cook like no one else I know. I can make my way around in the kitchen, but not nearly as well as Carolyn. In fact, some people accuse me of getting married solely for the culinary benefits. That's ridiculous. After all, there are countless income tax benefits as well.

Here's some advice for you: When you think of tax planning, think of it as a family affair. Just think of the fun it could be—you, your spouse, and your kids if you have any, sitting around the table sharing tax strategies. It's not something my family did when I was young. Too bad. I think my sisters would have enjoyed it. So, next time you're tempted to pull out the Monopoly board, think twice, and pull out this book instead!

You need to realize that any effective tax plan will involve your family members. And I realize that families come in all shapes and sizes. Some involve single parents, adoptive parents, common-law partners, or same-sex relationships. The strategies in this chapter apply, for the most part, to all families. I should mention, however, that those in same-sex relationships are not considered spouses under our tax law. Don't be offended. Being a spouse could work to your disadvantage for tax purposes in many situations.

Let's take a look at some of the best ideas available to make tax planning a family affair.

Splitting Family Income

Tim's Tip 8: **Split income for hefty tax savings.**

Maybe you've heard the term *income splitting* before. It's not a complicated tactic, but it's certainly one of the cornerstones of tax planning. Income splitting involves moving income from the hands of one family member who is going to pay tax at a higher rate, into the hands of another who will pay tax at a lower rate. The savings can be substantial. Check out Ron and Becky's situation.

If Becky earned $60,000 in 1998 in Ontario and was the only spouse earning income, the family's tax bill would amount to $16,037. But things change dramatically if both Becky and Ron each bring home $30,000. With two income-earners in this case, the family's total income remains at $60,000, but the family's tax bill drops to just $11,654, for savings of $4,383 *each year*. Why the tax savings? Simple. Think back to our talk about marginal tax rates in

THE VALUE OF SPLITTING INCOME			
	Becky's Income	Ron's Income	Total
One Income-Earner			
Employment income	$60,000	$ –	$60,000
Tax to pay	$16,037	$ –	$16,037
Two Income-Earners			
Employment income	$30,000	$30,000	$60,000
Tax to pay	$5,827	$5,827	$11,654
Tax saved annually			**$4,383**

Chapter 1, Tip 2. With each spouse earning just $30,000, nearly every dollar earned by the family is taxed at the lowest marginal tax rate possible for employment income— about 27 percent. When Becky earned all the money herself, every dollar over $29,590 was taxed at a higher marginal rate—about 41 percent—giving rise to a higher tax bill.

The Attribution Rules

The problem is this: The tax collector will not allow you to simply hand a portion of your income to your spouse or child to be taxed in their hands. If you try this, you'll be caught under the *attribution rules* found in our tax law. These rules say that, when you try to pass income to your spouse, children, in-laws, nieces or nephews, *you* will be taxed on the income, and not the person who you intended to pay the tax. By the way, spouses are defined to be those of the opposite sex

Did You Know?

You could be liable to pay a friend's tax bill in certain situations. If your friend owes taxes at a time when he or she gives any type of asset to you at all, you could be jointly liable for that tax owing to the extent you didn't pay for the asset transferred to you. Section 160 of the Income Tax Act says so.

who are legally married or who have been living together in a conjugal relationship for more than 12 months. Where the 12-month test is not met, you're still considered spouses if you're parents of the same child.

THE ATTRIBUTION RULES IN A NUTSHELL

	Type of Transfer		
Transfer To	**Gift**	**Loan with No Interest**	**Loan at Interest***
Spouse	Attribute all investment income back to transferor	Attribute all investment income back to transferor	No attribution
Minor Child	Attribute all investment income except capital gains to transferor	Attribute all investment income except capital gains to transferor	No attribution
Adult Child	No attribution	Attribute all investment income if loan made specifically to avoid tax	No attribution

Interest charged must be Revenue Canada's prescribed rate, or commercial rates if these are less.

Never fear. There are a number of ways to side-step the attribution rules. What follows is the *A to Z* of income-splitting strategies.

a. Lend money and charge fair interest.

Set up a loan between you and the family member you'd like to split income with. As long as you charge interest on the loan at Revenue Canada's prescribed rate or current commercial rates (you should choose whichever rate is lower), then you'll avoid attribution back to you of any income earned on the money you've lent. The interest must be paid to you by January 30 following any year the loan is outstanding, and will be taxable to you. Your family member can deduct the interest paid on the loan. One last thing: You'll be able to permanently set the rate on the loan at the time the loan is set up—which is great news if interest rates happen to be low at that time.

b. Lend money, then take repayment.

This idea works well if you'd rather not charge interest on money lent to family members. It works this way: Lend money to a family member for investment purposes—say $15,000—then take back those funds after five years. Those funds will earn, say, $1,500 each year which, in most cases, will be taxed in your hands because of the attribution rules. Here's the kicker: That $1,500 can be re-invested each year, and any second-generation income—in other words, income on income—will not be attributed back to you. By lending money to a family member for five years or more, there will be enough time for the second-generation income to grow and take on a life of its own. Soon, your family member will have a sizeable portfolio growing and facing tax in his or her hands—not yours. You'd be wise to transfer the income earned each year to a separate account to keep the second-generation income segregated.

Action Step

When you set up a loan between family members for the purpose of splitting income, be sure to properly document the loan. A promissory note signed by both parties should do the trick. The promissory note should detail: the date and amount of the loan; the interest rate charged (if any); the method for calculating interest (compounded daily, monthly, or annually); and the terms of repayment, including when interest will be paid. Remember: To avoid the attribution rules, pay the interest by January 30 each year.

c. Transfer money for business purposes.

You'll manage to avoid the attribution rules if you lend or give money to family members for use in a business. If it's a loan, there's no need to charge interest to avoid the dreaded attribution rules, but there are right ways and wrong ways to invest in a small business. I'll talk more about this issue in Chapter 5, Tip 50.

d. Transfer money to cover interest on investment loans.

The fact is, when you've transferred money to a lower-income family member, and those funds are used to pay for expenses and not to invest, the attribution rules won't apply. So, why not give cash to your family member in order to pay the interest on any investment loans? Giving that family member the cash to make those interest payments will make it much easier for that lower-income family member to borrow for investing. The result? Investment income is taxed at a lower marginal tax rate in the hands of your family member.

e. Swap assets with another family member.

We've been talking, so far, about splitting income by passing investment assets to other family members who are going to face a lower marginal tax rate than you. Why not swap assets to make this happen? Here's how: "Sell" some of your investments to your spouse or child in exchange for another asset you take back in return. The asset you take back should be worth at least as much as the

Caution!

When a family member borrows money to invest, make sure that a higher-income family member does not guarantee the loan or give the borrower funds to repay the loan principal! The problem? Quite simply, the attribution rules! These rules will cause any income earned on the borrowed funds to be taxed in the hands of the person guaranteeing or effectively making payments on the loan.

investments you're handing over, and should not produce an income of any kind. I'm talking about things like jewellery, artwork, a coin or other collection, or even your spouse's half of the family home—provided your spouse actually contributed to its purchase. If the house was purchased with your money alone, the attribution rules will catch up to you. Keep in mind that, for tax purposes, any swap is considered to be a sale at fair market value, so there could be tax to pay on any accrued gains when you make the swap.

f. Generate capital gains in the hands of your kids.

One of the most common ways to split income with the kids is to give or lend them cash to invest. Regardless of the age of your kids, there will not generally be attribution of capital gains on the invested money back to you. That is, your kids will pay the tax on any capital gains generated. The best part, of course, is that your kids may pay next to no tax on those gains if they have little other income. Besides cash, you could also transfer existing investments to your kids. But beware: When you give assets away, you are deemed to have sold those assets at fair market value. So, if those assets have appreciated in value, there could be some tax to pay on the gains. This tax cost, however, could pale in comparison to the taxes you'll save by splitting income with the kids.

g. Transfer any investment income to your adult child.

While you'll generally be able to move capital gains to the hands of your children and avoid attribution, it's a whole new ball game when we talk about interest, dividends, rents, royalties and other *income from property*. If you transfer money to your minor children for investment, you're going to pay the tax on any income from property. But there's good news. Any income generated on assets given to an adult child (18 years or older at the end of the year) will avoid attribution, no matter what type of income. The only catch is that your child now owns and controls the assets. To avoid having your child spend your hard-earned money on the finer things in life, consider setting up a formal trust to maintain control over the assets. One last point to note: If you transferred the money to your adult child as a loan rather than a gift, and the tax collector decides that your primary motive was to avoid tax, you're going to face the attribution rules.

h. Give funds to your adult child, then charge room and board.
When you give money to a child who has reached age 18 by December 31, you'll avoid attribution on any income earned. Of course, you may not want to give up the income you were enjoying on those investments, so here's a plan: Charge your child room and board for living at home. This will enable you to recover the income that you've given up by giving away your money. If you're not thrilled with the idea of handing over a sum of money to your semi-responsible 18-year-old, consider transferring the assets to a trust. This will allow you to accomplish the same thing, but will give you control over the money as long as you're a trustee (see Tip 9).

i. Make a corporate loan to a related student.
If you're a shareholder of a corporation, consider setting up a loan from the corporation to a student who is not dealing at arm's length with you. If the loan is not repaid within one year of your company's year-end, the loan is going to be taxed in the hands of the student. That's no big deal: The student will likely pay little or no tax on the amount if he or she has very little other income. But there's more. Once that student graduates and is earning a regular income, the loan can be repaid, and the student will be allowed a deduction for the amount of the repayment. Not a bad deal! Little or no tax to pay when the loan is included in income, but a healthy deduction when it's repaid later. This idea is great where the student doesn't work in the business and it would be tough to justify paying salary or wages.

Keep in mind that the company won't be entitled to a deduction for the cash paid to the student. After all, it's a loan.

j. Pay an allowance to your working child.

I know, I know, you've been looking forward to the day when your children are out working, earning their own spending money, if only because it will teach them responsibility. What if I were to tell you that paying your children an allowance makes sense once they're earning their own money? Here's why: Giving your children an allowance will free-up their earnings for investment. When they invest their own income, the attribution rules won't apply and you will have effectively split income. By the way, a child who has earned income will be entitled to RRSP contribution room, which will save tax down the road when the child starts contributing to that RRSP.

k. Pay an adult child to baby-sit the younger kids.

If you haven't got investments or cash to simply hand over to the kids to split income, try this idea on for size: Pay your adult child who was 18 or older in the year to baby-sit your younger kids who were age 16 or under in the year. Baby-sitting fees, like other child care expenses, may be deductible if they were paid out to allow you to earn income. Follow me now: You're entitled to a deduction for the payments to your adult child, and that child will report the payments as income. There's a very good chance, however, that your child will face little or no tax on those payments. In this case, you've managed to split income by moving income directly from your tax return to your kid's return. Oh, and there's another big benefit: This *earned income* will entitle your child to RRSP contribution room.

l. Pay an adult child to help in a move.

Where you're entitled to claim moving expenses, why not pay your adult child to help you with the move? Let's face it, someone's got to drive the truck or lift the furniture. It might as well be a family member. You'll not only keep the money in the family, but you'll be entitled to a deduction for the payment made—subject, of course, to the usual moving expense rules (see Tip 13). Your child will have to report the income, but may not pay much tax, if any, when his or her income is low. The payment will also entitle your child to RRSP contributions, since it's earned income. There's nothing quite like moving income directly from your tax return to your child's—and this is what you're accomplishing here.

m. Transfer assets before leaving the country.

Suppose that you and your spouse have decided to leave Canada. Did you realize that you could face an ugly tax hit when you leave? Here's why: When you leave, you are deemed to have "sold" everything you own at fair market value, and so you could face tax on any property that has appreciated in value. You could minimize this tax hit with a clever tactic used by Burt and Margaret.

After spending several winters in the sunny south, Burt and Margaret decided to retire in California in January 1998. At the time the couple decided to move, Burt owned stocks worth $20,000 that he had paid $5,000 for. Burt was due to face a tax bill on the $15,000 ($20,000 – $5,000) accrued capital gain when leaving Canada, thanks to the rule that deems him to have sold these stocks. In December 1997, just before leaving, Burt gave the stocks to his wife Margaret (with no tax effect to himself since assets transferred to a spouse generally transfer at original cost). On January 5, 1998, Burt left for California and became a resident of the U.S. Margaret left one month later to join Burt and became a resident of the U.S. in February 1998. When Margaret left, she owned the stocks with the $15,000 gain, and had to pay tax on that gain when leaving. Normally, the attribution rules would require the gain to be taxed in Burt's hands; but not in this case, since Burt is no longer a resident of

Canada. Instead, Margaret paid the tax on the $15,000 gain at her lower marginal tax rate. The couple successfully split income.

By the way, normally the tax collector will consider two spouses to have given up residency on the same day. In Burt and Margaret's case, Margaret had business reasons to stay behind. Be sure to visit a tax professional to talk over the residency issue before trying this idea.

n. Transfer capital losses to your spouse.
When I met Paul, he had a problem that may be more common than you might think. His wife, Esther, had sold some stocks for a $10,000 profit, and he owned shares in ABC corporation with an accrued loss of $10,000. You see, he had paid $25,000 for the ABC shares, but today they're worth just $15,000. Wouldn't it be nice if we could transfer Paul's $10,000 capital loss to Esther to shelter her capital gains from tax? The good news is, we can. There are four steps to take.

If you're leaving Canada, be sure to visit a tax professional who can help you to determine, in advance, whether or not you are properly giving up residency for tax purposes. Revenue Canada will make this determination for you if you complete Form NR73, but I never recommend sending a completed Form NR73 to the tax collector! You see, if there's any way to call you a resident of Canada—the tax collector will! In most cases, there's no need to send anything to the tax collector before giving up residency.

Caution!

Step 1
Paul is going to sell his ABC shares to Esther for their fair market value of $15,000. His loss on the sale will be $10,000, but the loss will be denied under the *superficial*

loss rules in the Income Tax Act. Instead, the loss that is denied will be added to Esther's cost of the ABC shares.

 Step 2 Esther will sell the shares on the open market. That is, she'll sell the shares for their current value of just $15,000. Although she paid $15,000 for the shares, her actual cost is considered to be $25,000 since the loss denied to Paul is added to her cost base. The result? She realizes a capital loss of $10,000 ($25,000 minus $15,000).

 Step 3 Esther will apply the $10,000 capital loss against her $10,000 capital gain and will avoid tax on that gain.

Step 4 Paul will file a special election with his tax return (this is a statement attached to the return) that says he elects that subsection 73(1) of the Income Tax Act not apply on his sale of ABC shares to Esther. You see, without making this election, the attribution rules will apply to pass Esther's capital loss back to Paul—something we want to avoid.

The moral of the story is this: Don't try this stunt at home. Visit a tax professional for help. You'll want to do it right.

o. Transfer personal tax credits.

There are a few non-refundable personal tax credits that can be transferred from one spouse to the next. The idea here is to transfer these credits to the higher-income spouse when possible. Overall, this will save the family taxes—largely due to the surtax savings you'll enjoy. Which credits can be passed by your spouse to you? Four in particular: the age credit (if your spouse was age 65 or older in the year); disability credit (where your spouse had a severe mental or physical impairment, supported by a signed Form T2201—see Tip 15); pension credit (where your spouse had pension income); and tuition and education credits (where your spouse attended a qualifying post-secondary school).

p. Pay household expenses through the higher-income spouse.

This is, perhaps, the simplest technique for splitting income. Let's suppose that you have a higher income and marginal tax rate than your spouse. If you pay for all or most of the household expenses, this will free-up your spouse's income for investment. You can even pay your spouse's income taxes. There won't be any attribution of income in this case, since you are not giving money to your spouse to earn income. The result? This will free up some of your spouse's income to invest, and your spouse will face the tax on those investment earnings at his or her lower marginal tax rate.

q. Invest inheritances in the right name.

Make sure that any inheritance received by the lower-income spouse is kept separate and apart from any joint accounts you might have as a couple. As long as the inherited money is invested solely in the name of the lower-income spouse, the investment income will be taxed in the hands of that spouse alone, which will spell tax savings for the family. Likewise, where money has been left to both of you, be sure to invest the lower-income spouse's half separately rather than keeping the money in a joint account. The tax savings on an inheritance properly invested could be enough to pay for a family vacation each year!

r. Invest Child Tax Benefits in the child's name.

It was in January 1993 that the tax collector replaced the old Family Allowance system with the Child Tax Benefit system. You know what I'm talking about. Child Tax Benefits are those payments that many Canadian families are entitled to receive on a monthly basis up until the children reach age 18. Did you realize that Child Tax Benefit payments can be invested in your child's name without the

Action Step

When investing Child Tax Benefits in the name of your child, your best bet is to open an investment account in the name of the child alone. Many financial institutions will do this for you. Obtain a Social Insurance Number (SIN) for your child and visit your financial institution armed with that SIN to open the account properly. This will avoid any confusion with the tax collector when it comes time to report the income on the child's tax return.

attribution rules kicking in? You better believe it. And it makes good sense. Ensure that the payments are deposited directly into an investment account for the child, and consider investing those funds for the long term—perhaps to help with your child's education.

s. Contribute to a spousal RRSP.

Your goal for retirement should be for you and your spouse to have equal incomes. Why? Because this will accomplish a perfect splitting of incomes. To make it happen, you may need to help your spouse by contributing to an RRSP for him or her. I'm talking about a spousal RRSP. It works this way: You'll contribute to an RRSP under which your spouse is the annuitant. This simply means that your spouse will be the one to make withdrawals from the plan, and your spouse will pay the tax on those withdrawals. The good news is that you'll be entitled to a deduction for the contribution you've made to the spousal RRSP. I'll take a closer look at spousal RRSPs in Chapter 6, Tip 72.

t. Consider an RESP for a child's education.

Registered Education Savings Plans (RESPs) are special plans registered with the government to help save for post-secondary education. Here's the deal: You won't be allowed to deduct your contribution to an RESP, but the funds will grow tax-deferred in the plan over the years. When the money is withdrawn from the RESP for education purposes, the income that had accumulated in the RESP will be taxed in the hands of the student. I like it—a perfect splitting of income. By the way, RESPs are much more attractive now than in the past. I'll be talking more about them in Tip 10.

u. Split the tax bill on your CPP benefits.

Here's an income splitting idea that the tax collector openly endorses. You're entitled to take up to one half of your Canada Pension Plan (CPP) benefits and report them on your spouse's tax return. The arrangement is actually reciprocal so that the same proportion of your spouse's CPP benefits will have to be reported on your tax return. As long as your benefits are higher than your spouse's, and you have a higher marginal tax rate, you're going to save some tax. Be sure to contact Human Resources Development Canada to arrange for this splitting of benefits.

v. Report your spouse's dividends on your tax return.

What if I told you that reporting someone else's income on your tax return could actually save you tax? You'd probably have me committed. The truth is, the idea can work. You see, you can elect to report all of your spouse's Canadian dividends on your own tax return. It can make sense if your spouse's income is quite low. By putting your spouse's dividends on your return, you'll reduce your spouse's income which may, in turn, increase the spousal tax credit you're entitled to claim. In fact, you'll

The tax rules say that, when you transfer dividends from one spouse to the next, you'll have to transfer *all* the dividends. You can't simply pick and choose which dividends to transfer. Watch out! Transferring all the dividends to the higher income spouse's tax return might increase that spouse's income enough to cause a clawback of Old Age Security benefits. In this case, you might want to avoid this type of transfer.

Caution!

only be allowed to make this election if it increases your spousal tax credit. Since you'll also be entitled to claim a dividend tax credit on the dividends reported, your family could save hundreds of dollars in tax by making this swap.

w. Pay family members a salary.

If you happen to run a business of any kind, you'll be able to pay your family members a salary or wage to work in that business. The only catch is that the amount you pay must be reasonable for the services provided. What's reasonable? Consider what you would pay an unrelated third party and this should give you a pretty good idea. Your business will claim a deduction, and your family member will report the income.

x. Become a partner with family members.

Did you know that a partnership does not pay taxes itself? Rather, the income or loss of the partnership is passed along to each of the partners, who are then responsible for reporting the income or loss to the tax collector. If you become a partner with your spouse or children, you'll split income by having some of your profits taxed in their hands, in accordance with your partnership agreement. By the way, a written partnership agreement is critical to avoid misunderstandings with family and to satisfy Revenue Canada of the partnership allocations.

y. Own a corporation with family members.

If you're a co-shareholder with your spouse or kids, you can split income with them in a number of ways. As shareholders, your family members are entitled to dividends from the corporation. In addition, they may be entitled to directors' fees if they are directors of the company, or salary if they are actively employed by the company. It's also common to see family trusts set up where the trust owns shares in the corporation, and the kids are beneficiaries of the trust.

Dividends can be paid to the trust and allocated out to the children to be taxed in their hands. A family member with no other income can receive up to $23,760 in dividends from a Canadian corporation in a year and not pay any tax, thanks to the dividend tax credit.

z. Use two corporations to transfer money.

The ugly attribution rules we've been talking about apply to transfers of assets between two individuals or between an individual and a corporation—but not between two corporations. If, for example, you and your spouse own separate corporations, funds can be lent from your corporation to your spouse's without attribution. If those funds were used in a business or invested inside your spouse's corporation, your spouse could access the funds by taking dividends. Your spouse will be able to take up to $23,760 in dividends from his or her corporation without paying any tax, thanks to the dividend tax credit, provided those dividends are your spouse's only source of income. Be sure to visit a tax pro before trying this idea. You'll have to set things up properly to avoid the anti-avoidance provisions in the Income Tax Act.

TO MAKE A LONG STORY SHORT:

- Splitting income involves moving income from the hands of one family member, who

Action Step

Making family members shareholders with you in a corporation can be a very effective way to split income. The ideal time to make family members shareholders is when the company is first set up, although it can be done at any time. Your best bet is to issue a separate class of shares to each family member, or at least a separate class to the kids. This way, you can pick and choose which shares will receive dividends each year, if any. This is what we call *dividend sprinkling*. If all family members had the same class of shares, every family member would receive equal dividends per share any time dividends are paid.

will be taxed at a higher rate, to the hands of another, who will face tax at a lower rate.

- The attribution rules prevent many attempts at passing income to other family members.

- Splitting income most commonly entails investing money in lower-income hands, making deductible payments to lower-income family members, and claiming deductions and credits on the most appropriate tax return.

Tim's Tip 9: Consider family trusts for income splitting.

Trusts can offer a ton of flexibility in managing your affairs and controlling the use of your property. And a trust can be as simple to set up as a visit to your lawyer. Sure, it's going to take some legal fees up front and some accounting fees each year to file the appropriate T3 information and tax return for your trust, but the costs could be well worth it.

How a Trust Works

A trust is simply a legal arrangement where one or more persons (known as *trustees*) hold legal title to certain assets (the *trust assets*) exclusively for the benefit of other persons (the *beneficiaries*). If you're the person creating the trust by putting the assets into the trust, you're known as the *settlor*.

William is elderly and has two sons, Scott and Jason. Jason is mentally impaired. William wants to ensure that Jason will always be provided for, so he gave $300,000 to Scott to hold in trust for Jason. A trust agreement was drawn up so that Scott is able to use the funds to provide for the needs of Jason. Scott is responsible for investing the funds until they are paid out for Jason's benefit. Scott is legally bound to use the funds for Jason's *benefit alone. In this case, the trust agreement provides that an annual fee is paid to Scott for his services. William is the settlor of the trust, Scott is the trustee, and Jason is the beneficiary.*

How is a trust taxed? Just like any other individual. That's right, the trust will have to file a tax return each year for any income earned in the trust. There's a way for the trust to avoid tax on its income, and that is to pay out to the beneficiary, or make payable to the beneficiary, any income earned in the trust each year. This way, the beneficiary will pay tax on the income instead.

Here's an important point: A trust that is set up while the settlor is alive is called an *inter vivos* trust and will face tax at the highest marginal tax rates going! All this means is that you'll want to ensure any income in an inter vivos trust is taxed in the beneficiaries hands, and not in the trust in most cases. A *testamentary* trust, on the other hand, is created through the will of a deceased individual. This type of trust is taxed just as you and I are, at graduated tax rates.

There are a number of uses for family trusts: to protect assets from creditors; to provide privacy over ownership of assets; to provide for the needs of dependents; or to achieve other non-tax goals. Let's talk about the most common use of family trusts.

You should remember that whenever you transfer any property to another individual or to a trust, you're deemed to have sold that property at its fair market value at the time of the transfer. What does this mean for you? It means that, if the property has appreciated in value, you could end up with some tax to pay on the capital gain. You won't have to worry about this with cash and near-cash investments, like guaranteed investment certificates and Canada Savings Bonds, because these generally don't appreciate in value.

Caution!

Trusts for Income Splitting

In Tip 8 we talked about the dreaded attribution rules which were designed to prevent you from passing income to the hands of lower-income family members in order to avoid tax. For the most part, the attribution rules will apply to any trust arrangement you might set up. For example, if you give $10,000 directly to your spouse to generate investment income, that income will be taxed in your hands, thanks to the attribution rules. Now insert a trust into the equation. If you give $10,000 to a trust of which your spouse is the beneficiary, any income earned on that $10,000 will still be taxed in your hands.

But there's a happy ending to this story. Remember strategies *A to Z* in Tip 8, designed to split income and side-step the attribution rules? Those same strategies can be applied to avoid the attribution rules when we insert a family trust into the story. And why introduce a family trust? There are a few good reasons. Consider Peter and Janice.

Peter and Janice are married and have two children, Tori age 21, and Lincoln age 18. The couple would like to pass some of their investment income to the kids to be taxed in the kids' hands. Rather than giving the funds directly to Tori and Lincoln, Peter and Janice decided to set up a family trust with Tori and Lincoln as the beneficiaries. Peter and Janice named themselves as trustees. This allows Peter and Janice to maintain control over the assets they gave to the kids. Because the kids are adults, the attribution rules will not apply to any income earned by the trust for the benefit of Tori and Lincoln (see Tip 8g). If Tori and Lincoln had been minors, Peter and Janice would focus on generating capital gains in the trust to avoid the attribution rules (see Tip 8f).

Did you catch the key benefit to using a family trust for income splitting? It's *control* over the assets—even after you've given them away. This is important, especially if you're transferring valuable assets to your kids but don't want them to take the money and run. I should also mention that Peter and Janice in our story no longer own the assets even though they do control them. But since they don't own the assets, the couple will by-pass probate fees on those assets when they die. Nice fringe benefit. And here's another benefit: If the beneficiaries are minors, you'll be able to use income from the trust to pay certain costs for their upbringing. Imagine paying for summer camp, piano lessons, sports equipment, and more out of money that has been taxed in the kids' hands!

You'll learn more about family trusts, particularly testamentary trusts, in Chapter 9.

TO MAKE A LONG STORY SHORT:

- Every trust has a settlor, trustee, trust assets, and beneficiaries.

- A trust can be used to implement many of the income-splitting ideas presented in Tip 8.

- The benefit of using a trust in splitting income is that you can maintain control over the assets after giving them away.

Educating the Family

When it comes to saving for education, there are a number of tax-efficient strategies you can consider. I want to focus here on the two most common: Registered Education Savings Plans and in-trust accounts. I also cover the subject of education briefly in other parts of the book. Refer back to Tip 8*i* if you're a shareholder in a closely-held corporation, or check out Tip 75 in Chapter 6 if you're wondering about using RRSP savings for education. Now let's talk about those two most common strategies I was referring to.

Tim's Tip 10: Use an RESP to save for your child's education.

Let's face it, our government has not exactly offered Canadians a smorgasbord of tax-saving opportunities. That's why I'm a firm believer that when the tax collector finally does offer some type of relief, every Canadian ought to sit up and take notice. Enter: Registered Education Savings Plans (RESPs).

The Old and the New

I've got to admit, RESPs were not so attractive as recently as 1995. In fact, they were really the laughing stock of the investment world. Why? For starters, it used to be that you could only contribute $1,500 annually to an RESP. Setting aside $1,500 each year wasn't likely to be enough to send the family dog to obedience school, let alone pay for four years of post-secondary education for the kids. In addition, it used to be that if your kids decided not to attend post-secondary school, you'd lose all the income that had been accumulating in the plan over the years. All you'd get back was your original contributions.

Things have changed—Big Time. Thanks to the 1997 federal budget, you'll be able to contribute up to $4,000 annually per beneficiary, to a maximum of $42,000 per beneficiary in a lifetime. Further, if the student decides that post-secondary education is not "cool," an RESP can now hand back to the contributor all the money inside the plan, including the accumulated income, provided the plan has been in place for at least 10 years and each beneficiary under the plan is at least 21 years old and ineligible to receive payments from the RESP—most likely because they're not attending school. If you're the contributor and you receive your money back, with the accumulated income, you'll face tax plus an additional 20 percent penalty on that income.

If you'd rather not pay the tax and penalty on the RESP income in the event your kids by-pass the yellow-brick road to post-secondary school, you now have the option of transferring the RESP assets to your RRSP, up to $50,000 in your lifetime. You will, however, need sufficient RRSP contribution room to make the transfer.

There's more. The 1997 budget made reference to *family plans* where each of the beneficiaries of the RESP is related by blood or adoption to the contributor. Under a family plan, the accumulated income inside the plan can be transferred to the other beneficiaries if one or more is not entitled to receive payments out of the plan.

By the way, you'll be entitled to use RESP funds for correspondence courses of a qualifying post-secondary school. This wasn't possible before the 1997 budget.

Canada Education Savings Grants

The 1998 federal budget improved RESPs even more with the Canada Education Savings Grant (CESG). The CESG works alongside any RESP. Beginning January 1, 1998, any contributions made to an RESP for a child who is age 17 or under in the year will net you a grant from the federal government, paid directly to the RESP. The grant is equal to 20 percent of the contributions made to the RESP, but only to the extent the child has CESG contribution room.

You see, the CESG is a distant cousin to your RRSP. Each child age 17 or under in the year is entitled to CESG contribution room of $2,000 per year. If

Action Step

If you're going to make use of an RESP, be sure to contribute enough to take maximum advantage of the CESG payments the government is offering. This will mean contributing at least $2,000 each year, or $4,000 every two years. The truth is, the more you can sock away the better, because post-secondary school is not going to be cheap.

no contributions are made to an RESP in a given year, that contribution room is carried forward to a future year. When you contribute to the RESP, you use up that amount of contribution room, and the RESP receives a grant equal to 20 percent of the contribution room used. Keep in mind, however, that you're restricted to maximum RESP contributions of $4,000 per beneficiary each year under the usual RESP rules, so the biggest CESG grant you'll receive in any given year will be 20 percent of $4,000—or $800. I should mention that any contributions over and above the CESG contribution room cannot be carried forward to attract a CESG payment in a future year. Confused? Consider Jake's story.

Jake is fours years old and his CESG contribution room for 1998 is $2,000. In February 1998, Jake's father contributed $800 to Jake's RESP. A CESG payment of $160 (20 percent of $800) is paid directly to the RESP. A few days later, Jake's grandmother made a $2,500 contribution to another RESP on behalf of Jake. Since only $1,200 of Jake's CESG contribution room is available at the time of Grandma's contribution (his dad used up $800 of it), only $1,200 of her contribution qualifies for a CESG payment. The remaining $1,300 of her contribution will not qualify for a CESG payment in the following year. By the way, if no contributions other than Dad's were made, the remaining $1,200 of Jake's CESG contribution room would be carried forward for use in a future year.

To ensure that Canadians are making use of RESPs on a regular basis, there's another catch to be aware of. If you're hoping to put money into an RESP for a child who is age 16 or 17 in the year, you're going to receive CESG payments only where one of two conditions are met:

- A minimum of $4,000 in RESP contributions must have been made on behalf of the child before the year he or she turns age 16; or

- A minimum of $300 in annual RESP contributions must have been made on behalf of that child in any four years before the year the child turns age 16.

Get the drift? Make an RESP a regular habit if you want the benefits of the CESG.

TO MAKE A LONG STORY SHORT:

- RESPs are much more flexible than they have been in the past.

- The new Canada Education Savings Grant (CESG) means a direct contribution by the government to a child's RESP, making these plans hard to resist.

Tim's Tip 11: **Set up in-trust accounts properly; otherwise stick to an RESP.**

In-trust accounts are more common than ever, and are often used by parents, grandparents or others to save for a child's education. The account is used to invest funds for a minor and, typically, an adult looks after the investment decisions on behalf of the child. These accounts are *informal* or *bare* trusts.

Normally, in-trust accounts are set up with the intention that the child, and not the adult, should pay the tax on any capital gains on the investment (see Tip 8*f*). After all, the child's income is usually so low that reporting the gains in the child's hands won't trigger a tax hit at all. Of course, any interest or dividends earned by the investment will be taxed in the hands of the adult under the attribution rules, so it's typical to invest in mutual funds or securities that will generate primarily capital gains.

Doing It Properly

Here's the problem: If the in-trust account is not set up properly, you could be in for a nasty tax surprise. In a nutshell, our tax law says that there must be a real and irrevocable transfer of property to the child. That's right, if you've set up the in-trust account with the belief that you can simply access that money down the road for your own benefit—maybe to buy a new car, or a set of golf clubs—you're mistaken. In the words of Revenue Canada, you have to "divest, deprive, or dispossess" yourself of title over the money you've transferred to the account.

If you fail to make this type of transfer, then you're considered to effectively own the assets still. And if you're still the owner, guess who pays tax on every cent of income from the investment, including capital gains? Right. You do. That will defeat the purpose of setting up the account in the first place!

Randy wanted to ensure he wasn't offside with the tax collector, so he took three steps to make sure the in-trust account for his daughter, Chloe, passed the smell test.

Step 1 Randy set up a true bare trust. Every true trust must have a trustee, property to be held in trust, and at least one beneficiary. Randy ensured these conditions were met for Chloe's in-trust account by placing an adult's name on the account along with Chloe's name. "Skye Doe, in trust" won't cut it, since no beneficiary is named.

Step 2 Randy ensured that the contributor (known as the settlor) of the account is not also the trustee. Since Randy contributed the money to Chloe's account, he ensured that someone else—his wife Skye—was named trustee. The account reads: "Skye

Doe, in trust for Chloe Doe." This provides some assurance to the tax collector that Randy has made a true transfer of assets when he set up the account.

Step 3 Randy signed an agreement providing that: (1) The property cannot revert back to Randy; (2) Randy will not require that the property be passed to persons to be named by him after setting up the account; and (3) Randy will not require that his consent or direction be obtained before the assets in the account are disposed of. Signing this agreement is not absolutely necessary to satisfy the tax collector, but it's going to help.

By the way, what you actually do with money in an in-trust account will speak volumes to Revenue Canada about whether there was a true transfer of property. Be sure that the funds in the account are reserved only for the beneficiary child. Let's take it a step further. You should realize that the in-trust account arrangement is really a *bare* trust: The trustee's authority is limited to holding those funds until the child reaches the age of majority, then passing those funds to the child at that time.

Hmm. Food for thought.

In-trust Accounts *v.* RESPs

There's only one question more perplexing than "Which came first, the chicken or the egg?," and that would be "Which is better for a child's educational savings, an in-trust account or an RESP?" Both are good questions. Neither has an easy answer. If you're looking for my opinion, I'm a fan of the RESP. Why? Three reasons:

• The 20 percent CESG is going to go far to multiply the assets in the RESP.

- If your child doesn't go to school, you can get your money back (after tax and penalties, unless you roll the assets to your RRSP).
- There are no annual tax filings until the child goes to school and takes money from the RESP.

TAKE YOUR PICK: REGISTERED EDUCATION SAVINGS PLANS OR IN-TRUST ACCOUNTS

	Registered Education Savings Plans	In-trust Accounts
Contribution Limits	$4,000 per beneficiary per year. Lifetime maximum of $42,000 per beneficiary.	No limit.
Investment Options	No restrictions under a self-directed plan. Investment or savings account plans generally offer one type of savings vehicle or mutual fund family. Group plans generally offer no options.	Generally no restrictions, although some have expressed concern due to provincial trustee legislation. These concerns will likely be put to rest over time.
Government Assistance	Canada Education Savings Grant. The grant is 20 percent of contributions made within the child's grant room—normally a maximum of $400 annually.	None.
Control over assets	The subscriber controls the investments and decides when to pay the assets to the beneficiary.	The trustee of the account controls where the money is invested. The assets, however, must be held for the child until age of majority; then the assets revert to the child.

continued

	Registered Education Savings Plans	**In-trust Accounts**
Use of assets	A beneficiary must use the plan assets for post-secondary education; otherwise, assets revert to the subscriber. If assets revert to subscriber, income tax plus a 20-percent penalty will be due on the accumulated income in the plan, unless the assets are transferred to the subscriber's RRSP.	Child may use the assets for any purpose once reaching age of majority. Contributor may not use the assets in any way, since the assets belong to the child.
Recovery of capital	Subscribers may receive a tax-free return of original capital at any time. Certain trustee or administration fees may apply.	Contributor has no right to recover the assets in the account since the assets belong to the child.
Taxation of assets	Assets grow tax-deferred over the years. When student withdraws this money to attend a qualifying educational program, student will pay tax on accumulated income in the plan.	Interest and dividends are taxed in the hands of the contributor annually. Realized capital gains are taxed in the hands of the child annually.
Tax filings	No annual filings are required until the student makes withdrawals from the RESP. Then student must file returns to report the taxable income.	Must file a tax return for the child to report capital gains. Technically, a trust tax return should be filed annually, but Revenue Canada has not, to-date, been enforcing these filings for in-trust accounts.

TO MAKE A LONG STORY SHORT:

- In-trust accounts are a popular method of saving for a child's education, but are often set up improperly. There are three steps to properly setting up an in-trust account.

- Once the money is in the account, forget about getting it back—it belongs to the child and he or she has a right to it at age of majority—for education or otherwise.

- I'm a fan of RESPs over in-trust accounts.

Heading for Home

When Dorothy returned from Oz, she declared, "there's no place like home." I'd have to agree, and not simply because home is a place to hang your hat. Your home can also provide tax savings. I want to focus here on the two most common tax matters related to the family home: the principal residence exemption and moving expenses. Virtually every Canadian homeowner will face these at some point. I cover some other home-related issues elsewhere in the book. See home office expenses in Chapter 4, Tip 40; the "mortgage versus RRSP" debate in Chapter 6, Tip 71; and the Home Buyer's Plan in Chapter 6, Tip 74.

Tim's Tip 12: Change the ownership of a second property to multiply tax savings.

My guess is that, unless you've been living under a rock for the last few years, you're probably already aware that when you sell your home at a profit it's going to be tax-free. You see, every family (which includes you, your spouse, and any unmarried kids under age 18) is entitled to one principal residence exemption. The exemption will shelter any gains on your home from tax. By the way, your home can include a house, condominium, cottage, mobile home, trailer, live-aboard boat, or a foreign property. Sorry, but vacant land or a rental property that you've never lived in won't qualify as your principal residence.

Sheltering Pre-1982 Gains

As I've already mentioned, your family is entitled to only one principal residence exemption. This simply means that, if you own more than one property that has appreciated in value, you may have to pay some tax at some point. There may be some good news for you, however, if you and your family have owned two properties since before 1982. You see, before 1982 your family was entitled to an exemption for each individual. As a result, it may be possible for you to change the ownership of one of those properties today to shelter capital gains that had accrued up to 1982. That's right, the tax collector will generally allow a current change in ownership to retroactively shelter pre-1982 gains from tax.

Jim and Angela own two properties, a home in Fredericton, New Brunswick, and a cottage in Gaspé, Quebec. Both properties were purchased back in 1975, and both properties have been jointly owned by the couple since that time. The home is worth $200,000 more today than when the couple bought it in 1975, and the cottage is worth $100,000 more than what they paid. They are selling the cottage this year. Although they'd like to shelter the $100,000 gain on the cottage from tax, they would rather save their principal residence exemption for the home—which they plan on selling in a couple of years. They can, however, take advantage of two principal residence exemptions for years prior to 1982. This means that they'll be able to shelter the pre-1982 gains on the cottage from tax. To do this, however, they'll have to separate their joint ownership of the cottage. They *first paid a visit to a tax professional before arranging for the ownership transfer with their lawyer.*

Many Canadians make the mistake of assuming that, just because they are able to sell a principal residence without paying tax on the capital gains, they should pour more and more money into that residence with the intention of enjoying tax-free returns. Folks, think of your home as an investment. If too much of your money is tied up in your home, are you well diversified? Maybe not. Let's face it, while real estate can provide decent returns on investment, it can also provide big losses too. There may be better places to invest your hard-earned money. Be sure to talk to a financial advisor about what investments make the most sense for you!

Caution!

Folks, this is not something to try in the comfort of your living room. The rules surrounding the principal residence exemption are complex! Be sure to visit a tax pro before getting yourself knee-deep into this tax strategy.

Multiplying the Exemption

Don't forget the tax collector's definition of a family unit for purposes of the principal residence exemption: You, your spouse, and any unmarried kids under age 18. This means that any children who have reached age 18, or are married, will be entitled to their own exemption. This can be great news for the family!

Consider transferring the ownership of a cottage or other property to a child who is eligible for his or her own exemption. This way, the property can be sold at some point in the future, and any gains on the sale can be sheltered by your child's principal residence exemption.

Of course, there could be some unwanted side effects here. First, when you give the property to your adult child, you will be deemed to have sold it at its fair market value at that time. The result? You could end up paying some tax on the gains to-date if the property is worth more than your original cost. This might not be so bad if the gain is small and if you expect the tax savings down the road to be that much greater when your child sells the property.

Second, keep in mind that when you give your property away to your adult child, the property then legally belongs to your child. The question is, can you trust your child to do with the property as you wish? Maybe. But if you're not comfortable with the idea of handing ownership over, you should consider the use of a family trust. (See Tip 9.) The trust will allow you to maintain control over the property while still effectively passing it to your child for purposes of multiplying the principal residence exemption.

In any event, it's going to be important to do things right, so be sure to visit a tax professional before taking your first step to transfer ownership!

TO MAKE A LONG STORY SHORT:

- Every family is entitled, for 1982 and later years, to one principal residence exemption to tax-shelter the profits on the sale of a home.

- Ownership of a second property can be transferred to multiply the available exemptions, but professional tax advice is going to be important here!

Tim's Tip 13: **Plan the family's move carefully to maximize tax benefits.**

If you're going to pack up your bags and move, you might as well do it properly—from a tax point of view.

Why Are You Moving and How Far?

The rules dealing with moving expenses are pretty clear. They say that you're entitled to deduct costs for making a move to start a business, begin working at a new location, or go to school. To boot, you're only entitled to claim expenses when your new residence is at least 40 kilometres closer to your new work location or school than

When you claim your moving expenses in the year of your move, report all eligible expenses on Form T1M and file it with your tax return. If you're not able to claim all your expenses because your income at your new location is not high enough, don't worry—file Form T1M anyway. The tax collector will keep a record of the costs you reported on the form and will allow a deduction in the following year. Be sure to keep all your receipts for the costs you claim. The tax collector may want to see them.

your old residence. By the way, that's 40 kilometres taking the shortest normal route of travel—not *as the crow flies*, which used to be the test.

Most importantly, you're only entitled to deduct costs up to the amount of income you've earned in the new location. Not to worry, if you can't claim all your moving costs in the year of your move because your income from the new location is too low, you'll be able to carry those expenses forward to claim them in the next year, subject to the same restrictions. The types of expenses you can deduct include:

• travelling costs, including meals and lodging
• moving and storage costs for your household effects
• lease cancellation costs
• selling costs for your old home, including real estate commissions
• legal costs on a new home purchase
• land transfer tax payable on the new home, if you've sold your old one
• costs of maintaining a vacant former residence (including mortgage interest and property taxes to certain maximums)
• cost of revising legal documents to reflect new address, replacing driver's licences, auto permits, and utility connections and disconnections. Want to maximize your claim? Here's my advice: Plan your move so that it coincides with a new work or school location, and make sure you meet the 40-kilometre test. If you're a student, don't forget that scholarships, bursaries, and research grants qualify as income in your new location, provided the amounts are taxable.

Moving to a New Province?

If you're going to be moving to a new province, keep in mind that you're considered to be a resident of the province where you lived on December 31. Why is this so important? Simple. You're going to pay tax to the province in which you reside on December 31. So here's your game plan: If you're moving to a province with lower tax rates, make the move before the end of the year if you can. This way, you'll take advantage of those lower rates sooner. If your new province has higher tax rates, consider waiting until the new year to make the move. You'll enjoy your current lower tax rates for an extra year.

TO MAKE A LONG STORY SHORT:

- You can deduct costs for moving as long as you're moving to a new work location or to school, and your new home is at least 40 kilometres closer than your old home.
- Plan your move so that it coincides with a new work or school location and meets the distance test.
- If you're moving to a new province, time your move to take advantage of lower tax rates.
- Remember that you can pay an adult child to help in the move and then deduct this as an expense. (See Tip 8/ earlier in this chapter.)

Claiming Family Care Costs

Tim's Tip 14: **Maximize the base for your child care expenses.**

By the time you're reading this, my wife and I will have had our first child! My first-hand experience with diapers, strollers, and child care expenses is bound to grow exponentially. Well, I have to admit, child care expenses are something I do happen to know about already—from a tax angle. Let me tell you about them.

Gimme the Facts

Child care expenses can be claimed when you've incurred them to enable you or your spouse to earn an income. In a two-parent family, the lower-income spouse has to claim the expenses in all but a few situations. If you're a single parent, you'll be allowed to make a claim as well. By the way, the tax collector changed the rules in the 1998 federal budget to allow child care expenses to be deducted where a single parent is in school full- or part-time or where both parents in a two-parent family are in full- or part-time study at a post-secondary school.

There has been talk that it's possible to deduct child care costs as a business expense. While there was some uncertainty around this issue in the past, this isn't the case any more! A 1993 Supreme Court decision (*Symes v. Canada)* made it clear that you won't be able to deduct these costs as a business expense. Too bad, really. Nevertheless, if you've claimed child care as a business expense in the past, you can expect a reassessment if the tax collector catches the write-off.

Caution!

You're not necessarily going to be able to deduct every dime of your child care expenses. There are some restrictions here, although the limits were increased in the 1998 federal budget. In a nutshell, you'll be able to deduct up to $7,000 of costs for each child under age 7 on December 31 or who suffers from a severe or prolonged physical or mental infirmity. The amount is reduced to $4,000 for kids age 7 to 16 in the year, or for those over age 16 suffering from a less severe infirmity who are still dependent on you. I should mention that the tax collector might further restrict your child care deductions. The tax collector will calculate two-thirds of your *earned income* for child care purposes (basically your employment and self-employment income) and, where this figure is less than the limits I've already mentioned, you'll be limited to two-thirds of your earned income.

CHILD CARE DEDUCTIONS: MAXIMUM CLAIM*			
		Child Is Infirm	
Age of Child on December 31	No Infirmity	Severe and Prolonged	Less Than Severe
Under Age 7	$7,000	$7,000	$7,000
Age 7 to 16	$4,000	$7,000	$4,000
Over Age 16	None	$7,000	$4,000

*The maximum deduction is two-thirds of earned income, or the amount in the table, whichever is less.

Child care expenses include payments for baby-sitters, day nursery services, boarding schools, and camps. You should know that deductions for payments to a boarding school or camp are limited to $150 per week of attendance for kids under 7 years of age, and $90 per week for kids 7 to 16.

So when, exactly, is the higher-income spouse allowed to claim the child care expenses? When the lower-income spouse was at school full- or part-time, in a prison or similar institution for at least two weeks in the year, certified to be incapable of caring for children, confined to a wheelchair or bed for at least two weeks, or separated due to a marriage breakdown. If you're the higher-income spouse claiming the child care expenses, you'll be limited to $150 per week for each child under age 7 or infirm, and $90 for kids 7 to 16. Hardly fair, is it?

Increasing the Base for Your Claim

The tax collector does not attach specific child care expenses to specific children. All that matters is that your total expenses deducted for all the kids not exceed the number of kids multiplied by the maximum expenses allowed for each child. Confused? Lindsay, Logan, and Jamie will help to make things clear.

*indsay is twelve years old. Her brother Logan is nine, and
sister Jamie is six. Their parents spent $13,000 on child care
this year ($8,000 for Jamie, $5,000 for Logan, and none for
Lindsay). Their parents figure they can deduct a maximum of
$7,000 out of $8,000 spent for Jamie, plus another $4,000 out of
$5,000 spent for Logan, for a total of $11,000. They were
mistaken. The tax collector doesn't attach costs to specific
children. Their parents were actually entitled to claim up to
$15,000 ($4,000 for Lindsay, $4,000 for Logan, and $7,000 for
Jamie). Since their total costs are just $13,000, they'll be entitled
to deduct the full costs incurred in the year!*

Here's the moral of the story: Remember to report all your
children age 16 or under, or those with infirmities, on your tax
return—even if you didn't incur expenses for some of them. This will
maximize the base for your child care deduction.

TO MAKE A LONG STORY SHORT:

- Claim child care expenses where they were incurred to allow you or your
  spouse to earn income.

- The amount deductible will be based on the age of your child and
  whether or not he or she has any infirmities.

- Maximize the base for your claim by reporting all your kids 16 or under on
  your tax return, even if you didn't incur child care expenses for some of
  them.

Tim's Tip 15: Challenge the tax collector if a disability credit is disallowed.

You know, there are certain tax breaks available to those who suffer
with disabilities. The problem is, it can be like pulling teeth to

convince the tax collector that the disability is severe enough to warrant tax help. You're entitled to a disability tax credit worth $720 annually, but only where you have a severe and prolonged impairment which "markedly restricts a basic activity of daily living." By the way, the impairment must have lasted or be expected to last for one year or more, and your disability will have to be verified by a medical doctor, optometrist, audiologist, occupational therapist, or psychologist, on Form T2201, which should be filed in the first year you make a claim for the credit.

You might be surprised at what will not qualify. In one case, a gentleman was unable to visit the washroom on his own because of a disability. His disability, however, was viewed by the tax collector as being less than severe, and no disability credit was allowed. Fair? Probably not. Especially when you consider that the government already admitted to the severity of his disability by qualifying him for Canada Pension Plan disability payments.

There have been a whole slew of court cases that have dealt with the issue of whether or not certain disabilities will qualify for the tax credit. And you'll be glad to know that the courts have found Revenue Canada to be wrong in disallowing the credit in some instances. So, if your claim for a disability credit has been disallowed and you believe you meet the criteria set out in the Income Tax Act, then consider filing a Notice of Objection or appealing to the Tax Court of Canada (see Chapter 1, Tip 7).

Now picture this: Your child is eligible to claim the disability credit, but doesn't have enough income to take advantage of it. Not to worry, the disability credit can be claimed by you—the supporting person. And there's more. If you support a dependent child who is over age 18 and suffers from a physical or mental infirmity, you'll be entitled to an additional federal tax credit of $400, which will be reduced by 17 percent of the dependent's income over $4,103.

TO MAKE A LONG STORY SHORT:

- You're entitled to a disability tax credit where you have a severe and prolonged disability that markedly restricts a basic activity of daily living.

- The tax collector has not been generous in allowing these credits.

- Consider filing a Notice of Objection or appealing to the Tax Court of Canada if you disagree with the tax collector's disallowance of your claim (see Chapter 1, Tip 7).

Tim's Tip 16: Choose carefully whether to claim attendant care as a deduction or a credit.

If you're disabled, you'll be entitled to claim attendant care costs that you incur to allow you to earn income. The limit for the deduction is two-thirds of your *earned income* which generally includes employment and self-employment income. It used to be that this deduction was limited to two-thirds of your earned income, or $5,000, whichever was less. Thanks to the 1997 federal budget, the $5,000 limit was removed and only the two-thirds test applies.

But before you claim the deduction, you should weigh another option first. You see, you're entitled to claim those attendant care costs as a medical expense credit instead, if you prefer. Recall that we talked about deductions versus credits in Chapter 1, Tip 3. Normally, a deduction will save you at least as much as the credit ever could, and probably more. But in this situation, there's another point to consider: You can claim all the medical expenses on the tax return of either spouse.

You may be better off classifying the attendant costs as a medical expense, particularly when your income is quite low. To figure out which method is better, your best bet is to use a tax software package. If any software package can ensure you're paying less, it's

QuickTax. The folks at Intuit, the makers of QuickTax, know exactly what Canadian taxpayers need. Other packages like HomeTax, CanTax, or TaxWiz do a fine job as well. Of course, you can always have a tax professional do the calculations for you.

TO MAKE A LONG STORY SHORT:

- You may be entitled to claim attendant care costs if you're disabled and require the care to earn income.

- Attendant care costs can be claimed as a deduction or as a medical credit. You'll have to do a calculation to figure out which is best for you and your family.

Surviving Separation and Divorce

It's a sad fact, but the truth is that a growing number of Canadian marriages end up in divorce each year. In fact, in 1967 there were just 55 divorces for every 100,000 marriages that year. Compare that to the 1994 figures, where there were 270 divorces for every 100,000 marriages. This represents an increase of almost 400 percent since 1967. The question is: How does divorce impact the family financially?

Statistics have shown that the median income for all families has increased by 2.9 percent since 1974. Let's break this down into two components: married-couple families; and families where a single parent is the head of the household. For married couples, the median income since 1974 has increased by 10.9 percent, while single-parent families have seen a drop in their median income of 3.4 percent since 1974. The conclusion is obvious: Staying married means greater financial health.

Did You Know?

Under Canadian tax law it's possible for a taxpayer to have more than one spouse! You may even be eligible to claim spousal credits for each of them. I can't recommend marrying more than one person though, this could land you in prison as a violation of other legislation!

Having said all that, I want to talk to those of you who, for one reason or another, are separated or divorced. There will be definite tax advantages to both you and your spouse or ex-spouse if you can agree to structure your affairs so that you're paying the least amount of tax possible.

Tim's Tip 17: Claim the equivalent-to-married tax credit, if applicable.

If you're separated or divorced (those who are single and widowed can also claim this credit) and you're supporting another family member living with you, then you may be entitled to the *equivalent-to-married* tax credit. How much tax can you expect to save? Up to about $1,450, depending on your province.

Specifically, you'll be entitled to claim this credit if you are supporting a person related to you who is living in your residence, and who is under age 18. You can ignore the age 18 requirement if the dependent person is your parent or grandparent, or suffers from a physical or mental infirmity.

TO MAKE A LONG STORY SHORT:

- Claim the equivalent-to-married credit if you are separated, divorced, or otherwise single, and you support a relative who lives with you.

- The credit could save you $1,450 in tax.

Tim's Tip 18: **Avoid a tax hit when splitting retirement plan assets.**

I know that things can get ugly when it comes time to divvy up the assets upon separation or divorce. For a lot of people, much of their net worth is tied up in their RRSP or RRIF. The good news is that the tax collector won't add insult to injury by forcing tax to be paid on RRSP or RRIF assets if they're transferred from one spouse's RRSP or RRIF to the other spouse's plan. As long as the payment is made in accordance with a written separation agreement, or a decree, court order, or judgment, then a tax-free transfer can take place without a problem. I should also mention that transferring assets from a registered pension plan (RPP) to an RRSP or another RPP can also be done on a tax-free basis in the event of a marriage breakdown.

> Upon a marriage breakdown, make sure that any transfers made from one spouse's RRSP, RRIF, or RPP to the other spouse's plan are made directly from one plan to the next to avoid tax on the transfer. That is, the plan assets should never actually pass through the hands (or the bank account) of either spouse, otherwise the tax collector will take a share of those assets as though they were taxable withdrawals from the plan.

Caution!

All of this invites the question: Who is going to pay the tax when the withdrawals are made from the RRSPs later? It's quite simple. The annuitant spouse will. If, for example, you transfer some of your RRSP assets to your spouse's plan upon a marriage breakdown, your spouse will be taxed on the withdrawals from his or her plan, and you'll continue to pay tax on any withdrawals made from your own plan. Make sense?

You'll also be glad to know that the rules that would normally apply to discourage withdrawals from a spousal RRSP (see Chapter 6, Tip 72) won't apply here.

TO MAKE A LONG STORY SHORT:

- When dividing up the assets after separation or divorce, avoid taxes on the transfer by splitting RRSP or RRIF assets in accordance with a written separation agreement or a decree, court order, or judgment.

Tim's Tip 19: Maximize Child Tax Benefits by applying for one-income status.

If you happen to have kids under the age of 18, you may be entitled to collect Canada Child Tax Benefits from the tax collector. Now these benefits won't make you rich, but they're better than a kick in the pants. Your benefits are based on the combined income of you and your spouse.

Currently, the benefits are $1,020 annually for each child, plus an additional $75 for the third and subsequent children, and $213 per child under age seven when no child care expenses are claimed. Once your family income reaches $25,921, these benefits are phased out.

There could be more in store for you. If your income is low, you may be entitled to a *National Child Benefit Supplement* of $605 for the first child, $405 for the second child, and $330 for the third and additional kids. This benefit is phased out beginning at $20,921 of income.

Since your benefits are based on the combined incomes of you and your spouse, the benefits will be clawed back quite quickly for many Canadians. However, when your marriage breaks down, the parent with whom the kids will be living is able to make a special election— within 11 months following the month of marriage breakdown—to base the benefits on the income of that spouse only. That is, the estranged spouse's income will be ignored in the benefit calculation. Making this election could put hundreds of extra dollars in the pocket of the spouse making the election.

TO MAKE A LONG STORY SHORT:

- Canada Child Tax Benefits are based on the combined incomes of both spouses and, as a result, often quickly disappear.

- Make an election within 11 months of marriage breakdown to have the benefits based on one income only. This may increase the benefits significantly.

Tim's Tip 20: **Consider splitting real estate when dividing up assets.**

I've already talked about the benefits of the principal residence exemption (see Tip 12). That's the exemption that allows you to sell your home at a profit without paying any tax on the gain. The problem, of course, is that each family is entitled to just one exemption. This is a problem, particularly where the family owns more than one property—perhaps a cottage or other vacation property in addition to the family home. Oddly enough, separation or divorce provides an opportunity to multiply the exemption. You see, once you're separated or divorced, you are considered to be your own "family," and you'll be entitled to your own principal residence exemption.

So, where two properties are owned, it makes a whole lot of sense from a tax point of view to give each spouse one property when splitting the spoils. That way, *both* properties can eventually be sold with any gains sheltered from tax.

TO MAKE A LONG STORY SHORT:

- Each family is entitled to just one principal residence exemption, but each separated or divorced person is entitled to his or her own exemption.

- Where the family owns more than one property at the time of a separation or divorce, it makes sense from a tax point of view to give each spouse one property, to multiply the number of exemptions that can be claimed.

Tim's Tip 21: Deduct legal costs incurred to collect support payments.

Legal fees are one of those things that everyone hates to pay. And the tax collector doesn't make things any easier because these fees are not often deductible unless you're running a business. There are certain situations, however, when legal fees can be claimed, and collecting alimony or maintenance payments may be one of those situations.

The rules say that where you've paid out legal fees to enforce the payment of alimony, maintenance or support, you'll be able to deduct those fees. This assumes, by the way, that those payments owing to you will be included in your income. To the extent that they are completely exempt from tax, don't expect the tax collector to allow you the deduction.

You'll be out of luck if you hope to claim legal fees paid in connection with a court application to increase or decrease your alimony or support (Quebec is an exception), or to establish a right to alimony or maintenance. There's an exception here. If you had to sue your spouse or former spouse in a Family Court, or under certain provincial legislation, to establish a right to maintenance, then the legal fees may be deductible.

TO MAKE A LONG STORY SHORT:

- Legal fees are not often deductible, but may be deducted when incurred to enforce your right to receive taxable alimony or maintenance payments.

Tim's Tip 22: **Consider preserving pre-May 1997 support agreements.**

Here's a situation where you're going to have to work closely with your spouse or ex-spouse to beat the tax collector. I know it might be a tall order when the tension between the two of you might be thick enough to cut with a knife, but do yourselves a favour and work together on this. Let me explain.

The Way It Was

There were key changes introduced in the 1996 federal budget that have changed the way child support payments are taxed. It used to be that the payor was able to claim a deduction for the payments made and the recipient spouse was taxed on those payments. While the arrangement may have been frowned upon by many who received the child support (because they were taxed on the payments), it had the advantage of reducing the amount of money ending up in the tax collector's coffers. Here's why: The payor spouse usually has a higher marginal tax rate than the recipient. So the deduction that was claimed usually saved the payor more in tax than it cost the recipient spouse.

Henry and Rosette are separated. Henry earns $70,000 annually and his marginal tax rate is 50 percent, while Rosette earns about $35,000 and has a marginal tax rate of 41 percent. Last year, Henry paid Rosette $10,000 in child support. He claimed a deduction, which saved him $5,000 in taxes ($10,000 x 50 percent). Rosette, on the other hand, reported the $10,000 as income and paid $4,100 in taxes. Combined, Henry and Rosette beat the tax collector by $900 ($5,000 less $4,100). Since the tax savings were in Henry's hands, he agreed to spend the $900 savings directly on his child.

The Way It Is

Things have changed. For any new child support agreements entered into after April 30, 1997, the payor is no longer able to deduct the payments made. On the flip side, the recipient is no longer required to report the payments as income. If you had an agreement in place before May 1997 that either provided for the deductibility and taxability of payments made, or was simply an agreement entered into prior to the federal budget of March 6, 1996, then your agreement escapes the new rules that exclude the payments from being deducted by the payor and taxed to the recipient. If, however, you vary the amounts in the agreement after April 30, 1997, then the new rules will apply. Follow me?

Who really wins under the new rules? The tax collector. If we go back to Henry and Rosette's story, the $900 savings enjoyed on a combined basis is gone under the new rules. Consider keeping pre-May 1997 agreements intact to avoid a windfall to the tax collector. The higher-income parent should consider spending the tax savings on the children to convince the lower-income parent to keep the pre-May 1997 agreement in place.

TO MAKE A LONG STORY SHORT:

- New rules say that child support agreements made or varied after April 30, 1997, provide for payments that are non-deductible to the payor and non-taxable to the recipient. The tax collector comes out ahead under the new rules.

- Consider keeping pre-May 1997 agreements intact to avoid the tax collector's win here.

Getting into the Game

It's time to turn to the Tax Planning Tip Sheet at the front of the book and review the strategies introduced in Chapter 2. Ask yourself, "Does this tip apply to me?" Each *Yes* or *Not Sure* could lead to big tax savings for you and your family.

SIGNING WITH THE TEAM: STRATEGIES FOR EMPLOYEES

*I'm not sure,
but I think my pay
deductions finally
caught up with my
salary.*

3

I f you happen to be one of the millions of employees in Canada today, then you know that Revenue Canada is not exactly bending over backward to provide you with tax relief. Sure, I'll be talking to you about the specific deductions that you're entitled to, but here's a tip for those of you who are employees: While it's important to claim all the deductions possible, you need to focus your energy on other tax planning opportunities. Why? Simply put, the deductions available to employees are very limited, except in special situations. You're going to do yourself a favour by reading this chapter and working with your employer to minimize your tax bill.

Optimizing Employment Benefits

Tim's Tip 23: Take non-taxable benefits as part of your compensation.

You know, I'd have to give most employers a 4 out of 10 on the creativity scale when it comes to compensating employees in Canada. I mean, most employees simply receive a flat salary or hourly wage for the work they perform, with no thought given to the tax bill that the employee is going to face. If employers and employees would give just a little more thought to the way compensation is paid, the results could be very tax-efficient. I'm talking about non-taxable benefits.

*A*llison works for a software company, Software Inc. She has one child, age 7, and her child care costs to enable her to work can be very high—about $6,000 annually after factoring in the tax savings from her child care deductions. How much additional salary does Allison have to earn just to pay for these child care costs? Since her marginal tax rate is 50 percent, the answer is $12,000. That is, an additional $12,000 in salary would leave Allison with just $6,000 after taxes—just enough to pay for the child care. Last year, Software Inc. decided to open a day-care facility right in the building for the benefit of employees. Allison no longer has to pay for day-care services. This benefit to Allison is worth the equivalent of $12,000 in additional salary! The best part, of course, is that Allison is not taxed on the value of the day-care provided to her. This is a non-taxable benefit.

The best part about non-taxable benefits is that they never show up on your personal tax return as income. Now, here's my question: Can you list all the non-taxable benefits you're currently receiving? If the list isn't long, consider negotiating with your employer the next time you take on a new job or are due for a salary review. The following *A-to-Z* list of non-taxable benefits will help you get started. It's divided into four categories: home benefits, family benefits, individual benefits, and workplace benefits. You'll find more information on many of these in Revenue Canada's Interpretation Bulletin IT-470R.

Home Benefits

a. Mortgage subsidies

Did you know that your employer can actually pay for part of your mortgage interest, and the benefit can be tax-free? It's true. Here's the deal: As long as your mortgage interest costs remain at or above Revenue Canada's prescribed interest rate each quarter, there will not be a taxable benefit to you. If, for example, your mortgage interest rate is 7 percent, and Revenue Canada's prescribed rate is just 5 percent, then your employer can pick up the tab for the 2-percent difference. Keep in mind that the benefit must generally be available to all employees.

Caution!

Thanks to the 1998 federal budget, any interest subsidies that your employer provides upon your relocation will now be taxable. I'm talking about situations where you relocate for work and take on a larger mortgage or higher mortgage rate as a result. Any help from your employer will now give rise to a taxable benefit, where it would not have in the past! Sorry for the news.

b. Relocation costs

If your employer requires you to relocate and reimburses you for costs associated with making the move, this reimbursement is not taxable in your hands. An allowance for your relocation costs is a different animal. An allowance is a cash payment to you for which you're not required to provide any receipts to your employer—and it's taxable! So be sure to provide receipts to your employer that cover the payments you receive for relocation.

c. Loss-on-home reimbursement

A woman I know found a new job last year that required her to move from Toronto to Vancouver. She had paid $250,000 for her home in Toronto, and she sold the place for just $235,000 when she made the move. Her new employer picked up the tab for the $15,000 loss she incurred on the sale. The best part is this: She wasn't taxed on this loss-reimbursement. Provided your employer requires you to relocate and doesn't reimburse you for more than $15,000 of losses, you won't face a taxable benefit. Thanks to the 1998 federal budget, you'll face a taxable benefit equal to one half of any loss-reimbursement over $15,000 for relocations after September 30, 1998. Reimbursements for relocations made before this date will be tax-free as long as they are paid before the year 2001.

d. Fair market value guarantee

Suppose for a minute that an employer asks you to relocate, and you're forced to sell your home fairly quickly for a lower price than you might otherwise receive if you weren't in such a hurry. Well, there's good news for you. Your employer can actually guarantee that you'll receive fair market value for your home—to a maximum of $15,000—and you won't be taxed on this benefit. For example, if it can be established that the true fair market value of your home is $175,000, and you're forced to sell quickly for $160,000, your employer can pay the $15,000 difference to you—tax-free. Not a bad deal. If your employer pays you more than $15,000 for a relocation after September 30, 1998, you'll be taxed on one half of the excess as a result of the 1998 federal budget. For relocations before that date, the payment will be tax-free as long as you receive it before the year 2001.

e. Employer home-purchase

I've seen a number of situations where an employer will buy a home from an employee to enable the employee to relocate to a new workplace. Typically, the company will then turn around and sell the home on the open market. This allows an employee to move right away, rather than wait for the right offer on the home. In this case, the benefit to the employee will be tax-free as long as the price paid to the employee does not exceed the fair market value of the home.

f. Remote location benefits

Do you work in a remote location? A remote location is called a *prescribed area*, and it includes many places far south of the Arctic Circle, not just spots where you'll find sub-zero temperatures in July! If you happen to work in a prescribed area, you may be eligible for tax-free benefits in the form of board and lodging, rent-free or low-rent housing, travel benefits, and allowances for a child's education—all paid for by your employer. Generally, it will have been necessary for you to reside in this prescribed area for at least six months.

g. Assets of personal value

Let's suppose for a minute that you've found a computer or a desk that you would really like to have. And what if your employer were to buy the asset for use in the business, and let you make use of the asset? This would be a definite benefit to you, but it would be a non-taxable benefit. Here's the best part: After two or three years, you could simply buy the asset from your employer for its fair market value at that time. Chances are pretty good that the asset will have depreciated in value enough to make the purchase very affordable. By the way, your employer doesn't need to buy the asset to make this idea work. Leasing the asset and allowing you to buy it at the end of the lease term can work just as well.

Family Benefits

h. Personal counselling

This is one of the lesser-known benefits that could really lend you a hand—not only financially, but mentally or physically as well. If your employer pays for counselling related to the mental or physical health of you or someone related to you, the benefit is non-taxable. This might include counselling related to stress management or an addiction, for example. Financial counselling related to your re-employment or retirement is also non-taxable, so if you're due for a severance or retirement package, be sure to negotiate a number of counselling sessions with a tax professional or financial advisor.

Looking for a non-taxable benefit? Consider buying from your employer the vehicle that your employer has been providing for use in the business. You'll manage to save a bundle by buying the vehicle used. Your employer may be willing to offer this opportunity if it's time to upgrade the vehicles anyway. And by the way, making this kind of purchase may minimize the tax cost of the dreaded stand-by charge that applies to you when an employer's vehicle is made available to you (see Tip 28).

i. Day-care services

If your employer provides in-house day-care services, this benefit will be tax-free. You should note that this is different from your employer paying for day-care provided by a third party. Third-party day-care paid for by your employer is a taxable benefit to you, although I should mention that, in this case, you'll still be entitled to claim a deduction for those child care expenses included in your income as a taxable benefit. The deduction is claimed under the regular rules for child care expenses, described in Chapter 2, Tip 14.

j. Transportation passes

If you're an employee of a bus or railway company, you'll be able to accept transportation passes from your employer—tax-free. Things work a bit differently if you're an employee of an airline. In this case, your passes will be tax-free as long as you're not travelling on a space-confirmed basis, and provided you pay at least 50 percent of the economy fare for the flight you're on. There's good news if you're a retired employee of any transportation company at all: You won't be taxed on any passes that you receive.

k. Group plan premiums

Most employees these days are members of a group plan for sickness, disability, or accident insurance. You'll be glad to know that the premiums paid by your employer to this type of plan are tax-free benefits to you. You'll want to make sure, however, that any premiums paid on a disability insurance plan are paid by you, and not your employer. You see, if your employer pays these premiums, any benefits that you receive under the policy will be taxable payments to you. Not so if *you* pay the premiums. Check out your plan at work to ensure that your disability payments would be tax-free if you had to collect.

l. Private health services plans

A private health services plan (PHSP) is a plan set up to cover certain costs not covered by public health insurance. I'm referring to costs like prescription drugs, hospital charges, and dental fees. Any contributions to a PHSP will be a non-taxable benefit to you. By the way, the government changed the rules in the 1998 federal budget to allow self-employed proprietors to deduct PHSP premiums from business income.

m. Disability top-ups

There are a number of Canadians who ran into some difficulty a few years ago when the life insurance company that held their disability policy could no longer make good on disability payments. Where your employer tops up disability payments made to you so that you receive all the benefits you were expecting under your disability policy, those payments will not be taxable to you. This applies to all payments made after August 10, 1994.

n. Death Benefits

Next time you're talking to your employer about non-taxable benefits, ask that a death benefit be paid to your heirs if you happen to die while in the employ of the company. You see, a benefit of up to $10,000 can be paid to your heirs tax-free once you're gone. It's not going to make your family rich, but hey, it's going to cover the cost of your funeral! How's that for practical? I'll talk more about this in Chapter 9, Tip 99.

Individual Benefits

o. Commissions on sales

Picture this. You're an insurance broker and you purchase a life insurance policy for yourself. The commissions owing on the sale are paid to you, just as though you had sold the policy to a third party. Are you taxed on the commissions you receive? No! In fact, any commissions on merchandise that you acquire for your own personal use will not be taxable. Evidently, commissions on sales of investment products to yourself are *not* tax-free. This hardly seems fair in light of Revenue Canada's position on life

It's an interesting fact that tips paid to a waiter or waitress are not caught under the definition of employment income in our tax law. But beware! This does not mean those tips you've received are tax-free. These are considered to be taxable employment benefits—and you're going to have to report them on your personal tax return every year. Revenue Canada has been targeting this industry in order to collect tax that has often been evaded in the past!

Caution!

insurance sales. If you happen to be an investment advisor, keep your eyes and ears open—I'll be pushing Revenue Canada on this issue. You should do the same.

p. Discounts on merchandise

If you're employer sells, say, soap or toothpaste, and you're able to buy those items at a discount, the benefit is not taxable to you. But this benefit doesn't apply to personal hygiene products alone. Any discounts offered by any employer to its employees will generally be a non-taxable benefit. The only catch is that these discounts must be generally available to all employees.

q. Membership fees

Perhaps you like to play golf, squash, or tennis—or just hang out at the social club? Membership fees paid by your employer for social or recreational clubs will generally be a non-taxable benefit so long as the membership is principally for your employer's advantage, rather than your own. Generally, your employer will not be able to deduct these fees for tax purposes. But that may not be a concern— particularly if your employer is a non-profit organization where tax deductions are not important.

r. Gifts

You're entitled to receive gifts from your employer for special occasions like Christmas, your birthday, or a wedding. If the gift is paid for by the company, you're allowed to receive up to $100 in gifts each year without facing a taxable benefit. And in the year you get married, those gifts can total $200. There's one catch here: Your employer will not be allowed to claim the gift as a tax-deductible expense. Talk about nickel-and-diming! Revenue Canada should be ashamed of this non-deductible policy. After all, keeping employees content through such gifts should be viewed as part of the income-earning process.

s. Education costs

There has been some controversy over this tax-free benefit recently. At the time of writing, education costs are still a non-taxable benefit, but you may want to check with a tax professional to ensure nothing has changed in very recent days. Having said this, if your employer pays for certain educational programs taken by you at your employer's initiative, these costs will be non-taxable to you. To ensure these benefits are non-taxable, it should be evident that your employer is benefiting from your education. Generally, if your employer is giving you paid time off to study or attend classes, it will be presumed by the tax collector that your employer is benefiting.

t. Vacation property use

How would you like a few days away at the company condominium in California? If you're required to spend a few days at the firm's property, in Canada or abroad, the benefit will not be taxable to you to the extent the trip is business-related. Be sure to keep an itinerary of scheduled meetings and events as evidence to the tax collector that business activities actually took place.

u. Out-of-town trips

Next time your employer sends you on a business trip, why not extend the trip and turn it into a personal vacation too? Once I was forced to spend a week in Whistler, B.C., learning about advanced tax issues. I thoroughly enjoyed extending that trip by another week just to relax. You see, turning a business trip into a personal vacation will mean that costs paid by your employer will be tax-free benefits to the extent the trip is business-related. This can really cut the cost of any vacation!

v. Host or hostess trip

I was asked to speak at a financial advisors' conference in Halifax last year. On that trip, a woman who worked for a financial planning firm was asked to come along to act as a hostess. The majority of her time was spent helping to organize events and to generally keep the event running smoothly. But she shared with me that she did have some time to relax and take in the scenery. While she was still able to enjoy her time there, the trip was a tax-free benefit to her because her hostess duties took up a substantial part of each day. If you happen to take a similar trip, you'll enjoy non-taxable benefits as well.

Workplace Benefits

w. Meal subsidies

Before you get too excited, I'm not talking here about your employer picking up the weekly grocery tab. But where your employer provides subsidized meals—most commonly at a workplace cafeteria—the benefit will be tax-free, provided you're still required to pay a reasonable charge.

x. Recreational and fitness facilities

More and more employers are recognizing the importance of having healthy employees. As a result, it's more common than ever for employers to provide in-house fitness and recreational facilities. I know of some corporations that go so far as to financially reward employees for maintaining a certain level of fitness. If your employer provides these facilities, the benefit is non-taxable.

Action Step

If your employer already provides a recreational facility at work, ask that a fitness instructor be present at the facility for a certain number of hours each week. It's well accepted that a fitness professional helps to increase the use of the facility at work, and provides for a healthier work force. Your boss might just be shocked at the increased productivity around the office! More and more companies are hopping on this bandwagon. And the best part is that the cost of the instructor will not be a taxable benefit if the instruction is available to all employees.

y. Special clothing and uniforms

Some employers are keen on presenting a certain image or look and, as a result, will provide uniforms or special clothing to their employees. If you're in this boat, you'll be glad to know that the clothing is a non-taxable benefit to you. I met a guy once who really enjoyed wearing his employer-provided pants and jacket out on the town. Let's just say that this guy enjoyed an extra benefit—non-taxable, of course.

z. Transportation to work

How would you like it if your boss insisted on sending a stretch limo to pick you up each morning? The truth is, where your employer provides you with transportation to or from work for security or other reasons, the value of that transportation is a non-taxable benefit. This is not the same, however, as your employer giving you an allowance or reimbursement for transportation that you provide yourself: You could be taxed on that type of benefit.

TO MAKE A LONG STORY SHORT:

- Most Canadian employers lack creativity when structuring employment compensation.

- Receiving a non-taxable benefit is the same as receiving salary or wages that will never show up on your tax return.

- Next time you change employers or re-negotiate your salary or wages, ask for non-taxable benefits to form part of your compensation package.

Tim's Tip 24: Calculate whether a taxable benefit works to your advantage.

There's no question that most benefits your employer provides to you will be taxable as regular income. Want some examples? If your employer pays the premiums on a life insurance policy for you, provides you with a company car, allows you to keep the frequent-flier air miles earned on business trips, buys you a home computer, or provides you with many other benefits—you can expect the value of the benefits to show up on your T4 slip at tax time.

Is this a bad thing? Not necessarily. In fact, where the taxable benefit involves something that you would have bought for yourself anyway, you come out ahead by having your employer pay for it, even if it's a taxable benefit. Consider Floyd's story.

F*loyd wanted very much to have a membership at the local golf club, and decided he was going to join last year. The fees are $5,000 annually. As part of his compensation package he asked his employer to pay for the membership. Floyd felt that he couldn't convince the tax collector that the membership was primarily for his employer's benefit, so he expected the membership to be a taxable benefit. But what was Floyd's true cost of this membership? Just $2,500! Here's why: The $5,000 cost of the membership is added to Floyd's income as a taxable benefit. At a marginal tax rate of 50 percent, Floyd will pay taxes of $2,500 on this benefit. This is a whole lot cheaper than paying for the $5,000 membership himself. Effectively, the taxable benefit cut Floyd's cost in half, given his marginal tax rate.*

If you're going to be taxed on a benefit received from your employer, exactly how much will be added to your income? Simple. You'll be taxed on your employer's cost of the benefit. In Floyd's example, the membership cost his employer $5,000, so Floyd's taxable benefit is $5,000. The good news is that your employer may be able to negotiate lower prices on certain things because of your employer's size and number of employees. If this is the case, the amount of your taxable benefit may be reduced—and your true cost will shrink even further.

TO MAKE A LONG STORY SHORT:

- A taxable benefit will still leave you better off than if you had purchased the item yourself, and is of most value when you would have purchased the item anyway.

- The value of the benefit added to your income is simply your employer's cost of the item—which could be a lower cost than you could have obtained yourself.

Tim's Tip 25: **Negotiate a loan from your employer instead of from a bank.**

Next time you're thinking of borrowing money from the bank for any reason, why not consider approaching your employer for a loan instead? Loans from your employer should be viewed by you—and your employer—as a perk that forms just another part of any creative and tax-efficient compensation package!

I've met more than just a few employees who have received taxable benefits without realizing it. In many cases, even your employer may not realize that you've received a taxable benefit. Do you suppose Revenue Canada will go easy on you if both you and your employer were oblivious to the benefit? Don't count on it! You could end up with a nasty tax reassessment. Consider carefully whether you might be receiving some of these benefits, and ensure you're paying tax on these through your regular tax withholdings.

Caution!

Interest Savings

You see, you could save interest costs if the loan is made at a lower interest rate than you'd pay to the bank. You may have to include a taxable interest benefit in your income, but you're still bound to enjoy savings. How much will your taxable benefit be? Simple. It's calculated as Revenue Canada's (or Revenue Quebec's) prescribed interest rate minus the actual rate of interest you pay. By the way, if you're paying interest to your employer, you've got to make those payments during the year or within 30 days following the end of the year (January 30).

*J*ohn wanted to buy a new car. He figured it would help him in his work since he is always driving clients to and fro. He needed to borrow $10,000 to make the purchase. John approached his employer, who agreed to lend John the $10,000 at an interest rate of 3 percent, although Revenue Canada's prescribed rate throughout the year was 8 percent. What is John's taxable benefit? It amounts to $500, which is simply 5 percent (8 percent minus 3 percent) of $10,000. This taxable interest benefit will appear on John's T4 slip. John's true cost of borrowing is just $550 ($250 in tax on the benefit plus $300 in interest paid to his employer). If John had borrowed from the bank at, say, 8 percent, he would have paid $800 in interest. John saved $250 ($800 minus $550), or 2.5 percent, just by borrowing from his employer.

It's worth mentioning that you won't face any taxable benefit at all if the rate of interest charged by your employer is equal to or greater than commercial rates available from your local bank or other financial institution. This is true even if these commercial rates are lower than Revenue Canada's prescribed rate.

Home Loans

If your employer lends you money to buy or re-finance a home, some special rules apply. And these rules will work to your advantage. In this case, the prescribed rate used to calculate your taxable interest benefit will be either the rate in effect at the start of the loan or the current prescribed rate, whichever is less. The loan is deemed to be a new loan every five years. As a result, the prescribed rate in effect at that time will be the maximum rate for the next five years.

There's more good news if the purpose of your loan was to buy a home because of a job relocation (rather than to re-finance your existing home). In this case, the tax collector will allow you to claim a deduction for the taxable interest benefit on the first $25,000 of the loan. This interest deduction is available only for the first five years of the loan and, to qualify, your relocation must have moved you at least 40 km closer to your new work.

Investment or Automobile Loans

There may be other situations where you'll be entitled to claim a deduction for all or part of the taxable interest benefit. In a nutshell, if you'd be entitled to an interest deduction had you borrowed from the bank instead, you'll also be entitled to a deduction for the interest paid to your employer. And by the way, even where you haven't paid your employer any interest, the amount of the resulting taxable interest benefit is considered by the tax collector to be interest-paid, and may entitle you to a deduction. So if you borrow from your employer to invest, to buy a car for use in your work, or for some other purpose that normally provides you with the ability to deduct interest, you'll reduce your taxable interest benefit.

If you're going to borrow for both deductible and non-deductible purposes, and your employer isn't willing to lend you money for everything, borrow the non-deductible funds from your employer and the deductible from your bank. Here's why: Your true interest cost when borrowing from your employer is likely to be less than the bank's interest, so borrow the funds from your employer that will otherwise cost you the most—the non-deductible funds. Since borrowing from your bank is going to cost you more interest, you might as well get all the breaks you can through deductions.

TO MAKE A LONG STORY SHORT:

- Borrowing from your employer rather than from a financial institution will normally save you interest costs.

- While you will normally have a taxable interest benefit to include in your income, there may be special relief from this taxable benefit if you are borrowing to buy or re-finance a home, or for a purpose that would normally entitle you to deduct interest.

Tim's Tip 26: Opt for stock options or similar tax-efficient compensation.

One of the more creative methods to compensate employees is the good ol' stock option plan. Not sure how this works? Let me explain. A stock option plan will entitle you to buy shares of the company that employs you—or shares of a related company. This purchase will take place at a pre-determined price—called the *exercise price*. Normally, you'd exercise your right to buy the shares only when the fair market value of those shares is higher than your exercise price. After all, why would you want to buy company shares for $10 if the shares are only worth $8? If the shares are ripe for the picking because the market value is higher than your exercise price, then your stock options are said to be *in the money*.

If you were to exercise your stock options for, say, $20,000 while the fair market value of those shares is $30,000, then you've received a benefit from your employment. In fact, you'll face tax on that $10,000 benefit in the year you exercise your stock options. But here's where stock options can be very attractive. Provided certain conditions are met, you'll be able to claim an offsetting deduction equal to 25 percent of the stock option benefit you've reported as income. In my example, you'd include $10,000 in income, but you may be entitled to an offsetting deduction of $2,500. This can make a stock option very tax-efficient.

What conditions have to be met to entitle you to the 25-percent deduction? There are two:

- The shares must be common shares, not preferred shares.
- The stock options cannot be in the money on the day the option is granted.

That is, the fair market value of the shares on the date the options are granted must be no greater than your exercise price. Otherwise, you could exercise your stock options right away and sell your shares that same day for a profit. This is no different than receiving cash, so the tax collector won't allow the 25-percent deduction.

ary's employer, Option Corp., set up a stock option plan for its employees. Cary was granted stock options in 1998 at a time when Option Corp. shares were selling for $10 on the stock market. Cary was granted options to purchase 1,000 shares of Option Corp. at a price of $10 per share—his exercise price. In early 1999, shares of Option Corp. were trading on the stock market for $15, so Cary decided to exercise all his options. Cary paid $10,000 for his Option Corp. shares ($10 x 1,000 shares), but they were worth $15,000 on the date he exercised them ($15 x 1,000 shares). In 1999 Cary will have to report the $5,000 difference as employment income. In fact, this amount will appear on a T4 slip for him. Since the conditions for the 25-percent deduction were met, Cary will also be entitled to claim a deduction of $1,250 (25 percent of $5,000) on line 249 of his tax return.

Things work a little differently if your employer is a Canadian-controlled private corporation (CCPC) and you buy your shares at arm's length from the company. In this event, you will pay tax on that stock option benefit only when you actually *sell* the shares, not when you exercise your options. What's more, you'll still be entitled to the 25-percent deduction I've been talking about, even if you haven't met the two conditions I noted above, as long as you held the shares for two years before selling them.

When you acquire shares under a stock option plan, there's always the risk that you could acquire too much stock in one company—your employer's. Make sure that your overall investment portfolio remains properly diversified. This may mean selling some of those option shares from time to time and reinvesting in other securities. Speak to your financial advisor about proper diversification!

Caution!

Are Stock Options Always a Good Idea?

Do stock options always make sense? Well, not always. You want to be confident of two things. First, you should feel confident that the shares in the company are going to increase in value over time. Only then will you be *in the money*. Second, you want to be confident that you'll be able to sell the shares later. Think back to Cary's example. Cary's purchase may look good on paper, but he won't actually realize a profit unless he sells those shares for a higher value than what he paid. You've got to be able to sell those shares. This can be a problem with private company shares in particular. Before exercising stock options in a private company, you'd better have a way out—in other words, someone to sell the shares to.

Phantom Stock Plans and Stock Appreciation Rights

A phantom stock plan works much like a stock option plan, except that you don't actually acquire shares. Rather, your employer will simply pay, in cash, the difference between your exercise price and the fair market value of the company's shares on the date you exercise your phantom stock options. With a phantom plan you don't have to worry about raising the money to buy the shares and, best of all, you don't have to worry about how you're going to sell the shares later. The drawback? You're not entitled to the 25-percent deduction against your taxable benefit.

A stock appreciation right (SAR) is a combination of a phantom plan and a stock option plan. When it comes time to exercise your SARs, you'll have two choices: buy shares in your employer; or take cash as you would under a phantom plan. Talk about flexibility! The best part of a SAR is this: So long as the employee has the right to choose between shares or cash, and this decision isn't influenced by the employer, then the employee should still be entitled to claim the 25-percent deduction against the taxable benefit reported as income. In my mind, this makes SARs a better choice than straight stock options or phantom plans.

TO MAKE A LONG STORY SHORT:

- Stock option plans can be a very tax-efficient source of compensation, since the plan may entitle you to a 25-percent deduction to offset the taxable benefits.

- These plans are best when you're confident that your employer's shares will increase in value and you'll be able to sell the shares down the road.

- Phantom plans and stock appreciation rights (SARs) are hybrids of a stock option plan, except that they don't require you to buy shares. SARs are especially attractive, since they still offer the potential for the 25-percent deduction.

Claiming Employment Deductions

The fact is, employees are provided very little in the way of deductions. Unless something is specifically allowed as a deduction, then don't count on claiming it. Nevertheless, you certainly don't want to pass up the opportunity to claim what you're entitled to.

Tim's Tip 27: Claim all the employment deductions you're entitled to.

Let's take a look at the things our tax law will specifically allow employees to deduct.

a. Commissioned employee expenses

If you're an employee selling a product or service and you're compensated partially or fully by commissions, you may be able to claim expenses against that commission income. Your employment contract must require you to pay your own expenses, and you must ordinarily be required to carry on your employment duties away from your employer's workplace. The types of expenses you can deduct are as varied as those available to a self-employed person (see Chapter 4), with some exceptions. Most notably, you can only claim expenses up to the limit of your commission income. That is, you can't create a loss with your expenses.

Action Step

Many of the employment deductions I refer to are available only if your employer requires you to pay for certain costs. To ensure you're entitled to claim the costs, your best bet is to put in writing the requirement that you pay for these things. This is done most easily before you start working for an employer.

b. Travel expenses

You can count on deducting any travel costs related to your employment if you were required to pay these costs and did not receive a reimbursement or tax-free allowance to cover those costs. I'm talking about costs such as taxis, trains, planes, buses, parking, or hotels.

c. Automobile expenses

If your employer required you to use your own vehicle in your employment and you did not receive a reimbursement or tax-free allowance to cover your automobile costs, you'll be entitled to claim a deduction for a portion of all your car costs. I'll talk more about this in Tips 28 and 29.

d. Aircraft expenses

If you provided your own aircraft for use in your employer's business, and you did not receive a reimbursement or tax-free allowance to cover your costs of flying the aircraft, you'll be able to claim a deduction for a portion of those costs. Your deductible portion is based on the percentage of flying hours that were spent on business in the year.

e. Cost of supplies

Did you incur any costs for supplies consumed directly in your employment activities? If so, you may be able to deduct these costs at tax time. Your employer will have to verify that you were required to pay these costs yourself and that you did not receive a reimbursement or tax-free allowance to cover them. By the way, supplies can include cellular phone air time and long distance calls, but won't include connection or monthly service charges.

f. Assistant's salary

If your employer required you to pay for an assistant, you'll be entitled to deduct the cost of hiring that person. This includes the wages or salary paid plus your share of any Canada Pension Plan and Employment Insurance premiums paid.

g. Home office expenses

In certain situations, you'll be entitled to claim costs for an office in your home. Before you deduct anything, you've got to meet some tests. First, your employer must require you to have an office in your home. Second, your home must either be your principal place of employment (meaning half your work is performed there), or it must be used on a regular and continuous basis to meet people as part of your work. Employees will generally be restricted to claiming a portion of any rent, utilities, repairs, maintenance, and supplies associated with the office space. Commissioned employees can add a portion of property taxes and home insurance to the list of eligible expenses. The deductible portion depends on the percentage of your home used as your office. I'll deal with home offices for the self-employed in Chapter 4.

h. Office rent

If your employer required you to pay your own office rent, you'll be able to deduct the cost of that rent. Sorry, this does not include rent for space in your own residence. See my previous point on home office expenses for more information on using your home as your workplace.

i. Attendant costs

When you have a severe and prolonged impairment and you need to hire an attendant in order to perform your duties of employment, you can claim a deduction for the attendant costs, up to a maximum of two-thirds of your earned income. See Tip 16 for more details.

j. Union and professional dues

You can deduct union or professional dues if you had to pay those dues to maintain your membership in a union or

to maintain your professional status in an organization recognized by statute. Sorry to disappoint you, but you can't claim a deduction for dues to a voluntary organization: Only the self-employed can write off those costs.

k. Musician's instruments

If you are employed as a musician and are required to provide your own instruments, you'll be able to claim a deduction for the cost of any rental, maintenance, or insurance on the instruments. In addition, if you own the instruments, you'll be entitled to claim capital cost allowance (depreciation) on your instruments. Keep in mind that your total deductions cannot exceed your employment income as a musician.

l. Artists' expenses

If you earn employment income from artistic activities, then you'll be entitled to claim a deduction for virtually any un-reimbursed costs incurred to earn that employment income. Your total deduction is limited to 20 percent of your income from artistic employment activities, or $1,000, whichever is less. Oh yeah, I should mention that this $1,000 limit is reduced by any interest or CCA claimed for work-related use of your automobile, or by any claim for musician's instruments.

m. Legal fees

If you had to pay a lawyer to collect or a establish a right to salary, wages, alimony, or maintenance payments, then those fees will normally be deductible. The general rule of thumb is this: If you pay legal fees to recover income that will be taxable to you, it's very likely you'll be entitled to a deduction for those costs. You'll also be entitled to claim a deduction for legal fees paid to file a Notice of Objection or Appeal against the tax collector. See Tip 7.

n. Clergy deduction

Are you a member of the clergy? If so, you may be entitled to a deduction equal to the fair market rent on your home. And this deduction is available even if you own your home. As you may be aware, anyone claiming this deduction can, at one time or another, expect some queries from the tax collector, who will want evidence that you're actually ordained or otherwise entitled to the deduction.

Last Thoughts

When claiming certain employment expenses, you must file form T777 (Statement of Employment Expenses) and form T2200 (Declaration of Conditions of Employment). The T2200 form must be signed by your employer. Ask your employer for a signed T2200 each January, and if you leave an employer part way through the year, get a signed T2200 before you go.

I should also mention that, when you make a claim for employment expenses and your employer happens to be registered for GST purposes, you'll generally be able to claim a GST rebate for the GST paid on the expenses you're deducting. To claim this rebate, you'll have to file form GST370. The GST rebate is taxable in the calendar year in which it's received.

Finally, always be sure to keep the receipts that support any expenses you claim, if the receipts are not filed with your tax return. The tax collector may ask to see them later.

TO MAKE A LONG STORY SHORT:

- Employees aren't given a lot of breaks in the form of deductions.

- Claim all the deductions you're entitled to, and make sure you obtain a signed form T2200 where necessary.

- Remember to claim a GST rebate where possible, using form GST370.

- Always keep your receipts on file in case the tax collector wants to see them.

Driving Automobiles on the Job

I was sitting in a restaurant in Red Deer, Alberta, not long ago, and I couldn't help but overhear a rancher from Red Deer bragging to the owner of a small farm from Lloydminster, Saskatchewan. "I can get in my car at six in the morning," he said, "drive for six hours, spend an hour eating lunch, drive for another six hours, and I still wouldn't have reached the end of my property." "Yeah," the farmer said, nodding sympathetically. "I had a car like that once."

Now there's a man using his car—regardless of its condition—for his work. Do you use your car in your employment? Now, I'm not talking about driving from home to work and back again. I'm talking about using your car for other employment activities on a regular basis. Perhaps you're one of the few who has been provided a car by your employer. What a perk that is! Or is it? Let's talk about automobiles and employment.

If you earn employment income from a prescribed international organization, including the United Nations or any specialized agency that has a special relationship with the United Nations, your employment income is likely 100 percent tax-free! Don't believe it? Check out subparagraph 110(1)(f)(iii) of the Income Tax Act!

Tim's Tip 28: Say "thanks, but no thanks" when offered a company car.

There's a definite misconception that an employer-provided vehicle is a sign that you've "made it." You've arrived. You're loved so much by the company that they insist on showering you with benefits, not the least of which is a luxurious company car.

Yeah, right.

If your employer provides you with a company car, your taxable benefit from the stand-by charge every year could be high enough that, after just four years, you will have effectively paid tax on the original purchase price of the car! How's that for a tax hit? Reduce the tax hit by keeping your personal use to under 12,000 km each year and to less than 10 percent of total time the car is available for use. If you can't manage this, then consider giving up the company car!

Caution!

In many cases, it's going to hurt you to have a company car at your disposal. Why? Because the tax collector may require you to pay tax on two separate benefits. The first is called a *stand-by charge*, and the second is an *operating cost benefit*.

Stand-By Charge

There's nothing uglier than a stand-by charge in my estimation. Here's how the rule works: A taxable benefit called a stand-by charge will be added to your income and reported on your T4 slip just for having a company car at your disposal. The government figures that there's got to be some personal benefit to you, so you ought to be taxed somehow. The stand-by charge is calculated as 2 percent of the original cost of the car (or two-thirds of the lease payments, if the car is leased) for each month that the car is available to you. That works out to be 24 percent of the original cost of the car each year! You'll be able to reduce this taxable stand-by charge only if two conditions are met. First, your business use must be over 90 percent of the total kilometres driven; and second, your personal use of the car must be less than 12,000 km in the year. Don't bother counting those trips straight from home to the office and back again as business kilometres: They won't generally qualify.

By the way, to add insult to injury, the tax collector will also add 7-percent GST to your taxable benefit (15-percent HST in Nova

Scotia, New Brunswick, and Newfoundland). In Quebec, the additional tax amounts to 7-percent GST plus 7.5-percent QST.

Operating Cost Benefit

If your employer pays for any operating costs on the car (insurance, gas, repairs, etc.), then you'll face an operating cost benefit. For 1998 the calculation is 14 cents per kilometre for each kilometre of personal use (11 cents per kilometre for automobile salespeople). If you reimburse your employer for all operating costs within 45 days after the end of the year (that is, by February 14 each year for the previous year's operating costs), then you'll avoid this operating cost benefit altogether.

There's another acceptable way to calculate your operating cost benefit where your business use of the car is greater than 50 percent. To take advantage of this second method, you've got to inform your employer in writing before December 31 that you'd rather use the alternative method of calculating the operating cost benefit. This method allows you to simply take 50 percent of your stand-by charge as your operating cost benefit. Which method is best for you? In a nutshell, you'll prefer this second method if the cost of the car is fairly low and your personal kilometres are close to 50 percent of the total kilometres driven. But remember: Not more than 50 percent is allowed here.

Know Your Options

Should you always say no thanks to a company car? Generally, I discourage employees from taking a company car. Here's why: The stand-by charge you're going to face is always based on the original cost of the car, even as the car depreciates in value over time. This is a bad deal if there ever was one. In most cases, it'll be better for you to provide your own car, and then take an allowance or reimbursement from your employer to cover the costs of using your car for work. I'll talk more about this in a minute.

If you're going to accept a company car, here are three things to keep in mind:

! Consider buying the car from your employer after two or three years to avoid a consistently high stand-by charge on a vehicle that has depreciated in value.

! Avoid company cars that cost over $26,000. You see, this will lead to a double-tax problem. Your stand-by charge will be based on the full cost of the car, but your employer will only be entitled to depreciate $26,000 (plus GST and PST) of that car. The excess over $26,000 is effectively taxed twice.

! Minimize the amount of time the car is available to you for personal use. If, for example, you park the car at your employer's place of business at the end of the work day, you could argue that the car is not available to you for personal use that day. If the car is only available to you 345 days each year, rather than 365, you'll effectively face a stand-by charge for just 11 months instead of 12 months because of the way the calculation is done.

TO MAKE A LONG STORY SHORT:

- You may face two different taxable benefits if your company provides you with a car: a stand-by charge and an operating cost benefit.

- In most cases, you'll be better off providing your own car to avoid these taxable benefits, and then taking an allowance or reimbursement from your employer for use of your car at work.

Tim's Tip 29: Claim automobile expenses that exceed your allowance or reimbursements.

So, you're convinced that providing your own car for use at work is better than using a company car. Great. Now how is this use of your car going to save you tax? The rules can be kind of tricky, but I'll walk you through them.

Reimbursements and Allowances

First, you need to understand the difference between a reimbursement and an allowance. A *reimbursement* is never taxable. If, for example, you incurred certain car expenses on the job and you submitted actual receipts to your employer for reimbursement, you would not be required to include that reimbursement in your income.

An *allowance* is different. It's a payment from your employer for which you are not required to provide actual receipts. That is, you're not required to account for the payments received. Is an allowance taxable to you? It all depends. Let me explain.

An allowance paid to you for using your own car for work will be non-taxable if it is considered *reasonable*. The allowance will generally be considered reasonable if it's based on actual kilometres driven for work. That means you'll need to keep a daily driver's log showing how many kilometres you've driven and the purpose of the trip. If you meet this test then the allowance is tax-free. If the allowance is not based on distance driven, then it is not considered to be reasonable, and it must be included in your income. In fact, this type of allowance is supposed to be reported by your employer on your T4 slip each year.

Claim Those Deductions

When do you suppose you're entitled to claim a deduction for automobile expenses? Well, you can forget about a deduction if you were fully reimbursed for your expenses, or if you received a reasonable allowance and you accepted that allowance as tax-free compensation.

You're entitled to a deduction if you received an allowance that's not reasonable—in other words, an allowance that is not based on distance driven and that is treated as taxable income. In this case, your deductible expenses help to offset the income.

But what if you received an allowance that is based on distance driven, and therefore would normally be considered reasonable, except that you feel the allowance is not reasonable at all because your actual business-related automobile expenses are greater than the

WHEN CAN YOU DEDUCT AUTOMOBILE EXPENSES?

	If you received a reimbursement	If you received an allowance
Amount received is reasonable	Reimbursements are always tax-free. You cannot claim a deduction for automobile expenses that have been fully reimbursed.	Allowances are considered reasonable if they are based on kilometres driven. In this case, the allowance is tax-free and you cannot claim a deduction for automobile expenses.
Amount received is not reasonable	If you were not fully reimbursed for your automobile costs, and no allowance was received, you may deduct the costs incurred over and above your reimbursements.	Allowances are not reasonable when they ignore kilometres driven, or when the employee otherwise considers the allowance not reasonable. In this case, the allowance is taxable and you can claim a deduction for actual expenses.

allowance? In this case, you have the option of including that "unreasonable" allowance in your income and claiming a deduction for your actual automobile expenses.

Here's the rule of thumb: If your allowance based on distance driven is less than your actual car expenses, then consider the allowance to be unreasonable, include it in your income, and claim a deduction for those actual car expenses. Likewise, if you have not been fully reimbursed for your actual car expenses, claim a deduction.

What to Claim—and How

You're entitled to claim a portion of all your operating costs. These costs include gas, oil, repairs, insurance, licence, cleaning, and auto club fees—to name a few. In addition, you can claim depreciation—called capital cost allowance (CCA)—on the cost of your car. Keep in mind, however, that the maximum cost you can depreciate is $26,000 (plus GST and PST) for 1998. If your car costs more than this, you won't be entitled to any tax relief for the excess.

Interest costs on a loan to buy your car are also deductible. But there are limits here. For 1998, the maximum that can be deducted is $250 per month.

Finally, if you lease your car rather than own it, you'll be entitled to claim a deduction for a portion of your lease costs. The maximum deduction in 1998 is $650 (plus GST and PST) for each month you leased the car.

To determine the portion of your automobile expenses that you can deduct:

Action Step

Be sure to maximize the employment use of your car to maximize your deduction. This can be done by visiting clients and suppliers, or making other business stops on the way to or from work. This will turn non-business kilometres into business kilometres. Also, consider using one car only for work to simplify your record-keeping.

add up the kilometres driven for work in the year, divide that by the total kilometres driven in the year, and multiply by 100. The result is the percentage of the expenses you can deduct.

As I mentioned at the end of Tip 27, you'll need to file form T777 with your tax return, and your employer will have to sign form T2200 to verify that you were required to use your automobile for work. I also talked about the GST rebate which you may be entitled to claim using form GST370.

TO MAKE A LONG STORY SHORT:

- A reimbursement and an allowance are different things. A reimbursement requires that receipts be provided to your employer, while an allowance does not.

- Reimbursements and reasonable allowances based on kilometres driven are not taxable. Unreasonable allowances are taxable.

- Claim a deduction for automobile expenses if you have not been reimbursed, or if your actual expenses are greater than your allowance received.

Deferring Compensation

You'll recall from Tip 4 that pushing your tax bill to a future year almost always makes sense. But given today's tax law, it's not so easy to take a portion of your employment income and arrange to pay tax on it a year or two down the road. You see, the Income Tax Act has rules to govern these salary deferral arrangements. For example, if you earn $75,000 in 1998 but agree with your employer that you'll take $50,000 in 1998 and $25,000 in 1999, you're going to face tax in 1998 on the full $75,000. Sorry about that. But don't fret. There are some ways you can escape the salary deferral rules. Wherever it's possible and practical, be sure to defer your income to a future year by taking advantage of these ideas.

Tim's Tip 30: **Defer tax with an RPP, RRSP, or DPSP.**

Registered Pension Plan (RPP)

A registered pension plan (RPP) at work operates much like your RRSP. Putting money into an RPP, however, will limit your ability to use an RRSP. The government imposes this limitation through something called your *pension adjustment*. You see, the tax collector doesn't want you to have an unfair advantage over those who save through an RRSP alone for retirement. An RPP allows you to defer tax on your employment income by providing a tax deduction for the money you contribute to the plan. You'll face tax when funds are paid to you out of the pension plan, but this won't likely be for a number of years.

I'll make this one comment: I'm not a big fan of company pension plans in many situations. The reason? If you don't plan on staying with the same employer for the better part of your working career, you may actually lose a portion of your retirement savings every time you move from one employer to the next. Since the average Canadian is likely to change jobs a number of times in a lifetime, a lot of people could be short-changed in saving for retirement. I prefer an RRSP alone in many—but not all—situations. You may want to talk this issue over with a tax professional or a financial advisor.

Registered Retirement Savings Plan (RRSP)

I suppose that registered retirement savings plans (RRSPs) are one of the more familiar tax-deferral vehicles available today. I won't go into much detail on these now because I've devoted Chapter 6 to retirement savings. Suffice it to say that your RRSP may be the most effective method to push the tax on your employment income to a future year. It's no secret how this works. If you earned $40,000 and had accumulated RRSP contribution room of $10,000, you could contribute the full $10,000 to your RRSP and deduct that amount from your income for the year. In effect, you'd pay tax on only $30,000 of your employment income. And the $10,000 would grow tax-deferred in your RRSP. In fact, you won't pay tax on those funds until you make withdrawals later in life. Can't get a better or more direct deferral than that.

Deferred Profit Sharing Plan (DPSP)

With a deferred profit sharing plan (DPSP), your employer may contribute up to 18 percent of your income or $6,750 (for 1999), whichever is less. You can't make contributions to a DPSP—only your employer can. As a result, you're not entitled to a deduction for DPSP contributions. These contributions are based on your employer's profitability, and so there may not be any contributions in years where the company loses money.

How are these contributions taxed? The funds will grow inside the DPSP tax-deferred, and you'll pay tax on the amounts paid out of the DPSP to you. With most DPSPs, taxable payments can be made to you over a maximum ten-year period which, by the way, is going to result in a longer deferral of tax than simply paying the funds out in one lump sum. You might even consider rolling some of the payments out of your DPSP into your RRSP, RPP, or a term annuity not exceeding 15 years—just to defer tax even longer. Money contributed to a DPSP will reduce the amount that you can contribute to your RRSP in a manner similar to RPPs. By the way, some of the proceeds out of your DPSP may be tax-free if they represent your pre-1991 contributions made at a time when employees were allowed to contribute to DPSPs.

TO MAKE A LONG STORY SHORT:

- A registered pension plan (RPP) can provide a deferral of tax on your employment income, although in many cases I prefer an RRSP to an RPP when given a choice.

- An RRSP is the most common tax-deferral vehicle in Canada and, like an RPP, provides a direct deferral of tax on employment income.

- A DPSP is a plan to which your employer alone can contribute.

- Contributions to RPPs and DPSPs will reduce the amount you can contribute to your RRSP.

Tim's Tip 31: Push the tax on your bonuses to a future year.

If you're entitled to a bonus for work performed in a given year, you'll be able to defer receipt of that bonus for up to three years, and you won't face tax on the bonus until you actually receive it. How much tax will this save? That depends on the rate of return you can generate on the money you would otherwise use to pay the tax. Consider Eileen's case.

*E*ileen *earned a $10,000 bonus from her employer in 1998 and is due to face a tax bill of $5,000 on that bonus, at her marginal tax rate of 50 percent. Instead, she arranged with her employer to defer receipt of that bonus until December 31, 2001. The result? She's going to face that $5,000 tax bill three years from now when she receives the bonus. Here's her game plan: Eileen expects that she can earn 5 percent after taxes on her money between now and the time her tax bill is due in three years, so she's going to set aside $4,320 today. At her estimated rate of return, that investment will grow to be worth $5,000 in three years. She can then use the funds to pay her tax bill at that* *time. Did Eileen's tax bill really cost her $5,000? No! It cost her just $4,320 thanks to the deferral. That's right, her tax bill cost her just 86 cents on the dollar.*

....

Is there a downside to this idea? Sure. If you're hurting for cash, you may not want to wait for three years. And your employer won't be able to deduct the bonus until the year it's paid.

TO MAKE A LONG STORY SHORT:

- You're entitled to defer a bonus for up to three years. You won't face tax until the year the bonus is paid.

- Deferring the bonus for three years and investing the money you would otherwise pay in taxes will reduce the true cost of that tax bill.

Tim's Tip 32: Consider a leave of absence or sabbatical plan to defer tax.

Who says you have to be a teacher or professor to take advantage of a leave of absence or sabbatical plan? With the help of your employer, you can set up a similar plan. It works this way: You can set aside up to one-third of your salary each year for up to six years. You won't have to pay tax on the portion of your income set aside. Your leave of absence or sabbatical must begin no later than six years after the deferral begins, and must be at least six months long (three months if you are taking the leave to attend an educational institution full-time). For the plan to qualify, you'll have to return to your workplace for at least as long as your leave, and you'll have to pay tax on the deferred income no later than the seventh year whether you take the leave or sabbatical or not.

TO MAKE A LONG STORY SHORT:

- A leave of absence or sabbatical plan will allow you to defer tax on up to one-third of your income for a full six years.

- Certain other conditions must be met for the plan to qualify, and you'll pay tax on the deferred income no later than six years after the deferral begins, whether or not you actually take the leave or sabbatical.

Calling It Quits

There's going to come a day when you won't be working for your employer anymore. Perhaps this is by your own choice—you've put in your dues, and it's time to start a new chapter in life. Maybe it's by your employer's choice—the company might be down-sizing, right-sizing, or whatever you want to call it. In any event, you'll do yourself a real favour by working with your employer to make your departure a tax-efficient one.

For a deferred-salary leave or sabbatical plan to be accepted by Revenue Canada, you must make sure that your employer documents the plan in writing, and that the main purpose of the plan is to fund a leave of absence and not, for example, to provide retirement benefits. If the tax collector looks at the plan as some kind of attempt to defer tax without really funding a leave of absence, you'll face tax on the full amounts as if they were regular salary.

Caution!

Tim's Tip 33: Roll as much as possible of your retiring allowance to your RRSP or RPP.

I met a gentleman about two years ago. After we talked over his financial affairs, it became evident that he had been given a bum steer. You see, the gentleman had one thing on his mind: paying down his mortgage with his retiring allowance. When he retired from

When you receive a retiring allowance, it's not critical that the allowance be transferred directly to your RRSP when it's paid out. But be sure to contribute those funds to your RRSP within 60 days following the end of the year that you received the payment—that is, by March 1, 1999, for retiring allowances received in 1998, or February 29, 2000, for allowances received in 1999. See Tip 68 for more.

his last job, a "counsellor" in his former workplace somehow forgot to inform this man that he was able to roll a good portion of his retiring allowance to his RRSP or RPP. It seems that this "counsellor" liked the idea of paying down the mortgage as well. As a result, this man took his $60,000 retiring allowance, handed $30,000 to the tax collector, and used the remaining $30,000 to pay down his mortgage.

It takes a lot to get me angry folks, but this type of misguided advice makes me steam. Remember this: There is no better option for your retiring allowance than to roll it to your RRSP where you'll defer tax until you make withdrawals. Yes, this is your best option in virtually every case, even if you have a mortgage outstanding. If you don't make this rollover, you're going to face tax, all at once, on any retiring allowances you receive. The gentleman in my story could have made regular withdrawals from his RRSP to meet his mortgage payments, and the mortgage still would have been paid off by the time he was 63 years of age. In the meantime, he would have avoided that $30,000 tax hit, and those assets would have grown tax-deferred in his RRSP.

How much of your retiring allowance can you roll to your RRSP? The answer is $2,000 per year of service prior to 1996. In addition, you'll be able to roll $1,500 for each year or part year of service prior to 1989 in which you had no vested interest in any employer's contributions to an RPP or DPSP.

TO MAKE A LONG STORY SHORT:

- Your best option when receiving a retiring allowance from your employer is to roll as much of it as possible into your RRSP or RPP to defer tax as long as possible.

- This rollover must be made within 60 days following the year you receive the payment.

Tim's Tip 34: Consider a non-competition payment for potential tax savings when leaving your job.

A woman that I met worked for a successful office furniture wholesaler. She and her employer came to disagree on a number of issues, and it was agreed that she would leave the company. Her employer was concerned that she might open a similar operation close by, so she agreed not to do this for a two-year period, in exchange for a non-competition payment. How do you suppose this payment should be taxed?

In a recent court case, *Fortinos v. The Queen* (1997), it was held that a non-competition payment was not taxable at all to the recipient. Now, before you get overly excited about this, you should realize that the facts surrounding each case are usually very different, and just because the non-competition payment was not taxable in the Fortinos case does not necessarily mean you'll enjoy the same treatment.

Having said this, it would seem from the arguments put forth in the Fortinos case that if the non-competition payment were in fact taxable, it would most appropriately be taxed as a capital gain, and not as regular income. Think about it for a minute. When you accept a non-competition payment, you are actually disposing of a right that you possess—the right to compete. This right is most certainly an asset of yours, and it would appear to be a capital asset. As a result, if you were to sell or dispose of this right, it makes sense that the payment should be taxed as a capital gain. The benefit, of course, is that capital gains are just 75-percent taxable. Compare this to regular income which is fully taxable, and the tax savings could be significant.

At this point, it's not clear how Revenue Canada will treat non-competition payments in the future, given the outcome of the Fortinos case. Will the payment be tax-free? It's possible. Will the payment be taxable? This is more likely, particularly where you've structured it as a non-competition payment strictly to avoid tax. If the payment is taxable, will it be taxed as a capital gain? This, too, is likely. And in a worst case scenario, you'll be taxed on the non-competition payment as though it were regular income.

General Anti-Avoidance Rule (GAAR)

Now is probably a good time to introduce the concept of the general anti-avoidance rule (GAAR). In a nutshell, our tax law contains a provision known as GAAR that effectively provides Revenue Canada with the ability to shut down any tax planning strategy if the tactic violates the intention or the spirit of Canada's income tax legislation. This means that, even where your strategy is within the letter of the law, it may be shot down if it violates the intention or spirit of the law. Pretty sweeping powers for the tax collector, wouldn't you say? The good news, however, is that there have been very few reassessments under GAAR since its introduction back in 1988. And it's quite a chore for the tax collector to invoke GAAR: Your case has to be transferred to the GAAR committee in Ottawa for review and a decision. And if you don't like the result, you can always file a Notice of Objection or Appeal (see Chapter 1, Tip 7). Nevertheless, a non-competition payment, among other more aggressive strategies, could be subject to GAAR.

Here's my advice: Before entering into a non-competition agreement and taking payment, be sure to visit a tax professional. This is critical. You'll want to talk over the benefits, risks, and any new developments on this issue.

TO MAKE A LONG STORY SHORT:

• A non-competition payment made to you may be very tax-efficient. It would appear, based on the Fortinos case, that the payment will either be tax-free, or taxed as a capital gain. In a worst-case scenario, it'll be taxed as regular income.

• Before entering into a non-competition agreement and taking payment, be sure to visit a tax professional to talk about the benefits, risks, and any new developments on this issue.

Getting into the Game

Whether you're leaving an old job, starting a new one, or heading into this year's performance review, make sure you know all the ways you can maximize your after-tax employment income. Turn now to the Tax Planning Tip Sheet at the front of this book and review the strategies introduced in Chapter 3. Ask yourself, "Does this tip apply to me?" With a little planning, each *Yes* or *Not Sure* might mean more dollars in your pocket.

BECOMING A FREE AGENT: STRATEGIES FOR SELF-EMPLOYMENT

To be successful:
Rise early, work late,
and strike oil.

4

I can still remember those long hot summers when I was a kid—
you know, after school finished at the end of June each year. In
those days, two months of care-free living seemed like an
eternity. I laugh now. Two months these days feels more like two
weeks!

When it got too hot to play outside, my friends and I would
retreat to the rec room. And if it was up to me, we'd pull out a game
like Monopoly—something with lots of strategy, luck, and money.

From the time I was young, I guess I was destined to be an entrepreneur. It's in my blood.

Now, I'm not going to suggest that if you happen to love Monopoly (even the long version) you're destined to be self-employed. But I will say this: If you have the inclination to run your own business—either full-time or part-time—you will significantly increase your tax planning opportunities. Make no mistake: Self-employment is one of the last great tax shelters.

And, like winning a good game of Monopoly, winning the tax game through self-employment can leave you feeling on top of the world.

Jumping on the Bandwagon

No doubt about it, a growing number of Canadians are turning to self-employment for their livelihood. Some out of necessity, but many simply because they recognize the benefits—tax and otherwise. But is self-employment for everyone?

Tim's Tip 35: Count the costs before leaping into self-employment.

The benefits of self-employment are pretty evident: tax breaks, control over your time, and the opportunity to make more money than you ever have before. But hold on a minute. Life isn't always so cheery. Self-employment also brings long hours, a shift in family priorities, and the risk of financial loss. Before jumping into self-employment, you need to evaluate your willingness to do what it takes to be successful at the venture and, just as important, evaluate your likelihood of success.

Let me start by saying that there's nothing more important to the success of a business than experience. I recently asked a very wealthy man how he had made his fortune. He replied, "I became the partner of a rich man. My partner had the money and I had the experience." Then with the slightest pause, he added: "Now he has the experience and I have the money!"

Experience definitely goes to the top of the list. But you'll need more than that. Before leaping into self-employment, consider whether you have these other assets on your side:

• start-up capital

• good business sense

• the drive to succeed

• high energy

• willingness to work long hours

• the education and credentials for your field

• contacts in the industry

• above-average skills with people

• a good credit rating

• the support of your family.

If you come up short in some of these areas, is your business doomed to fail? Not necessarily. And in any case, even if full-time self-employment isn't for you, working for yourself on a part-time basis can provide many of the same tax breaks.

TO MAKE A LONG STORY SHORT:

• Self-employment can offer benefits—not the least of which are tax breaks—but it's not for everyone.

• Know what resources you have, and what you need, before committing to full-time self-employment.

Tim's Tip 36: Structure your work so that you're self-employed, not an employee.

From a tax point of view, it can make a lot of sense to do your work on a contract basis as a self-employed worker, rather than as an employee. You may want to approach your current employer with the idea of resigning and being hired back on this basis. But you'll have to dot your i's and cross your t's here. Just because you call yourself self-employed doesn't mean the tax collector will agree with you. You see, Revenue Canada is more concerned about the true substance of your business relationships than whether you call yourself self-employed. Consider Anwar's story.

If full-time self-employment is not for you, perhaps because the risk is too great or because you have a job you really don't want to give up, consider part-time self-employment instead. Turn that hobby into a legitimate business to make money *and* cut your tax bill.

*A*nwar worked as a software programmer for Acme Software Inc. for seven years. In order to provide Anwar with more tax breaks, and to save the company certain costs, his employer agreed last year that Anwar would resign and the company would hire him back on a contract basis. Anwar still performs most of the work at Acme's offices, and he's still enrolled in Acme's benefits plan. Last year, Anwar claimed a number of expenses against his self-employment income from Acme that he wouldn't have been able to claim as an employee. Revenue Canada took a close look at his relationship with Acme and decided that he's really still an employee of the company. The tax collector has disallowed Anwar's deductions, and reassessed Acme for its share of the CPP and EI premiums that should have been paid. Sadly, the tax collector is likely right in this case.

You see, Revenue Canada looks at four tests to determine whether you're truly self-employed, or just an employee. You'd do well to look at these, too—before the tax collector comes knocking.

- *Control Test.* Do you control when, where, and how you work? If you're in control, this is evidence in your favour that you may be self-employed.

- *Integration or Organization Test.* How vital are you to the organization you're working for? Can it survive without you? The further removed you are from being critical to the company, the easier it will be to convince the tax collector that you're actually self-employed.

- *Economic Reality Test.* Do you assume any financial risks in your work? Do you supply your own tools of the trade? Do you assume any liabilities in your work? Do you perform services for different organizations or at least have the right to do so? If your answers to these questions is generally "yes," this is a stroke in your favour when claiming that you're self-employed.

- *Specific Results Test.* Is there an end in sight to the particular project you've been engaged to work on? Or is your arrangement with the company one where no specific result or end is contemplated? To convince Revenue Canada that you're truly self-employed, you'll need to show that you've been hired to complete a specific task, and that your relationship is not simply ongoing.

Action Step

Make sure that you sign a written contract with any organization that you work for as a self-employed individual. The contract should clearly spell out the nature, extent, and duration of your services. Set up the contract so that you pass the four self-employment tests: control, integration, economic reality, and specific results.

TO MAKE A LONG STORY SHORT:

- Arrange your work relationships so that you're considered self-employed rather than an employee.

- You'll need to pass four tests to convince the tax collector that you're truly self-employed and not simply an employee in disguise.

Tim's Tip 37: **Make sure you have a reasonable expectation of profit.**

You should realize that if you report losses from your business on your personal tax return, these losses are going to offset any other type of income you might report, including employment income, interest or other investment income, or pension income. This is going to save you tax. And reporting losses can be easier than you might think—especially when you're claiming a deduction for a portion of your home costs, such as mortgage interest, against your business income.

Here's the problem: It has been a favourite pastime in recent years for the tax collector to attack taxpayers based on the assertion that there is no reasonable expectation of profit from the business. This same *reasonable expectation of profit* test applies to those with rental properties as well. And where there is no reasonable expectation of profit, our tax law will allow the tax collector to disallow the deductions you've claimed. Most commonly, the tax collector will disallow enough deductions to wipe out that loss you claimed. Trust me, it's an uphill battle fighting Revenue Canada on this issue.

If you're in the middle of a heated battle with the tax collector already, be sure to get professional tax advice, because you're virtually guaranteed to lose the battle on your own. A tax pro will be familiar with the many court cases that apply to your situation. Your best bet, however, is to avoid a problem in the first place. How? In two ways:

Step 1 Prepare a forecast from the start of your business to establish that you do have an expectation of profit. In many situations, Revenue Canada wins the battle simply because it was evident from the start that there was no possible way to make money.

Step 2 Avoid reporting losses year after year. There's nothing that creates a red flag on your tax return like recurring business or rental losses. There's no set number of years that you're allowed to claim losses. Generally, the tax collector will expect you to have some losses in your first year or two as the business gets off the ground. Once you report losses for three or four years, it may become a problem.

Avoid recurring losses by cutting costs. The most common culprit is a deduction for mortgage interest. Commit to paying down that mortgage as soon as possible to minimize the losses created by interest deductions. You might also consider delaying discretionary deductions—like capital cost allowance (CCA). CCA does not have to be claimed in a given year if you prefer not to claim it. You don't lose the CCA deduction, you simply push it to a future year.

TO MAKE A LONG STORY SHORT:

- Claiming losses from your business will save you tax since those losses are applied against other sources of income.

- While claiming losses for a couple of years is not likely to be a problem, recurring losses for three years or more could be a red flag on your tax return.

- Avoid problems with Revenue Canada by preparing forecasts today to support your claim that you have a reasonable expectation of profit, and try to avoid recurring losses.

Choosing Your Business Structure

An important question that you'll face when entering the world of self-employment is this: What business structure are you going to choose? There are three common business structures available to you: a proprietorship, partnership, or corporation. Let's take a closer look at them.

Proprietorship

A proprietorship is you, in business for yourself. A proprietor may have employees, but owns the business alone. Last week I passed some kids at the side of the road selling lemonade, and since I'm always interested in supporting entrepreneurial efforts, I stopped for a drink. Although the kids seemed a little confused when I explained that they were operating a proprietorship, they'll appreciate the education later in life, I'm sure.

The real benefits of a proprietorship are these: There is little or no cost involved to set up your business as a proprietorship; it's as easy as hanging up a shingle or putting up a sign; and there is little government regulation. The only requirement you might have is to register the business name with the provincial government (for example, "John's Heating and Cooling"). And even this requirement can be waived if you simply operate the business under your own name (for example, "John's" or "John Doe's").

Of course, there can be some drawbacks to a proprietorship, too. First, you'll face unlimited liability for the debts and obligations of the business—effectively, you and the business are one and the same. Second, it may be more difficult as a proprietor to raise financing if you need capital to start or expand the business. Third, there's less flexibility when it's time to plan for the succession of your business. Finally, there's the question of image. Is there a risk that others will view your business as a small, unsophisticated operation? Maybe. But in most cases, the fact that you're a proprietorship will have no effect on whether someone retains your services or buys your products.

If you're a proprietor, the profits of your business are yours personally. You must report all the income and expenses of your business on your personal tax return each year (form T2124 for

Operating as a proprietorship could leave you vulnerable to creditors and lawsuits if your business involves significant financial or other risks to you or other people, including your employees. Protect yourself with business insurance, and consider operating through a corporation to limit your liability.

Caution!

business activities or T2032 for professional activities). You don't pay yourself a salary; instead, you simply take cash out of the business for personal use. This is called a *draw*. Of course, if you draw too much, the business may not have enough cash to operate. If you incur losses as a proprietor, those losses are also reported on your tax return, and can be applied against the other sources of income (see Tip 37 for more).

Partnership

A partnership works much like a proprietorship, except that there is more than one business owner. A partnership is really just a group of proprietors joining forces to carry on business together with the idea of generating profits. The benefits to a partnership are these: You're able to share the risks of being in business; you may have greater access to capital; and you can pool your skills.

The truth is, a partnership can also bring new challenges. Think of these as drawbacks if you want. First, you and your partners may not always agree on how the business should be run, and resolving these differences can be tough at times. Second, getting rid of a partner that isn't working out is not exactly an enjoyable task. And finally, a partner is generally liable jointly for the debts and obligations of the partnership.

If you're a partner, you'll be required to pay tax on your share of the partnership's profits. In fact, as with a proprietor, partners are required to report their profits or losses on their personal tax returns. The partnership itself is required to file a partnership information return annually with Revenue Canada.

If you're going to enter into a partnership, even with family members, be sure to visit a lawyer to write up a partnership agreement. This is critical. The agreement should cover issues such as these: how and when the profits of the partnership will be allocated to each partner; how to handle disputes; what to do when a partner dies or leaves the partnership; and whether insurance will be purchased on the lives of each partner.

Corporation

A corporation is a separate legal entity. In fact, a corporation is considered to be a separate *person* for tax purposes. And, just like you, a corporation has to file its own tax returns and financial statements with the tax collector. You can usually tell which businesses are set up as corporations because you'll see the terms *Inc., Incorporated, Corp., Corporation, Company, Ltd.,* or *Limited* after the name of the business.

There are two key benefits to a corporation, and one of these is tax-related. First, a corporation generally offers limited liability protection to its shareholders (the owners). That is, the debts and obligations of the corporation do not become obligations of the shareholders. I should mention that, in some circumstances, a director of a corporation may be liable for certain obligations of the company.

The other benefit is a *tax deferral*. You see, most small Canadian corporations are entitled to an attractive rate of tax on the first $200,000 of *active business income*. That rate is generally 23 percent, although this varies slightly by province. Passive income—generally from investments—in that same corporation will face tax at over 50 percent. Quite a difference! It's the low rate of tax on active business income that provides the opportunity to defer tax. Notice that I didn't call this a permanent tax reduction. This is a tax deferral that lets you push taxes to a future year. And this is great tax planning (see Chapter 1, Tip 4). Consider Astrid's case.

strid's corporation expects to generate $100,000 in income this year. Astrid's going to pay herself $60,000 in salary, which keeps her income below the highest marginal tax bracket. If she were to receive any more salary, each additional dollar would face tax at about 50 percent in her hands (see page 272 for actual rates). The remaining $40,000 will be left in her corporation, where it will be taxed at just 23 percent. Her tax deferral in this case is about 27 percent (50 minus 23 percent). Once Astrid pays the remaining $40,000 out of the company, she'll face tax personally and the tax deferral will be over. But until that point, she saves herself tax dollars.

There are two drawbacks to a corporation. The first is the cost of setting it up and maintaining it. For the set-up, you're looking at paying between $400 and $1,500. Usually a lawyer is best for this, although you can do it yourself. There's also the cost of paying an accountant to prepare your corporate financial statements and tax returns each year—a job best left to a professional, where corporations are involved. Accounting fees can vary widely, depending on the nature of your business and the neatness of your records.

The second drawback is *trapped losses*. You see, if your business loses money from its operations, it will have what we call *non-capital losses*. These losses can be carried back three years or forward seven to offset taxable income in those years. If losses are incurred by your corporation in its first few years, they will be trapped in the corporation and will only be available to offset income earned by the corporation in the following seven years. Beyond seven years the losses expire. This is not nearly as good as if you had incurred those losses personally as a proprietor or partner. As a proprietor or partner, the losses could be applied to offset your other personal income, and could even be carried back three years to recover taxes you may have paid personally in those prior years.

Tim's Tip 38: Consider incorporation once your business has grown, but not before.

I know, I know. You're looking forward to the day when you can incorporate your business and move to a whole new level of sophistication. Besides, it sounds great to be called a founding shareholder of a corporation. Well, hold your horses for a minute.

Remember what I said earlier about the benefits of a corporation? The two key benefits are these: (1) limited liability for shareholders; and (2) opportunities for tax deferral. There's a good chance that you may not even benefit in these ways if you incorporate too soon. Think about it. Will you benefit significantly from the limited liability offered by a corporation? It depends on the industry and the nature of your business. If, for example, you're in the desktop publishing business, your potential liability is likely much lower than if you're in the construction industry. But as your business grows in size, your need for protection from liability will also grow.

Action Step

What about the tax-deferral issue? If you're not going to leave any of your business earnings in the company, then you won't benefit from the tax deferral I've been talking about. Refer back to Astrid's story. If she had paid the full $100,000 of corporate earnings to herself rather than leaving $40,000 in the company, she would have lost the benefit of the tax deferral. In many situations, it's not until the business has grown in profitability that the owner is in a position to leave some of the earnings in the corporation and really benefit from a tax deferral.

If you're operating as a proprietorship or partnership and decide to incorporate your business, visit a tax pro to arrange for your business assets to be transferred to the new company on a tax-free basis. This is normally done under Section 85 of the Income Tax Act. In exchange for transferring those assets to the company, you'll receive payment and/or shares from the company.

And remember, as I discussed earlier, setting up a corporation from the start of your business could leave losses trapped inside the corporation that could have been used to recover taxes paid personally in previous years.

The general rule, then, is that you should wait until the business has grown in size and profitability before you incorporate. As with all tax planning, your circumstances will be different from others', and seeking the advice of a tax pro who's familiar with your situation will help you to make the best decision regarding your business structure.

TO MAKE A LONG STORY SHORT:

- The key benefits to setting up your business as a corporation are *limited liability* and the opportunity for *tax deferral* on corporate earnings.

- Normally, you'll experience these benefits most once the business has grown in size and profitability, and so it's often preferable to wait until that time to incorporate.

- Setting up a corporation too soon could result in *trapped losses* in the corporation.

Tim's Tip 39: Choose the right year-end for your business.

Brace yourself, we're now dealing with a very complex area of tax law—choosing a year-end for your proprietorship or partnership. Before 1995 it was fairly easy to pick a year-end for your business. It used to be that you could effectively defer tax for a full year by choosing a non-calendar year-end. Not so any more. While you'll generally be able to choose any year-end you want for your business, all proprietorships and partnerships are now required to report income on a calendar-year basis. As a result, if you choose a non-calendar year-end, you'll have to adjust your business income each year to reflect a December 31 year-end. Follow me?

In many cases, since you must report your income as though you have a calendar year-end anyway, it may not be worth the hassle to choose a non-calendar year-end. It'll only mean extra work in preparing your tax returns. There may, however, be an opportunity for you to defer tax. Here's the general rule of thumb: If your business is growing and you expect your business income to continue increasing for a number of years, then choosing a non-calendar year-end will provide a tax deferral.

Let's briefly look at how the calculation works. Suppose your proprietorship has an October 31 year-end. On your personal tax return for 1999, you'll have to report your income for the 12 months ended on October 31, 1999. But you'll have to convert this to a December 31 year-end. This means you'll have to calculate your income from the business for November and December 1999 as well—called the *stub period*—and add this to your October 31 income. When you do this, you will now be reporting income for a 14-month period (the 12 months ended October 31, 1999, plus income for the 2-month stub period). It hardly seems fair that you should report 14 months of income on your tax return each year. Don't panic. You can now deduct from that 14-month income the stub-period income added in the prior year. This brings your income back to a 12-month figure. Make sense?

By the way, the stub-period income that you add each year is not your actual income

Did You Know?

If you are resident in Canada for tax purposes, you must pay tax to the Canadian government on your worldwide income, regardless of whether that income comes from legal or illegal sources. If you fail to pay tax on your income from illegal sources, you could be subject to penalties, interest, and possible imprisonment for evading tax!

for those months. It's based on a formula. In my example, we need to add two months' worth of income, so we'd simply take 2/12ths of the October 31 fiscal year income and call this our stub period income.

If you changed to a December 31 year-end back in 1995, as so many business owners did because of new rules, you would have calculated your income for the stub period that fell between your former year-end and December 31, 1995. The tax collector has allowed you to report those stub period earnings over a ten-year period. If you cease or significantly change business operations, give up Canadian residency, or incorporate— watch out—you'll be taxed on the full balance of your stub period income in that year.

Caution!

If your business is losing money, either because it's new or because it's simply on the decline, you'll be better off with a December 31 year-end. You're able to change to a December 31 year-end at any time, but once you've made this decision, you can't go back to a non-calendar year-end. As you can see, the rules are confusing, and I've only touched the surface here. Be sure to visit a tax pro before making a decision about which year-end is best for you.

TO MAKE A LONG STORY SHORT:

- It can be a difficult decision to choose between a non-calendar and a calendar year-end.

- Generally, if your business income is expected to rise consistently over the next few years, a non-calendar year-end will offer tax-deferral opportunities.

- Be sure to visit a tax pro before making a final decision on a year-end.

Claiming Business Deductions

Why in the world is self-employment such a great tax-shelter anyway? Deductions! In fact, our tax law will allow you to claim a deduction for virtually any costs, so long as the costs were incurred for the purpose of producing income from the business, and provided the expenses are reasonable. Let's take a look at the most common expenses you'll be able to claim.

Tim's Tip 40: Maximize your deductions for home office expenses.

There's no getting around it—you've got to pay for a place to live, so why not make a portion of the costs tax deductible? There's nothing like self-employment to make this a reality. However, there are some rules to be aware of. You'll be entitled to claim a deduction for home office expenses where you meet one of two criteria: (1) Your home is your principal place of business; or (2) you use a specific area in your home exclusively for earning income from your business and you meet clients there on a regular and ongoing basis.

Once you've met the criteria, there are a number of expenses to consider deducting. The key here is not to forget deductions that you might otherwise overlook. Here's a list to try on for size:

- rent
- mortgage interest
- property taxes
- utilities (heat, hydro, water)
- home insurance
- repairs and maintenance
- landscaping
- snow plowing
- capital cost allowance (but this is not advisable)
- telephone (100-percent deductible if it's a separate business line).

There are a couple of things to note here. You won't be able to deduct the full cost of these expenses I've listed. Rather, you'll be able to deduct the business portion only. If, for example, your office in the house is 200 square feet in size and your home is 2,000 square feet in

I generally tell folks not to claim capital cost allowance (CCA) on the portion of a home used for business. If you do claim CCA, the tax collector will consider that portion of your home to be a business asset. This will jeopardize your ability to claim the principal residence exemption on that portion of your home—which could leave you open to capital gains tax if you sell your home later at a profit.

Caution!

total, then 10 percent of these costs would be deductible. By the way, residents of Quebec will find their deductible home office expenses reduced by 50 percent thanks to changes in Quebec's 1996 budget. Be sure to maximize your deductible expenses by maximizing the business percentage of your home. You can do this by including a portion of your hallway and washrooms as business space if they are used in the business, or by excluding certain non-useable space (an unfinished basement, for example) from the calculation of your total square footage of the home.

Telephone expenses are fully deductible if you have a separate business line, and even where you don't have a separate line, a portion of your personal line (based on time usage) will be deductible. Any additional home costs that were incurred solely because you are running your business from home—additional insurance, for example—are fully deductible.

TO MAKE A LONG STORY SHORT:

- Claim a portion of all eligible home costs when your home is your principal place of business or is used to meet clients on a regular and ongoing basis.

- Maximize the business use of your home by choosing carefully the areas to include in the calculation.

Tim's Tip 41: **Maximize deductions related to business use of your automobile.**

If you're self-employed, you'll be entitled to a deduction for using your car in the business. The rules work basically the same for employees and the self-employed, so I'll refer you to Tip 29 in Chapter 3, where I talk about deducting automobile costs. Keep in mind, you can deduct a portion of a vehicle's costs, based on the percentage of your driving that was business-related.

To satisfy the tax collector, you'll need to keep a log book for each trip, and you'd be wise to maximize your business usage. This can be done, for example, by making stops for business on the way home from work or on the way to work. And don't forget about the wide range of expenses to deduct, including auto club costs, car washes, licence fees, and the more obvious: gas, oil, repairs, insurance, loan interest, lease costs, and capital cost allowance.

A little boy once asked his mother: "Mom, what happens to a car when it's too old to run anymore?"

"Someone sells it to your father," the mother replied.

Folks, if this sounds familiar, take this once piece of advice: Use that old jalopy in your business instead of your newer car! Since repair costs may be high, you'll save more tax by making those repairs deductible.

TO MAKE A LONG STORY SHORT:

- Maximize business use of your car by stopping for business reasons on the way home from work, or on the way to work, and keep a log book of distances driven for business during the year.

- Use your jalopy with the most costly expenses for business purposes.

- Refer to Tip 29 in Chapter 3 where I talk about automobiles at greater length.

Tim's Tip 42: Categorize your meals and entertainment expenses to maximize tax savings.

Leave it to Revenue Canada to come up with a way to make any simple subject complex! The rules around meals and entertainment are a perfect example. Generally, 50 percent of any meals and entertainment costs will be deductible if the costs were incurred to earn income from your business.

There are some situations, however, where those costs are 100-percent deductible. In fact, there are four of these situations: (1) when the meal or entertainment has been provided to all your employees (a Christmas party, for example, to a maximum of three such occasions each year); (2) when the meal or entertainment costs were incurred by an employee who had to travel out of your metropolitan area to do work; (3) when the meal costs were built into the price of a rail, airplane, or bus ticket; or (4) when the cost of the meal or entertainment is billed to a client and separately disclosed on your invoice to the client (in this case, your client is subject to the 50-percent restriction).

Given that some meals and entertainment costs are 50-percent deductible and others are fully deductible, you'd be wise to keep track of the categories separately. If you don't, the tax collector could restrict all meals and entertainment to 50-percent deductibility.

Did You Know?

If you're a golfer, you'll be glad to know that Revenue Canada has recently changed its opinion on meals purchased at a golf course. You see, the tax collector used to enforce the policy that those meals were not deductible, forcing many to finish a round of golf and then head elsewhere to eat. Talk about dumb. The policy has now changed. Food purchased at a golf course is now deductible, subject to the usual 50-percent limitation.

TO MAKE A LONG STORY SHORT:

- Meals and entertainment costs are generally 50-percent deductible when they are incurred to earn business income.

- In some situations these costs are fully deductible.

- Keep track of the categories separately to ensure maximum deductibility.

Tim's Tip 43: Maximize your eligibility to claim capital cost allowance.

You've seen the term capital cost allowance (CCA) now and again as you've browsed the pages of this book. CCA is simply our tax law's term for *depreciation*. And CCA is one of the more attractive tax deductions for any self-employed taxpayer. Here's why: There are a number of things that you have probably purchased which will now become tax deductible in the form of CCA because you're running a business.

Want some common examples? Take your home computer. If that computer is now used in the business, even part-time, then it becomes an asset that you can depreciate through the CCA system. Your printer, software, desk, bookcase, fax machine, car, boat, trailer, and tools are all good examples of depreciable assets—provided they are used in the business.

There are different *classes* of assets for CCA purposes, and each asset used in your business will fall into one class or another. Each class has an opening balance at the start of every business fiscal year, and that balance can be depreciated at the specified rate for that class. For example, your computer hardware is a class 10 asset in which the undepreciated capital cost (UCC) can be deducted each year at the rate of 30 percent.

In the year you acquire an asset, you're generally entitled to just 50 percent of the CCA you'd otherwise claim. This is called the *half-year rule* because you're only entitled to CCA for half of that first year.

Here are some pointers for dealing with CCA. First, if you're going to acquire new assets, consider buying them before the fiscal year is over and make sure those assets are available for use by the end of the fiscal year. This will provide a CCA claim sooner than if you waited until the start of the next fiscal year. Second, delay the sale of an asset until early in the next fiscal year to permit a CCA claim this year. Third, recognize that CCA is not a mandatory deduction. If you don't want to claim it in a given year, you don't have to. This does not mean you give up that deduction forever. It simply means you're pushing it to a future year. This can make sense, for example, when your business is not yet profitable and you don't need the CCA deduction to bring your taxable income to nil. If you want more information on claiming CCA, Revenue Canada's *Business and Professional Income Tax Guide* can offer help, as can a number of Interpretation Bulletins that can be accessed on Revenue Canada's Web site at **www.rc.gc.ca.**

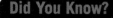

Revenue Canada calculates its prescribed interest rate each quarter by determining the average rate on 90-day treasury bills sold during the first month of the preceding quarter. This figure is then rounded up to the nearest percentage point. The rate charged on overdue taxes is 4 percent above this figure, while interest paid on refunds and overpayments is just 2 percent above this figure.

TO MAKE A LONG STORY SHORT:

- It's possible to claim CCA on assets that you might already own and are now using in the business.

- Maximize your CCA claim by buying new assets before the end of the fiscal year or by selling old assets after the current fiscal year.

- Your CCA claim is not mandatory each year, and it may make sense to postpone the deduction in certain situations.

Tim's Tip 44: Pay salaries to family members for a number of tax benefits.

There's no situation quite like self-employment to allow for effective income splitting between family members. I talked about this strategy briefly in Chapter 2, Tip 8*w*. The idea is this: Your business will be entitled to claim a deduction for any salaries or wages paid to family members, provided the compensation is reasonable for the services provided.

Tai *runs his own carpet cleaning business. Last summer, he hired his daughter Kim to work in the office booking appointments and doing various other tasks. Tai paid $6,500 to Kim for her work last year. Kim used the money to help pay for her college education, but she paid absolutely no tax on the $6,500 since it was her only source of income and it's below her basic and supplementary personal amounts of $6,956. If the $6,500 had not been paid to Kim, it would have been taxed in Tai's hands as business income, and would have cost Tai $3,250 in taxes at his marginal tax rate of 50 percent ($6,500 x 50 percent). These taxes were saved by splitting income through the payment of a salary. In addition, the $6,500 is earned income to Kim, which provides her with RRSP contribution room. A great deal all around.*

Did you catch the benefits of paying a salary to family members? First, if the salary is paid to a family member who will face no tax, or less tax than the business would have attracted, there are permanent tax savings. Second, the salary provides RRSP contribution room to the family member on the receiving end. Third, the money stays in the family, as opposed to being paid to an unrelated third party. You'll also notice that this strategy works very well when a child needs money for school. Think about it. Tai was able to support his daughter's education in a manner that was tax-deductible to his business and tax-free to Kim.

TO MAKE A LONG STORY SHORT:

- Paying salaries or wages to family members with a lower marginal tax rate can result in permanent tax savings, and a perfect splitting of income.

- The compensation will provide RRSP contribution room to your family member.

- This strategy makes for a great way to cover education costs for children in school.

Adding Up the Tax Hits

Don't be fooled into thinking that income taxes are your only tax burden as a business owner. In fact, there are a number of different "taxes" that your business will be subject to, and while I'm not going to talk about these in detail here, it's important that you're aware of what they are.

Tim's Tip 45: Understand the various "taxes" affecting your business.

In case the income tax burden you'll face on your business profits is not enough to faze you, try a few of these other "taxes" on for size. I call these taxes and, in most cases, that's precisely what they are. In other cases, these are more akin to premiums owing. There are four categories worth talking about.

Canada/Quebec Pension Plan and Employment Insurance

I've got good news and bad news for you. The good news is that, as a self-employed individual, you won't be required to pay any Employment Insurance (EI) premiums on your own earnings. This will save you over $2,527 in 1998 when factoring in both the employee and employer portions, although you won't be entitled to collect EI if you decide to try. The bad news is that you'll have to make Canada/Quebec Pension Plan (CPP/QPP) contributions on your self-employment earnings, and you'll have to pick up both the employee and employer portions, amounting to a maximum of $2,138 in 1998. And CPP/QPP contributions can only get uglier in the future. In fact, these contributions are scheduled to rise to 9.9 percent of income by the year 2003. This will mean an increase in annual contributions for self-employed individuals of over $1,400!

Provincial Payroll Taxes

Provincial payroll taxes originated in Manitoba, and have spread like wildfire across the country. These payroll taxes normally apply to employment income, and in some cases extend to self-employment income. A case in point: Ontario's Employer Health Tax (EHT) currently applies to the self-employed. The good news, however, is that the EHT is being phased-out and will disappear by 1999. In 1998, incomes under $300,000 will be exempt from EHT.

In a family-run business, it may be possible to consider certain family members exempt from Employment Insurance (EI) premiums. This will save you the cost of the premiums, but it means that these family members won't be eligible to collect EI down the road if they find themselves unemployed. If you choose this route, make sure that the salary paid to these family members is reasonable, since the tax collector is more likely to examine the salaries of persons who are EI-exempt.

Caution!

Workers' Compensation

Many businesses are required to pay premiums to the Workers' Compensation Board. The amount of the premiums depends on the type of work that is being undertaken. Be sure to look into this when you start your business.

GST and HST

Every consumer knows first-hand about the GST (the HST in Nova Scotia, New Brunswick, and Newfoundland and Labrador). Your business will need to register for the GST/HST if your taxable sales of goods or services exceed $30,000 in a fiscal year. Once your sales reach this level, you'll be required to register for GST/HST and start charging the tax in the following month. You'll be required to file GST/HST returns, normally on an annual basis, although some businesses will be required to file more often. In any event, you may be required to remit quarterly installments of GST/HST.

TO MAKE A LONG STORY SHORT:

- Income taxes are not the only type of tax that your business will have to deal with.

- Take the time to understand your obligations related to CPP, EI, provincial payroll taxes, workers' compensation, and the GST/HST.

Getting into the Game

If self-employment is in your game plan, there's plenty you can do to minimize the taxes you pay. Turn now to the Tax Planning Tip Sheet at the front of the book and review the strategies introduced in Chapter 4. Ask yourself, "Does this tip apply to me?" Every *Yes* or *Not Sure* could add dollars to your bottom line. When you've finished reading this book, take your Tip Sheet to a tax pro for help in setting up your tax-savvy proprietorship, partnership, or corporation.

BULLS, BEARS, AND BASEBALL: STRATEGIES FOR INVESTORS

To become a millionaire: Start with ten million then invest in a hot tip.

5

All right, I'll be the first to admit it. My life is a little one-tracked. Here's proof: My career is taxation, and my hobby is investing. Being one-tracked makes me good at what I do, but—according to my wife—something far less than exciting at the dinner table. In fact, my wife Carolyn and I were at a friend's place for dinner recently when the conversation turned to investment issues. I was in my element. Evidently, everyone else wished they were in bed.

After dinner, Carolyn said to me privately: "Tim, for the first time in my life, I envied my feet—they were asleep. Why can't you take up another hobby, like insect collecting or something?"

"Insect collecting," I replied. "Great idea! I could liquidate some of my South American holdings, and reassess my short position in that small resource play out west to free up some cash. Then I could undertake a fundamental analysis on any insect-related securities that I can locate in the market. Of course, I'd want to check the price-volume histories and look at other technical analyses. Heck, I could even take a long position in some bug-related futures contracts through my broker in Chicago. Carolyn, you're a genius. We could make millions!"

"Tim," my wife replied, "forget what I said about starting a new hobby."

At this point, I want to talk to those of you who, like me, are investors. And this will include just about everyone. In fact, you can consider yourself an investor for our discussion here if you have any money at all invested outside your registered retirement savings plan (RRSP), registered retirement income fund (RRIF), or other tax-deferred plan—or if you expect to have these types of investments down the road. These are called *non-registered assets*, also referred to as your *open money*.

Let's look at some strategies that are sure to keep the tax collector away from your open money. It's time for investors to step up to the plate, because these pages contain some guaranteed home runs.

Reducing Taxable Investment Income

Tim's Tip 46: Deduct as much of your interest cost as possible.

Generally, the tax collector will allow you a deduction for your interest costs when you've borrowed for business purposes, or to make investments.

Convert to Deductible Debt

A sure-fire way to make your interest deductible is to swap your non-deductible debt for deductible debt when you have debt-free investments at your disposal. Consider Grant.

Grant has $30,000 invested in mutual funds. In addition, he has $25,000 of debt outstanding on his line of credit. The interest on this debt is not deductible since the borrowed funds on his line of credit were used for personal purposes, and not for business or investment purposes. Grant swapped this non-deductible debt for deductible debt. Here's how: Grant sold $25,000 of his mutual funds and used the cash to pay off his $25,000 line of credit. He then borrowed $25,000 to replace those mutual funds he had sold. Because he is borrowing for investment purposes, he's entitled to deduct the interest on the borrowed money.

Keep this in mind: When you liquidate some of your investments to swap non-deductible for deductible debt, you could face a taxable capital gain when you sell those investments. It might still be worth your while to make the swap if the tax bill is going to be less than the taxes saved from the interest deduction over the long haul.

You're entitled to claim a deduction for your interest costs if you've used the borrowed money to invest in a business or to earn income from property. Income from property most commonly includes interest, dividends, rents, and royalties—but not capital gains. If you're investing primarily to generate capital gains, the tax collector could disallow your interest deduction. But relax: If you're investing in stocks or equity mutual funds, there's usually the potential for dividends, which normally would allow you to deduct your interest. If you're not expecting much in the way of interest or dividend income, you could have a problem deducting your interest costs.

Caution!

Keep It Deductible

If you're not careful, you could lose your interest deduction in future years. You see, the tax collector is going to trace your borrowed money to its current use to determine whether the interest remains deductible year after year. Let's say, for argument's sake, that you borrow $100,000 to invest in units of a mutual fund, and your units grow to a total of $150,000. At that time, you sell $50,000 of those units. If your loan remains outstanding after this sale, what portion of your interest will remain deductible? The tax collector will look to where your sale proceeds are today. If you were to re-invest those proceeds of $50,000, you'd be entitled to continue deducting the full amount of the interest on your loan. If, however, you took that $50,000 and used it for personal purposes—to take a vacation, renovate your home, pay down debt, or even pay down interest on your debt—you'd lose the ability to deduct one-third ($50,000 of $150,000) of your remaining interest costs.

Consider these ideas to keep your interest deductible:

Skim the interest, dividends or other income from property (but not capital gains) from your leveraged investments before these amounts are re-invested, and spend this income in any way you'd like. This won't jeopardize your interest deduction because you're not dipping into your principal, or *invested capital*. However, once this income is re-invested in additional units or shares, it forms part of your capital, and you may run into an interest deductibility problem when you make withdrawals later.

Pay down your investment loans with the interest or dividends you've skimmed from your investments, or with another source of cash. Do not, however, use a portion of the capital you've invested with borrowed money to pay down the debt or interest on the debt, unless you're willing to lose a portion of your interest deduction on the balance of the loan. Of course, if you liquidate your investments to pay off your investment loan in one shot, the interest deduction is no longer an issue, since the debt is gone.

! **Beware of certain advice** being passed around today that could leave you with a nasty tax surprise. The strategy is this: Take out a home equity loan, invest the money in mutual funds, liquidate some of those mutual fund units monthly to make payments to the bank on that home equity loan, and then claim a deduction at tax time for the full amount of the interest paid on the loan. Sorry, the interest deduction part of the story doesn't work as advertised. You see, you're using the proceeds from the mutual fund redemptions for a non-income-producing purpose—to pay down debt or interest on the debt. The result? You can expect to lose a portion of your interest deduction.

Action Step

If you borrowed to make an investment that subsequently turned sour, then sold this investment at a loss, be sure to continue deducting a portion of your interest costs. You see, Section 20.1 of the Income Tax Act says that you'll be able to continue deducting the interest on your *loss portion* of the investment. This applies to dispositions after 1993 (except for sales of real estate or depreciable assets). But the rules are complex enough to leave your head spinning, so visit a tax pro for help.

TO MAKE A LONG STORY SHORT:

- Interest is normally deductible when the money borrowed is used for business or investment purposes.

- Consider swapping non-deductible for deductible debt where possible.

- The tax collector will look to your current use of borrowed money to determine whether your interest costs will remain deductible.

Tim's Tip 47: Call your profits capital gains and your losses business losses.

Sometimes you're going to make money on your investments, and sometimes you're going to lose it. But are you going to call your profits *capital gains* or *business income*? Similarly, are you going to call your losses *capital losses* or *business losses*? This issue can be as clear as mud. No doubt about it, this is one of the very gray areas in our tax law. And whenever there's gray, you should generally take the position that is going to give you the biggest tax breaks.

Saya loves to invest. In fact, she closely follows the stock market. In an average month, Saya makes about eight trades on her brokerage account. Last year, she generated $35,000 in profits from her investing. But investing is not Saya's primary source of income. She has a job working as a technician in an architect's office, and she earns $45,000 each year as an employee there. Should Saya's profits from investing be considered capital gains or business income? She could argue either way.

Here's the rule of thumb: Where you have the ability to argue either way, call your profits capital gains. Here's why: Capital gains are just 75 percent taxable in Canada, while business income is fully taxable. Have you incurred losses? You'll be better off calling these business losses than calling them capital losses. After all, capital losses can only be applied against capital gains to reduce tax, while business losses can be applied against any source of income at all.

Keep in mind that, in many cases, it will be clear whether your profits and losses are capital or income in nature. Consider the analogy of the tree and its fruit. If you bought a tree for the purpose of growing and selling fruit, then the tree is a capital asset to you. So, if you were to sell the tree itself at a profit, that profit would normally be considered a capital gain. The profits from selling the fruit would be considered business income.

Want a more life-like example? Suppose you bought a condominium for the purpose of renting it out, and someone offered a good price to buy the condo from you. Because you bought the condo to generate rents (your "fruit" in this case), the condo is a capital asset, and any profit on the sale is likely a capital gain. If however, you bought the condo largely to sell it at a profit, and not primarily to rent it, then you could argue that the transaction was income in nature. It's what we call an "adventure in the nature of trade." If you had lost money flipping the property in this case, it's arguable that the loss is a business loss.

In any event, it's important to document your reasoning for the position you take when reporting your gains and losses. And be consistent! That is, don't treat your stock profits as capital gains and your losses from similar investments as business losses. The tax collector doesn't really have a sense of humour in this regard.

Here's one last point: Any profits or losses that you generate from short-selling a stock, or from trading in options or futures, will generally be considered business income or losses. It only makes sense. You see, these securities don't provide the opportunity for any "fruit from the tree" such as interest, dividends, royalties, or rents. No fruit? Then these

You can make a special election to treat all your gains and losses from trading securities as capital gains and losses. Those who are considered *traders* cannot make this election (although a trader is not defined in the Income Tax Act). Normally, I don't recommend making this election. The reason? It's irrevocable: You'll be stuck with it for life. Besides, your profits and losses from trading securities will almost always be considered capital gains and losses anyway, so there's no need to make the election. Why tie your hands when you don't need to?

Caution!

securities are more akin to an "adventure in the nature of trade" and will be treated as income.

TO MAKE A LONG STORY SHORT:

- It may not always be clear whether you should treat your investment profits and losses as capital or income.

- Where possible, you'll want to argue that your profits are capital gains and your losses are business losses.

- Document your reasoning and be consistent from one transaction to the next.

Tim's Tip 48: Claim a capital gains reserve to spread your tax bill over time.

Ah yes, one of the mysteries of the universe—how to avoid tax on capital gains when an asset has appreciated in value. It's not an easy question to answer. I wish there were more magic available here. Your best bet in this situation is to push the expected tax bill as far off into the future as possible. You can do this by simply not selling the asset. But if you're determined to sell, you can at least minimize the tax hit by spreading it out over a maximum five-year period.

You see, the tax collector will allow you to claim what is called a *capital gains reserve*—a deduction—when you have sold something at a profit but have not yet collected the full amount of your proceeds from the sale.

L isa decided last year to sell the family cottage. She had bought it for $75,000 and was offered $125,000 for it—a $50,000 profit she couldn't refuse. She wasn't able to shelter this $50,000 capital gain in any way, so she decided to take payment from the purchaser over a five-year period—$25,000 each year. This way, the $50,000 taxable capital gain was not taxed all at once last *year. Rather, Lisa will pay tax on the gain over the five-year period—just $10,000 each year. She reported the full $50,000 capital gain last year, but claimed a capital gains reserve for 80 percent (four-fifths) of the gain. The gain will be taken into income slowly over five years.*

You'll have to take any capital gains into income at a rate not less than 20 percent (one-fifth) each year. If you're not keen on the idea of taking payment over five years because you're giving up use of the proceeds today, there's a simple solution. Build an interest charge into the selling price so that you're compensated for the time delay in collecting payment. For example, Lisa could have collected, say, $27,500 each year rather than $25,000—for a total selling price of $137,500. The additional $2,500 each year is effectively interest income, but the good news is that it will be taxed as a capital gain since it's built into the selling price!

TO MAKE A LONG STORY SHORT:

- It's very difficult to avoid paying tax on accrued capital gains on assets you own.

- Your best bet is to push the tax bill as far into the future as possible.

- A taxable capital gain can be spread out for up to five years by taking payment of the proceeds over an extended period. This is called a capital gains reserve.

Action Step

Selling an asset and taking payment over a period of up to five years could provide you with a capital gains reserve, allowing you to defer tax on your gains. If you're going to take payment over a period of time, make sure you maintain a claim on the assets in case the purchaser defaults on the payments. You can do this by entering into a written purchase and sale agreement that gives you a claim on the assets until the last payment is received.

Investing in Private Corporations

Tim's Tip 49: Consider an investment holding company in certain situations.

Many tax pros say that there's no use in setting up a corporation to hold investments any longer, because there's no real opportunity to defer tax by earning income in the corporation as there was in the past. What do I say? I say it's time to think outside the typical tax box.

There are four potential benefits to setting up an investment holding corporation. They are:

- to minimize clawback of OAS benefits
- to minimize taxes on death
- to minimize probate fees
- to provide a source for earned income.

Is this idea for everyone? Absolutely not. But if you have significant open money (investments outside your RRSP or RRIF)— generally $300,000 or more—then the idea could be for you. Consider Ruth.

*R*uth *is 67 years young and makes withdrawals from her RRSP every year, but her main source of income is the interest she earns on $500,000 worth of investments. Because of this interest income, she suffers a clawback of her Old Age Security (OAS) benefits.*

Here's what she did: Ruth transferred the $500,000 of investments to a new holding company. This was set up as a loan by Ruth to the company. Now, the interest income earned on the investments is no longer reported by Ruth on her personal tax return—it's taxed in the corporation instead. As a result, her clawback problem is minimized. Next, the company is going to declare—but not pay—a dividend to Ruth each year equal to the

*after-tax earnings of the company. Since Ruth needs the
investment earnings to meet her costs of living, she withdraws
the after-tax income earned by the company each year as a tax-
free repayment of the loan the company owes her. Alternatively,
she could take a director's fee or salary from the corporation
each year, which would count as earned income—providing her
with RRSP contribution room.*

*Upon her death, two things may happen. First, the dividends
still owing to her (that were declared but not paid) will be taxed,
but may be reported on a separate tax return called a* rights or
things *return—which will save her tax. Finally, Ruth may be able
to pass the shares in her private company to her heirs without
probate, by way of a separate will, since the family won't require
probate on these shares.*

Whoa. Did you catch all that? Let's look at the benefits of an
investment holding company once again—in slow motion.

First, you may be able to minimize or eliminate a clawback on
OAS benefits by removing income from your personal tax return.
You see, when you put your assets into the corporation, the company
will report the income and pay the tax from that point forward.

Second, you can minimize taxes upon death. By having the
company declare dividends each year equal to the after-tax earnings
of the company, but not pay those dividends, you create an asset for
yourself—a dividend receivable. Upon your death, this asset can be
reported on a separate tax return called a *rights or things* return. This
separate return entitles you to the basic personal and supplementary
exemptions of $6,956 ($6,707 in 1998) all over again and a lower
marginal tax rate on the first $29,590 of income.

By the way, if you need cash flow during your lifetime, you can
withdraw cash from the company as a repayment of the loan you
made when you transferred your investments to the company. Once

If you're going to set up an investment holding corporation, keep in mind the following:

- You won't be able to transfer your RRSP or RRIF assets to the company.
- The company will pay taxes at about 50 percent on its investment income, so you're not likely to save any income tax on an annual basis, but the other benefits may still make the idea worthwhile.
- There will be costs to set up the corporation and annual accounting fees for filing tax returns and financial statements.

The moral: Don't try this idea at home. Visit a tax pro!

this loan has been repaid, the company could make good on the dividends it owes to you.

Third, probate fees may be minimized. Here's how: Since family members are shareholders of the company, directors of the company, and heirs of any shares, it's possible to pass these shares to your heirs through a separate and non-probatable will. After all, who in your family will require probate in this case? Probably no one. But these shares must pass to your heirs outside of your original will, which will have to go through probate. Speak to your lawyer about this idea. It will have to be set up properly.

Finally, the corporation can be a source of earned income for you. Earned income is most commonly paid in the form of director's fees or salary, and will provide you with RRSP contribution room that will benefit you while you're under age 69—and sometimes beyond (see Chapter 6, Tip 67.)

TO MAKE A LONG STORY SHORT:

- A corporation may be used to reduce clawbacks on OAS, minimize taxes on death, reduce probate fees, and provide a source for earned income.

- You'll need enough open money to make this idea worthwhile—generally over $300,000. If you're interested, visit a tax pro to talk this idea over, since it won't be for everyone.

Tim's Tip 50: Consider buying shares in a CCPC for a capital gains exemption—and more.

If you're tired of paying tax on your investment income and you don't mind taking on some added risk, consider investing in a *Canadian-controlled private corporation* (CCPC). A CCPC is simply a corporation that is not controlled by a public corporation or by non-residents, and is not listed on a prescribed Canadian stock exchange or certain foreign stock exchanges. Typically, these are small to medium-sized companies and normally include most Canadian businesses—maybe even the one next door, or your own business. There are a number of tax benefits to owning shares in this type of company.

Enhanced Capital Gains Exemption

If you own shares in a small business, and those shares increase in value over time, there's a strong possibility that you'll be able to shelter up to $500,000 of that increase from tax—through the $500,000 enhanced capital gains exemption. To be eligible, your small company shares will have to be *qualified small business corporation* (QSBC) shares. Using the full $500,000 exemption could save you $187,500 in taxes if your marginal tax rate is 50 percent.

What in the world are QSBC shares? In general, these are shares that you (or a

If you haven't yet used up your enhanced capital gains exemption, consider making use of it today! A study on business taxation was undertaken on behalf of our government, and a document known as the *Mintz Report* was released in the spring of 1998, recommending that the exemption be eliminated. Don't delay! Visit a tax pro to determine whether it's worth your while and whether you're able to claim the exemption.

related person) must have owned for a two-year period. In addition, the company must be a CCPC. Finally, the company must be using 90 percent or more of its assets to carry on an active business primarily in Canada, and the same must hold true for 50 percent or more of its assets throughout the two-year period you've owned the stock. Sound complex? The truth is, the definition has been simplified here. Be sure to have a tax pro review the company's financial statements to determine whether it qualifies for the $500,000 exemption.

Allowable Business Investment Losses

Okay, so you're still not convinced that shares in a small business are worth owning—despite the enhanced capital gains exemption. Too risky, right? But consider this: Your investment in that small business could also offer greater downside protection than other investments if the investment goes sour. Again, the company has to be a CCPC, and 90 percent or more of its assets must be used in an active business that operates primarily in Canada.

If it becomes evident that you'll never recover your investment in the small business, you'll be entitled to claim an *allowable business investment loss* (ABIL). This ABIL equals three-quarters of the invested money you've lost, and can be deducted on your tax return against *any* source of income. Normally, when you lose money on shares you own, you've incurred a capital loss which can only be used to offset capital gains. You should also be aware that, where you've lent money to a small business instead of buying shares, you may still be eligible for ABIL treatment.

The Canadian Dealing Network

This has got to be one of the best hidden secrets in the world of Canadian investing. I'm talking about the Canadian Dealing Network (CDN). The CDN is Canada's over-the-counter equity market. It's essentially an electronic bulletin board for stock quotes that a network of securities dealers use to make bids and offers. The trades are generally made over the phone.

The CDN has one very special attraction from a tax perspective: Stocks listed on the CDN are not considered to be public companies under Canadian tax law. The benefit? You may be entitled to make use of the enhanced $500,000 capital gains exemption to shelter gains from tax when you sell shares listed on the CDN at a profit— or claim an ABIL if your investment turns sour.

Don't get me wrong—any shares listed on the CDN are still public shares under provincial securities legislation, but we're talking about income tax legislation, and the tax collector has decided to call these *private* shares from a tax perspective. Not every share traded over-the-counter on the CDN will qualify for the enhanced capital gains exemption or ABIL treatment, but many will. And by the way, there are some reputable companies to be purchased on the CDN—just have your investment advisor provide some information.

Qualified Farm Property

I talked about the enhanced capital gains exemption to shelter any gains on qualified small business corporation shares. This exemption is extended to shelter any capital gains on qualified farm property— which normally includes most family farms or farm quotas. There are some conditions that the farm property must meet to be eligible, so visit a tax pro to determine for sure whether you'll be eligible.

TO MAKE A LONG STORY SHORT:

- Owning shares in a Canadian-controlled private corporation can offer tax benefits in the form of an enhanced capital gains exemption if the shares increase in value, and an allowable business investment loss if the investment turns sour.

- Qualified farm property and shares purchased on the Canadian Dealing Network can also enjoy some of these benefits.

Investing in Real Estate

Tim's Tip 51: Use real estate properly to generate wealth and minimize taxes.

If you're looking to build wealth and maximize your tax savings through real estate, there are some things to think about.

It can make sense to borrow against the equity in your home to invest. Be sure to focus on safer equities when investing the borrowed money. Focusing on fixed income or other interest-bearing investments doesn't make the most sense, since your returns on these investments are not likely to be as high over the long term as equities you might buy. And you'll want higher returns to fully offset any interest expense you're incurring. The less volatile the equities, the better. After all, you don't want the value of your equities to fall below your outstanding loan balance.

Leverage Your Real Estate

I'm a firm believer that, in the long run, you're going to make more money by investing in the stock market than by investing in real estate. So, if you have equity in your home or a second property, consider using that equity to your advantage. I'm talking about borrowing against the property and using the loan to invest in the stock market, either directly or through equity mutual funds. If you structure things right, you'll also be entitled to claim a deduction for the full interest on that loan (see Tip 46 for important information!).

Is this idea for everyone? Absolutely not! Generally, it may make sense to borrow when the following statements are all true:

- You have the cash flow to make principal and/or interest payments on the debt.
- You're borrowing no more than 20 to 30 percent of your net worth.
- Interest rates are low.

- The interest is going to be tax-deductible.
- Strong investment opportunities exist in blue-chip stocks and equity mutual funds.
- You can sleep at night with the debt.

Avoid Unprofitable Rental Properties

When it comes to rental properties, make sure that you have a reasonable expectation of profit from the property. If you're claiming rental losses year after year, the tax collector might disallow those losses (see Chapter 4, Tip 37 for more). You'd be stuck with a bad investment and no relief for your grief. If you're in this boat, consider the following strategies.

- **Re-evaluate the investment.**

If you're expecting rental losses again this year, consider whether you might be better off choosing another type of investment instead. Talk to your financial advisor and get some solid advice. Don't be duped into believing that the tax savings from your losses will wipe out your poor return on investment.

- **Prepare a forecast.**

If you've decided to keep your rental property and you're going to report yet another rental loss this year, prepare a forecast to see if you really have a reasonable expectation of profit. This forecast will be critical to winning your case if the tax collector attacks the losses you've been claiming. And since most rental losses arise because of mortgage interest deductions, do yourself a favour—pay down that mortgage as soon as possible to avoid a problem with the tax collector.

- **Choose your CCA claim carefully.**

If you rent out a portion of your principal residence, your best bet is to avoid claiming depreciation—called capital cost allowance

If you had no other income to report, you could earn up to $23,760 ($9,755 in Quebec) in dividends from Canadian corporations, and not pay a cent in tax! The reason for this is that you're entitled to a dividend tax credit equal to 16.67 percent (11.08 percent in Quebec) of the actual dividend earned.

(CCA)—on the property. If you claim CCA on the rental portion of your residence and later sell your residence at a profit, Revenue Canada may disallow the principal residence exemption on the part of your home for which you've claimed CCA. As a result, you could find yourself with an unwelcome tax bill.

- **Obtain your own financing when buying a property with others.**
When you borrow the money as a group, and one person is denied rental losses because of excess mortgage interest, the entire group will face the same fate. I've seen the tax collector go easy on other partners when they could establish that their own mortgage interest was significantly less than the amount claimed by the others—perhaps because they were paying down their own mortgage more quickly.

TO MAKE A LONG STORY SHORT:

- Build wealth and minimize taxes by leveraging your real estate to invest in the stock market—but do this prudently!

- Make sure you have a reasonable expectation of profit from your rental property; otherwise you could be burdened with unexpected taxes *and* an investment dud.

Choosing Conventional Securities

Tim's Tip 52: Participate in REITs or royalty trusts for tax-efficient cash flow.

If you need a steady cash flow from your investments, and you're looking to minimize your taxes at the same time, real estate investment trusts (REITs) and royalty trusts can be a great option.

Real Estate Investment Trusts

I can think of no better way to participate in the benefits of owning real estate than to buy units of a real estate investment trust (REIT). With a REIT, there are no rental losses, tenant problems, repairs, or maintenance to worry about—and the units are affordable.

A REIT works like a mutual fund. Investors pool their money by buying units in the REIT. The funds are used to invest in income-producing real estate like office buildings, shopping malls, and industrial properties. Here's the best part: Each investor will receive his or her share of rental income from the properties on a tax-efficient basis. You see, you might receive $1,000 from your REIT in the year but only pay tax on, say, $250 of that cash flow because of depreciation—capital cost allowance (CCA)—claimed against the income. The tax-free portion will vary by REIT and by year. Your adjusted cost base will then be reduced by the amount of the CCA claimed.

*W*hen Alice told her investment advisor that she wanted a steady income from her investments but didn't want to be highly taxed, he recommended that some of her money be invested in REITs. So, Alice invested $10,000 in a well known REIT. Last year, the REIT paid out $1,000 in distributions to her. The REIT also allocated to Alice her share of the capital cost

allowance (CCA) on the properties purchased—a total of $750.
Alice received a T3 slip from the REIT and was required to
report $250 ($1,000 minus $750) on her tax return last year.
Alice's cost of the REIT was $10,000, but this cost base was
reduced by the $750 in CCA that was allocated to her, so that
her new adjusted cost base is $9,250 ($10,000 minus $750).
Now, if she were to sell the REIT units for $10,000, she would
realize a $750 capital gain ($10,000 proceeds minus $9,250
adjusted cost base).

When you invest in a REIT, two important tax benefits arise. First, you'll receive cash flow from the REIT that is likely to be very tax-efficient, thanks to the CCA on the properties that offsets a portion of the income. Second, while you'll still face tax when you sell the REIT, this may not happen for a few years, and when you do face the tax, it's going to be capital gains tax, not tax on rental income. And capital gains are not fully taxed—they're just 75-percent taxable! In a nutshell, a REIT allows you to defer to a future year the tax on a portion of the distributions received, and converts that rental income to capital gains.

Royalty Trusts

A royalty trust works much like the REIT. In fact, the concept is nearly identical, except that the funds in a royalty trust will typically be used to buy proven oil and gas properties (no risky exploration or development properties here). As an investor, you can then expect to receive your share of the royalties generated from the sale of oil and gas from the properties. Like a REIT, the royalties received from the royalty trust will be very tax-efficient. Each distribution you receive from a royalty trust will be partially sheltered from tax by certain deductions available to the royalty trust.

And There's More

If you need a steady cash flow from your investments, you're a good candidate for investing in a REIT or royalty trust. One of the most efficient ways to participate in these types of investments is to buy units of a mutual fund that, in turn, invests in these things. BPI's High Income Fund is a great example of a fund that provides tax-efficient cash flow through investment in royalty trusts, REITs, and preferred and common shares. This is just one of many examples. Be sure to speak with your investment advisor about others.

By the way, if you happen to have capital losses available, REITs or royalty trusts can be effective tools precisely because these investments generally offer capital gains when you sell them. Your capital losses can be used to offset some or all of these gains.

REITs and royalty trusts do have some risks. Specifically, interest rates and hard-asset prices can cause your units in these trusts to fluctuate in value. If interest rates rise, then other interest-bearing investments may become more attractive relative to these trusts, causing your trust units to fall in value. Similarly, if real estate prices or resource prices fall, the distributions offered by these trusts could fall, which would cause your units to drop in value. Like any investment, weigh the costs and benefits before jumping in.

Caution!

TO MAKE A LONG STORY SHORT:

- REITs and royalty trusts provide tax-efficient cash flow for those who need a steady income from their investments.

- Purchasing REITs or royalty trusts through a mutual fund is a great way to go.

- Both investments are ideal for those who need to generate capital gains to use up capital losses.

Tim's Tip 53: Think twice before you buy into a mutual fund at the end of the year.

As a mutual fund investor, who do you suppose pays the tax on any income and profits generated by your favourite mutual fund? Right— you do. How does this work? Quite simply, your share of any interest, dividends, or capital gains earned by the mutual fund will be reported on a T3 slip each year to be taxed in your hands if these funds are held outside your RRSP or RRIF.

Consider this common scenario: It's near the end of the year, and you've just purchased 1,000 units in XYZ mutual fund at $25 per unit (a total investment of $25,000)—and you're pleased as punch about it. After all, the fund has done very well over the last few years, and you're expecting this performance to continue. Little did you realize, however, that this year the XYZ fund sold some of its profitable stocks that it had been holding for the last few years. The time was right for the fund to take some profits. The result? Those capital gains realized by the fund—amounting to, say, $5 per unit in this case—are going to be taxed in your hands this year. In this example, your recent $25,000 investment will give rise to a $5,000 capital gain, and a tax bill of up to $2,000.

This tax bill might not be so bad if you had been in the fund over the last few years as it grew in value. Here's the problem: Since you've only been in the fund for a short time, is it fair that you should pay tax on profits that accrued long before you owned the fund? Maybe not.

Whose profits are these anyway? They belong to those investors who had been in the fund while the stocks were growing in value, but because you're a unit holder at the end of this year, you'll be taxed on the profits along with the others. In effect, you're paying tax on someone else's profits—a gift you can do without.

Does this mean that the fund company has somehow done something wrong? Absolutely not. If the company uses a buy-and-hold strategy that makes money for investors, the company will eventually pass a taxable distribution to those investors. If it's the right time for your fund company to take profits, then this will translate into a tax bill for you. If you face a tax hit on profits that really belong to other investors, it's because you're in the right place at the wrong time.

You might wonder how in the world a year-end distribution can be a bad thing. After all, isn't a distribution—a payment from the fund company—a good thing, even if some of that distribution will disappear to taxes? Not exactly. You see, the distribution you receive will give rise to a tax bill. Generally speaking, you're no better off as a result of the distribution, because the distribution also causes a drop in the per-unit value of the

Action Step

Speak to your financial advisor or mutual fund company in late November each year to determine what distributions, if any, you can expect from the mutual funds you have purchased. This will help you to plan for those taxable distributions. Once the distributions have been paid at the end of December, it will generally be too late to plan for the tax hit.

mutual fund. The result? You now have more units in the mutual fund, because the distribution is generally reinvested to purchase more units, but each unit is now worth less. The total value of your investment in the fund remains about the same—but you're worse off because you now have a tax bill to pay, thanks to the distribution.

Soften the Blow of Year-End Fund Distributions

Let's look at some ways to soften the tax blow when you anticipate a year-end distribution of interest, dividends, or capital gains from a mutual fund.

If you expect a large taxable distribution from a mutual fund that you bought recently, consider transferring the investment to a money market account before the taxable distribution at the end of the year. You'll avoid the ugly tax hit I've been talking about. You can always re-purchase the fund in early January. If, however, the fund has appreciated in value since you bought it, you could face a tax hit when making this transfer, so beware.

 In your personal records, keep track of all re-invested mutual fund distributions that you're taxed on. Add the re-invested amounts to the original cost of your investment. This will boost your adjusted cost base and minimize your taxable capital gains when you finally dispose of the units. If you don't do this, you will effectively be paying tax on the same gains twice.

 If the expected distribution is primarily in the nature of capital gains, consider offsetting these gains by triggering a capital loss before year end through the sale of another investment that has dropped in value since its purchase.

 When you filed your 1994 tax return, you may have created an *exempt gains balance* by electing to use up your $100,000 capital gains exemption. Don't forget to apply this exempt gains balance to offset any taxable mutual fund distributions you might receive.

If you expect a significant taxable distribution, and you have RRSP contribution room, consider transferring your fund to your RRSP today. This may trigger a taxable capital gain, but that gain will be offset by the deduction available for the RRSP contribution. Once inside your RRSP, you'll be protected from any taxable distributions.

TO MAKE A LONG STORY SHORT:

- Buying mutual funds near the end of the year could subject you to taxable distributions normally made at the end of December.

- Paying tax on this distribution could mean that you're effectively paying tax on someone else's profits.

- Consider buying your fund units at the start of the calendar year, or try some of the other strategies I've noted to minimize the tax hit on the annual distributions.

Tim's Tip 54: Avoid index-linked GICs outside your RRSP or RRIF.

As a tax professional, I have a lot to say about index-linked guaranteed investment certificates (GICs)—and most of it is not exactly complimentary.

In a nutshell, indexed-link GICs will offer you the downside protection of a GIC because you're guaranteed to get back your original capital, and if equity markets rise between the purchase date and maturity date of your linked GIC, you'll benefit from those returns. Sounds like a great deal doesn't it? The deal may not be as attractive as you first thought.

Consider this: While your returns may be based on gains in certain stock indices, your tax bill won't be. You see, your investment returns will be taxed as interest income—at your highest marginal tax rate. Normally, when your returns are based on capital appreciation, the tax collector treats the profits as capital gains, with the result that just 75 percent of those gains are subject to tax.

*J*enny *invested $10,000 in a five-year index-linked GIC and the market rose an average of 10 percent annually over those five years. She ended up with cash in her pocket, after taxes, of*

$13,050 thanks to that 10 percent return and a marginal tax rate of 50 percent. If instead she had invested that $10,000 in an equity mutual fund and generated that same 10 percent return, her profits would have been taxed as capital gains, and she would have had $13,820 in her pocket after taxes. This may not seem like a big difference in dollars, but the effective after-tax return over that five-year period works out to be a full 1.21 percent higher with the equity funds than the return offered by the index-linked GIC.

You might be convinced that you can't lose with an index-linked GIC since these generally provide the option of locking-in your returns before the GIC's maturity if you're happy with the performance of the underlying stock index. Here's the problem: Locking in is a taxable event. That's right, the gain that you lock in will be taxed—as interest income—in the year you make that decision.

Caution!

The question you have to ask yourself is this: Are you willing to take a lower effective return on your money for the security of a guarantee on your capital? Don't make your decision just yet—there's more.

You're guaranteed to pay tax in the year the GIC matures. Would this have happened if you had invested in an equity or index mutual fund? Not necessarily. In the latter case, there's the potential that you would not pay tax until you actually sold the investment, particularly if you choose a fund that focuses on long-term appreciation—and this tax hit might not rear its head for a number of years.

TO MAKE A LONG STORY SHORT:

- Index-linked GICs can offer stock market returns, but these returns are taxed as interest income—not capital gains.

- You'd do better for yourself by investing in an equity mutual fund that generates market returns. In this case, your profits will be taxed, appropriately, as capital gains.

- The additional tax savings with the equity fund is your reward for giving up the security of guaranteed capital offered by an index-linked GIC.

Tim's Tip 55: Invest in labour-sponsored funds for tax efficiency and good growth potential.

Let's not get greedy, but when it comes to investing, there's absolutely no reason why you can't have your cake and eat it too. In my mind, this is what a labour-sponsored venture capital corporation (LSVCC) accomplishes.

What's an LSVCC?

An LSVCC is a special corporation designed to provide venture capital to, and promote investment in, small and medium-sized Canadian businesses. And most LSVCCs do a good job at searching out companies with good growth potential. No doubt, an LSVCC is a higher risk investment than your blue-chip stocks or mutual funds, but there's a place in most portfolios for them.

To encourage investment in LSVCCs, the federal and provincial governments

If you want to increase the amount of foreign content that you're entitled to hold inside your RRSP or RRIF, consider investing in an LSVCC. Although you're only entitled to hold 20 percent of the book value of your plan assets in foreign securities, holding certain small business properties in your plan will allow you to increase that foreign content by $3 for every $1 of small business property owned, to a maximum 40 percent foreign content inside your plan. The shares of LSVCCs will generally qualify as small business property, and provide you with this 3-to-1 additional foreign entitlement.

provide healthy tax credits to investors. And the tax credits are worth writing home about. You'll be entitled to a federal credit equal to 15 percent of your investment, and a provincial credit equal to, in most provinces, another 15 percent. In most provinces, then, your total credits will equal 30 percent of your investment, to a maximum of $1,050. This means that the first $3,500 invested in an LSVCC each year will net you the maximum tax credits being offered. But there's sad news for you folks in Alberta, New Brunswick, and Newfoundland: You won't receive any provincial credits.

By the way, if you bought your LSVCC units after March 5, 1996, you'll have to hold those units for eight years from the date of purchase before selling them, otherwise you'll have to repay the generous tax credits you received. Units bought before that date must generally be held for five years.

It's important to know that LSVCC units are RRSP-eligible. You could, for example, contribute new funds to your RRSP to be used to buy LSVCC units. You'll increase your tax savings this way because you'll be entitled to a deduction for the RRSP contribution, plus the tax credits I've talked about. Keep in mind, however, that you could have contributed that same amount to your RRSP to make any other investment instead of the LSVCC, and you'd still receive the tax savings from the RRSP contribution. As a result, your true tax savings from the LSVCC investment will simply be the 30 percent credit generally available.

Make the Most of LSVCCs

Because LSVCCs are higher risk than some of your other investment alternatives, keep these strategies in mind:

- Contribute a maximum $3,500 annually. The attractive tax credits that mitigate some of the risk are only available on the first $3,500 of LSVCCs purchased each year, so don't invest more than this annually.

- Make another RRSP contribution. Use your tax savings from the LSVCC credits to make another RRSP contribution for added tax savings.
- Invest the tax savings in a good-quality equity mutual fund. Your LSVCC investment, while providing very attractive tax savings, is a higher-risk investment. Investing your tax savings in a good-quality, lower-risk, equity mutual fund may enhance the returns and mitigate some of the risk attached to the LSVCC.

TO MAKE A LONG STORY SHORT:

- LSVCCs offer generous tax credits to investors, usually worth up to $1,050 annually in most provinces, and are RRSP-eligible.

- Keep your annual LSVCC investment down to $3,500, since you won't receive credits for amounts over this.

- Use your tax savings from an LSVCC investment to make another RRSP contribution or to invest in a good-quality equity mutual fund.

Taking a Different Route

Tim's Tip 56: Consider an exempt life insurance policy for tax-sheltered growth.

There's no doubt about it: Life insurance can be confusing—and downright intimidating. But don't let this stop you from considering life insurance as an investment tool. Is this for everyone? Nope. This idea works best when two conditions are met: (1) You have already maximized your RRSP contributions; and (2) you need life insurance.

As an investment tool, an exempt life insurance policy can provide a tax shelter offered by little else. You see, under an exempt policy, a portion of each premium that you pay will cover the cost of your insurance, and the balance will be deposited in a growing pool of investments. The policy is called *exempt* because the investment component of the policy grows exempt from tax. That's right, tax-free growth can be yours—much like what you experience with your RRSP. The best part of all this is that, upon your death, the face value of the policy, plus the accumulated investments, are paid out on a tax-free basis to your beneficiaries.

I know what you're probably thinking: "Tim, the problem is that I can't enjoy those investments during my lifetime. I have to die for anyone to benefit here." Not true. You'll be able to access those investments in a number of ways.

For example, you can simply make withdrawals of the accumulated investments during your lifetime, although there could be a tax bill to pay when you do this. Alternatively, you could borrow using the investments in the policy as collateral. Upon your death, the life insurance proceeds would be used to pay off the debt. This last idea is called *leveraged life insurance*, and I like the idea in some cases, but you do run the risk of having your loan plus accrued interest at a level higher than you hoped for at the time of your death. This could leave your beneficiaries worse off than you had intended.

Where will you find an exempt life insurance policy? Most whole life and universal policies are set up to be exempt, but not all policies are created equal. It's important to find out your investment options. Make sure you're able to invest in equities to maximize your investment growth

Did You Know?

In the 1970's, Guaranteed Investment Certificates (GICs) provided returns averaging 9.1 percent annually before taxes and inflation. After taxes and inflation, these GICs showed negative returns of 3.12 percent. In the 1980's, the return was 11.4 percent before taxes and inflation, and negative 0.89 after. In 1996, the return was 4.5 percent before, and 0.78 percent after.

over the long term. Speak to a financial advisor licensed to sell life insurance.

TO MAKE A LONG STORY SHORT:

- An exempt life insurance policy will allow the tax-free growth of investments inside the policy.

- The face value of the policy plus the accumulated investments will be paid out tax-free to your beneficiaries upon your death.

- There are ways of accessing the investments in the policy during your lifetime, although there may be tax or interest costs involved in doing this.

Tim's Tip 57: Use offshore trusts for big tax savings in three scenarios—legally.

Offshore investing often catches the interest of Canadians. But before you get too excited, let me just say that I'm only going to deal with three clearly legal scenarios where an offshore trust could save your family tax. I'm not going to talk about other more aggressive offshore strategies that could, in many cases, offend the tax collector. There's a common thread that runs through each of the scenarios I'm going to talk about: Each involves a non-resident of Canada somehow.

Inheritance Trust. This is the perfect tool when you expect an inheritance from outside Canada. It works this way: Your non-resident relative who plans to leave assets to you upon death, or who wants to make gifts to you during his or her lifetime, should consider placing those assets in a trust located in a low-tax or no-tax jurisdiction. The trust will face little or no tax in the tax haven, and won't face any tax in Canada if the trustees are non-residents for Canadian tax purposes. Payments of tax-free capital can be made from the trust to any Canadian beneficiary. That's right—tax-free! See Chapter 9, Tip 98 for more details.

! **Emigration Trust.** Thinking about leaving Canada? If so, consider setting up a non-resident trust in a tax haven before leaving. While the trust will face taxes in Canada initially, the reach of Revenue Canada will end 18 months after you've given up Canadian residency. The beneficiaries can be Canadian residents, and tax-free payments of capital can be made out of the trust to those beneficiaries.

! **Immigration Trust.** Before coming to Canada, an immigrant can set up a non-resident trust offshore. Any assets in the trust can grow without Canadian taxation for the first 60 months of the immigrant's residency here. This is the case even if the beneficiaries of the trust are Canadian residents.

Foreign Reporting Requirements

The federal government has introduced new rules, effective in 1998, that will require certain Canadian residents to tell the tax collector about certain offshore interests. While I won't delve into the many details here, suffice it to say that anyone transferring or lending funds to a non-resident trust, or anyone receiving distributions from a non-resident trust, may have to file Form T1141 or T1142 each year. In addition, anyone owning foreign property with a cost base of $100,000 or more will be required to file Form T1135, and those with foreign affiliates (a foreign corporation) must file Form T1134.

TO MAKE A LONG STORY SHORT:

- There are three scenarios in which offshore trusts can clearly be used to avoid income tax in Canada.

- Each scenario involves a non-resident of Canada for tax purposes.

- You may be subject to the foreign reporting requirements if you're involved with an offshore trust.

Tim's Tip 58: Defer tax with a commodity straddle, but beware of GAAR.

If you want to really impress your friends, tell them you're using a commodity straddle to shift income from one year to the next. They'll think you're an investment whiz-kid. It's really not difficult to understand, but it's not for the faint-hearted because there's always the chance that Revenue Canada could apply the general anti-avoidance rule (GAAR). GAAR is that provision in our tax law that prevents the use of certain strategies if those strategies violate the intention or spirit of the tax law. GAAR can be applied even where the tactic is well within the wording of our tax law. Still, it could be fun to take a shot at this idea.

Here's how it works. You'll buy two futures contracts: one that offers the right to sell a particular commodity at a certain price within a certain time (a sell position); and another that offers the right to take delivery of that same commodity at a certain price

Don't think about ignoring the new foreign reporting rules. The penalties for failing to file the appropriate information can be steep. Generally, forms T1135, T1134, and T1141 carry maximum penalties of $12,000 ($500 per month for up to 24 months) plus 10 percent of the foreign property beyond 24 months. Form T1142 carries a maximum penalty of $2,500 ($25 per day for up to 100 days). Visit a tax pro for more information on filing requirements.

Caution!

within a certain time (a buy position). By the end of the year, the price of the commodity will have changed, and one of the futures contracts will have dropped in value while the other will have increased in value. Your next move is to sell the losing futures contract before the end of the year, and sell the profitable contract just after year-end. This will provide a deduction on your tax return in the current year, and taxable income next year. In other words, you will have shifted income from this year to next. Nifty idea, isn't it?

In July 1999, Ahmed purchased a futures contract for $4,000, giving him the right to deliver a certain amount of silver at $5 per ounce in March 2000 (a sell position). At the same time, he bought another futures contract giving him the right to take delivery of a similar amount of silver at $5 per ounce, also in March 2000 (a buy position). Toward the end of 1999, silver took a big drop in price and could be purchased for just $3 per ounce at the end of the year. Ahmed's sell position contract increased in value significantly, which makes sense because the contract allows him to sell silver for $5 per ounce when it's currently worth is just $3. On the other hand, his buy position dropped in value since it gives him the right to buy silver at $5 at a time when it can be purchased on the open market for just $3. Ahmed sold his buy position before the end of 1999 and realized a business loss of $2,000. In January 2000, he sold his other futures contract at a profit of about $2,000. Ahmed deferred income tax by shifting income from one year to the next.

TO MAKE A LONG STORY SHORT:

- A commodity straddle is an aggressive tactic that lets you shift income from one year to the next. It involves buying two opposite futures contracts.

- Be aware that the tax collector could potentially invoke GAAR.

Getting into the Game

From mutual funds to commodity straddles, investing properly can make you a clear winner in the tax game. Turn now to the Tax Planning Tip Sheet at the front of the book and review the strategies you've read about in Chapter 5. Ask yourself, "Does this tip apply to me?" When you've finished this book, take your Tip Sheet to a tax professional if you'd like more information on each strategy, or help in implementing the ideas.

EARNING THE GOLD GLOVE: STRATEGIES FOR RETIREMENT

"If you don't know where you're going you might not get there."
~ Yogi Berra

6

I n major league baseball, the Gold Glove is a coveted symbol of achievement. It's awarded to the best fielders in the game—those who rarely make mistakes when the ball comes their way. To earn it, you've got to keep your head up and your errors down. Most important, you've got to know the turf.

You know, retirement planning is a lot like that. If you want to make the most of your golden years, you've got to be alert, keep your mistakes to a minimum, and understand the world of retirement planning. It's going to take some perseverance and good coaching.

Tell you what: You provide the perseverance and I'll provide the coaching. Sound good? Great.

Understanding RRSP Basics

A registered retirement savings plan (RRSP) is a plan registered with Revenue Canada that is designed to encourage and help you save for your retirement. And make no mistake, an RRSP should be the cornerstone of any effective tax plan.

Tim's Tip 59: Contribute to an RRSP for tax deferral and tax-free growth.

Your RRSP offers two attractive benefits that can't be ignored: a tax deferral, and tax-free growth of your investments.

A Tax Deferral

Your RRSP contributions offer a deferral of tax because you'll be permitted to push a portion of your taxable income to a future year. No kidding. When you contribute to your RRSP within your contribution limit, the amount of that contribution may be deducted on your tax return, reducing your taxable income. You won't face tax on those funds until they're withdrawn from your RRSP—usually in a much later year.

For example, suppose you contribute $5,000 to your RRSP at age 35. So long as this is within your contribution limit, you'll be able to deduct the full amount from your earned income. If your marginal tax rate is 50 percent, your tax saving will be $2,500 in the year you make the contribution. Now let's say you leave the $5,000 to grow in your RRSP until you reach age 65 and then withdraw $5,000 from your plan. In that year—a full 30 years later—you'll face a $2,500 tax bill. Here's what you could do now to pay that $2,500 tax bill 30 years down the road: You could take $578 today, invest it for 30 years at an after-tax return of 5 percent annually, and watch it grow to be worth $2,500 in 30 years. You could then pay your tax bill with that money. Because of the tax deferral resulting from your RRSP deduction, your tax bill would really cost just $578, not $2,500. Effectively, you would have reduced your tax bill by pushing it to a future year. This is the value of tax deferral.

Tax-Free Growth

Your RRSP offers another significant benefit. I'm talking about tax-free growth inside the plan. Unlike investments held outside your RRSP (your *open money*), the investments inside your RRSP will not be taxed as they grow each year, regardless of how much you earn inside the plan.

Don't underestimate the value of this tax-free growth! Just look at how much more you'll have by investing inside your RRSP than outside. If you socked away $200 each month for thirty years and enjoyed annual growth on your money of 10 percent, you'd have $200,900 at the end of that period if you invested outside your RRSP, assuming an effective tax rate of 40 percent. But what if you made those same monthly contributions for the same length of time, earned that same 10 percent, but invested *inside* your RRSP? When all is said and done, your investments would be worth a whopping $452,100—more than double what you'd have outside your RRSP.

Action Step

To take full advantage of the tax-free growth offered by your RRSP, start a "pay yourself first" plan. It's not complicated. Each month, simply transfer a fixed dollar amount to your RRSP. Think of it as a mandatory payment, like a car loan or mortgage payment. Set up this automatic contribution plan with your financial advisor or financial institution and watch your RRSP grow!

Sure, you're going to pay tax on these RRSP assets once you withdraw the money from your plan, but this won't happen in a single year—it's going to take place slowly over time—so your tax deferral and tax-free growth may continue for your lifetime.

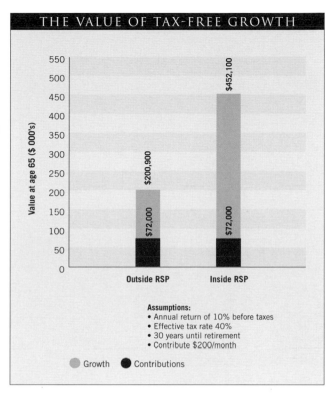

THE VALUE OF TAX-FREE GROWTH

Assumptions:
- Annual return of 10% before taxes
- Effective tax rate 40%
- 30 years until retirement
- Contribute $200/month

Growth ● Contributions

And the earlier in life you start your contributions, the more you'll benefit from the tax-free growth. For example, suppose that you contributed $3,000 to your RRSP each year for 10 years, starting at age 30, and then left those funds to grow at 10 percent each year until you were 65. How much would you have at age 65? The graph below shows a value of $518,030. Not bad on total contributions of just $30,000! But what if you waited just five short years until age 35 before making any RRSP contributions, and then contributed $3,000 every year until age 65—a total of $90,000 in contributions? At age 65 you'd have just $493,480. That's right, you'd end up with *less* by waiting five years, even though you would have invested more of your money.

The moral of the story is simple: The earlier you start your RRSP savings, the better off you'll be in retirement.

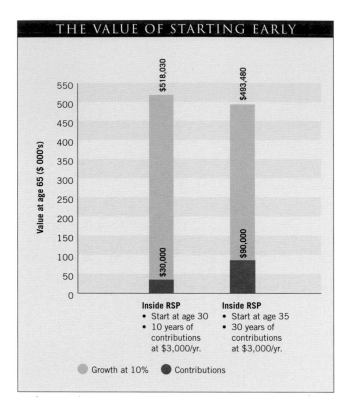

THE VALUE OF STARTING EARLY

Value at age 65 ($ 000's)

$518,030

$493,480

$30,000

$90,000

Inside RSP
• Start at age 30
• 10 years of
  contributions
  at $3,000/yr.

Inside RSP
• Start at age 35
• 30 years of
  contributions
  at $3,000/yr.

⬤ Growth at 10%   ⬤ Contributions

TO MAKE A LONG STORY SHORT:

• An RRSP offers two significant benefits: a deferral of tax and tax-free growth inside the plan.

• The earlier in life that you start, the greater the benefit to you in retirement.

• You'll face tax on your RRSP assets once you make withdrawals from your plan, but these withdrawals will be made slowly over time and won't begin for a number of years, multiplying the benefits of the deferral and the tax-free growth.

Tim's Tip 60: Understand whether your RRSP assets are protected from creditors.

Traditionally, it's been held that your RRSP is fair game when settling your debts, unless your RRSP is held by an insurance company. With an insurance-type RRSP, the RRSP assets will be protected from creditors, as established in a recent court case (*Royal Bank v. North American Life*, 96 DTC 6157).

Does this mean, then, that RRSPs held at other financial institutions are at risk if a creditor decides to chase those assets? The answer is not clear, and may depend on the facts in your situation. You see, another court case (*National Trust Company v. The Queen*, 96 DTC 1832) could provide you with some hope of protection. Here's the deal: National Trust was the carrier of a self-directed RRSP, and a beneficiary was named by the contributor of the RRSP to receive the assets of the plan on the death of the contributor. The contributor owed some tax dollars to Revenue Canada, so the tax collector asked National Trust to hand over the RRSP assets to satisfy the unpaid tax bill. National Trust told the tax collector to take a hike. When the trust company refused to hand over the funds, Revenue Canada assessed the trust company directly for the taxes owing, for failing to comply. In the end, the court sided with the trust company.

If you're going to withdraw money from your RRSP, be aware that these funds will become fair game for creditors, even if your RRSP turns out to be creditor-proof itself. And if you're thinking of declaring bankruptcy and you make an RRSP contribution with the hope of sheltering those assets from creditors, think again. There are laws designed to prevent this kind of sheltering.

Caution!

The court decided that the funds held under an RRSP are in fact held in trust. The beneficiary in this case did not request payment from the RRSP trust, so the trust company was not required to make payment.

TO MAKE A LONG STORY SHORT:

- RRSPs administered by insurance companies are generally protected from creditors.

- It has traditionally been believed that other RRSPs are vulnerable to creditors, but a recent court decision would suggest that your RRSP might be protected.

Tim's Tip 61: Pay your RRSP fees from outside your plan up to age 69.

Talk about confusing. I need two hands and a foot to count the number of times the tax collector has changed opinions on how your RRSP and registered retirement income fund (RRIF) fees will be treated for tax purposes. You may recall that, back in 1996, the rules were changed to disallow any kind of deduction for RRSP or RRIF fees. This rule still holds today. Regardless of whether it's your annual administration fee (typically between $40 and $125), or investment management fees (often a percentage of your assets), the fees are not deductible.

If these fees happen to be paid from inside your RRSP or RRIF (that is, paid using assets inside your plan), these payments *will not* be considered taxable withdrawals by you, which is great news. Likewise, if you pay these fees from outside your plan, the payments *will not* be considered a contribution to the plan anymore. This too is great news.

Here's the game plan: Pay these fees from outside your plan up to age 69. This will allow your plan assets to grow untouched, and will result in more assets in your plan at retirement. However, once you've reached age 69, start paying these annual fees from inside your plan. This makes sense because, at age 69, you've got to start making withdrawals on a regular basis, and each fee payment is like a tax-free withdrawal from the plan.

Action Step

If you pay a single fee (sometimes called a *wrap* fee) to your financial advisor each year for managing your investment accounts, keep in mind that the fee will be deductible if the account is non-registered. You'll have no such luck deducting the fee for your RRSP or RRIF. If your advisor can make a reasonable allocation of the fee to one account or the other, you'll come out ahead if the greater portion of the fee is allocated to the non-registered account, since this fee will be deductible.

TO MAKE A LONG STORY SHORT:

- Administration and investment management fees for your RRSP or RRIF are not deductible for tax purposes.

- Pay these fees from outside your plan up to age 69 to preserve the growth of your plan assets. From age 69 onward, pay the fees from inside the plan as a way to make tax-free withdrawals from the plan.

Contributing to Your RRSP

Tim's Tip 62: Know your RRSP contribution limit each year, then avoid an accumulation of contribution room.

How much are you entitled to contribute to your RRSP each year? Well, that depends on your earned income in the previous year. You're entitled to contribute up to 18 percent of your earned income from the previous year, to a yearly maximum amount. If, for example, you had $75,000 of earned income in 1998, you'd be entitled to $13,500 ($75,000 x 18 percent) of RRSP contribution room in 1999.

What is *earned income?* Basically, it includes employment income, rental income (minus losses), self-employment income (minus losses), royalties if you're an author or inventor, and alimony or separation payments received (subtract these payments if you made them). But the following don't qualify: investment income, pension income, RRSP or RRIF income, Old Age Security (OAS) or Canada Pension Plan (CPP) income, retiring allowances or death benefits, scholarships or bursaries, or income from limited partnerships.

The most obvious place to find out how much you're entitled to contribute to an RRSP is your Notice of Assessment—that form you get in the mail each year after filing your tax return. Your assessment will detail the amount of your contribution room and is usually accurate. But if you disagree with yours, don't hesitate to get a tax pro involved, since you don't want to rob yourself of contribution room.

By the way, if you don't make the maximum contribution to your RRSP in a given year, your contribution room will be carried forward for use in any future year. But don't get in the habit of allowing that room to accumulate for too long. After all, if you had trouble making a $5,000 contribution this year, it's going to be that much harder to make an even larger contribution next year! Besides, you could be enjoying a deferral of tax and that tax-free growth I spoke about earlier.

	MAXIMUM RRSP CONTRIBUTIONS	
Year	**18% of earned income from the prior year, to a maximum of:**
1998 to 2003	$13,500
2004	$14,500
2005	$15,500
2006	indexed to inflation

TO MAKE A LONG STORY SHORT:

- You're entitled to contribute 18 percent of your earned income from the prior year to an RRSP, to a yearly maximum.

- Even though unused contribution room can be carried forward, don't let this happen, since you'll be giving up a valuable tax deferral and tax-free growth of your money.

Tim's Tip 63: **Make a contribution in-kind to your RRSP if you're low on cash.**

Who says that your RRSP contributions have to be in the form of cash? It's just not true. In fact, you'll be able to contribute a whole host of qualifying assets to your RRSP, including:

- cash
- guaranteed investment certificates
- most mutual funds
- government-guaranteed debt obligations
- corporate bonds or other debt obligations
- shares listed on a prescribed stock exchange (Canadian and foreign)
- shares of certain private corporations
- mortgages secured by real property in Canada
- certain annuities
- certain life insurance policies
- certain rights and warrants
- other less common investments.

If you're going to contribute *in-kind* rather than in cash, there are two tax consequences:

First, you'll be entitled to a deduction just as you would with any RRSP contribution in cash. The value of the contribution simply equals the fair market value of the assets being contributed to your plan.

Second, you'll be deemed to have sold those assets when you contribute them to the plan. So, where those assets have gone up in value, you might face a taxable capital gain. Of course, the RRSP deduction will usually offset any taxable gain. On the flip side, if the asset you're contributing has gone down in value, the tax collector won't let you claim a capital loss on this transfer to your RRSP. Sorry.

Make sure that you don't contribute a non-qualifying asset to your RRSP—the effect could be ugly. In fact, you could face tax on some of the earnings inside your RRSP, tax on the value of those non-qualifying assets, or deregistration of your plan. Do you know what deregistration means? It means you could pay tax on the full amount of your RRSP assets in a single year! While this is not likely to happen, it's a possibility.

Make sure you've got enough RRSP contribution room available before making any contribution, including one in-kind. By the way, you'll generally have to set up a self-directed RRSP in order to make a contribution in-kind.

TO MAKE A LONG STORY SHORT:

- If you haven't got the cash, contribute in-kind to maximize your RRSP contributions.

- You'll be deemed to have sold any investment that is contributed in-kind, which could mean a taxable capital gain; but you'll also be entitled to a deduction for your contribution in-kind, within your contribution limits.

- Set up a self-directed RRSP to make a contribution in-kind.

Tim's Tip 64: Maximize your RRSP contributions, even if you have to borrow the money.

Truthfully, in most situations you'll be better off borrowing to make your RRSP contribution than not contributing at all, or than making that contribution two or three years down the road. You won't be entitled to claim a deduction for the interest on your RRSP loan; but don't worry, it still works to your benefit to borrow because that money is working for you by growing tax-free. If you have investments outside your RRSP, you may be better off to contribute those to your RRSP and then borrow to replace the non-registered investments. That way, the interest will be deductible. This is a contribution in-kind, as I discussed in Tip 63.

TO MAKE A LONG STORY SHORT:

- Borrowing to contribute to your RRSP makes sense when your other choices are to make no contribution or to delay the contribution for even two or three years.

- The interest on your RRSP loan will not be deductible.

Tim's Tip 65: **Have your employer contribute directly to your RRSP.**

What if I told you that there's a way to nearly double your ability to contribute to your RRSP? Arranging for your employer to send a portion of your pay directly to your RRSP could accomplish this. These are called *employer-direct contributions*. All that's necessary is enough contribution room and some cooperation from the boss.

Action Step

Let me buck a trend here. It's been commonly held that you should borrow for your RRSP and pay back that loan over a period of no more than one year. I don't buy this advice. Even a five- or ten-year loan can leave you better off in the long run when it lets you use up more of your contribution room. Besides, many Canadians have accumulated so much room that it would be impossible to borrow and pay back the loan over one year.

*R*ob's employer was due to pay him a bonus of $10,000 at the end of last year. If the bonus had been paid directly to Rob, his employer would have been required to deduct withholding tax for remittance to Revenue Canada. This would have left Rob with about $5,000, which he planned to contribute to his RRSP. But Rob managed to contribute much more. Rather than taking payment of the $10,000 bonus in his own hands, Rob arranged for his employer to send the amount directly to his RRSP carrier. As a result, his employer was not required to deduct the withholding tax; only Canada Pension Plan (CPP) and

Employment Insurance (EI) contributions were required. (Coincidentally, $10,000 is the most Rob's employer is able to send to his RRSP and still avoid the withholding tax.) Because almost all of the $10,000 was contributed to his RRSP, Rob effectively doubled his RRSP contribution without even borrowing to make it happen!

Maybe your situation is a little different from Rob's. He received a bonus. But if you're not slated to receive a bonus of any kind, the employer-direct idea still works well where your employer deducts a set amount from each pay, or simply sends one or two pay cheques each year to your RRSP. I like the idea better than most group RRSPs because it will give you more flexibility.

If you do receive a bonus from your employer, there's one other trick you can play. It worked well for Rob. He arranged for his employer to send his 1998 bonus directly to his RRSP carrier, but also arranged for this to happen in the first 60 days of 1999. The result? Rob gets a deduction on his 1998 tax return for the RRSP contribution, but he won't be taxed on the bonus until 1999, since it wasn't paid out until 1999. In short, he has managed to defer tax on the bonus for a year *and* claim a deduction for the amount of that income a year earlier.

Action Step

Your employer may wonder how in the world an employer-direct RRSP contribution works. It's really quite simple. Your employer will write a cheque to your RRSP carrier for a portion of your pay. That portion of your pay must still be reported on your T4 slip, but there's no need for your employer to withhold income tax on the amount. Regulation 100(3) of our tax law says so. There are no special forms to fill out to allow for these contributions.

TO MAKE A LONG STORY SHORT:

- Employer-direct RRSP contributions can significantly increase the amount you're able to contribute to your RRSP without borrowing.

- Your employer will simply send a portion of your pay directly to your RRSP carrier, and will avoid income tax withholdings (although CPP and EI will still be payable).

- Your employer should keep the payment at or below $10,000 to avoid tax withholdings.

Tim's Tip 66: Over-contribute $2,000 to your RRSP if you can leave it for 10 years.

For the most part, you can expect to face some penalties if you contribute too much to your RRSP. In fact, this penalty equals 1 percent of the excess amount per month. The good news, however, is that the tax collector will allow you a $2,000 cushion. That's right, the first $2,000 of over-contributions to your RRSP will not attract a penalty. You won't be entitled to claim a deduction for this over-contribution, but the money will still grow tax-free while it's in the plan.

Some argue that the over-contribution doesn't make sense because you're going to be taxed on that $2,000 when you eventually withdraw it from your RRSP, without having ever received a deduction when you put it into the plan. In other words, you'll face double tax here. I agree that the over-contribution doesn't make sense if you make the contribution and then withdraw the money in the very near future. But if you've got 10 years or more before you start making withdrawals from your RRSP, then the growth on that money inside the plan will outweigh any double-tax problem you might face. And that $2,000 will grow to be worth nearly $35,000 over a 30-year period if you earn 10 percent on your money each year. By the way, you're only entitled to this $2,000 over-contribution once you've reached 18   so your minor children can't take advantage of this.

TO MAKE A LONG STORY SHORT:

- Excess contributions to an RRSP attract a monthly penalty of 1 percent of the excess amount.

- You're entitled to a $2,000 over-contribution and should take advantage of this when you have 10 years or more before you'll be making regular withdrawals from your RRSP.

If you're 69 this year and you have earned income, making next year's RRSP contribution before winding up your RRSP this year can make great sense. But don't get greedy. You might be tempted to make not only next year's contribution, but contributions for the next number of years—all just before winding up your plan. If you do this, you run the risk that the tax collector may take offence and close this strategy to everyone. Two or three years of RRSP contributions before winding up your plan should be the max.

Caution!

Tim's Tip 67: Over-contribute to your RRSP just before winding up the plan at age 69, if you have earned income.

While an RRSP is going to help you save for retirement, you won't be able to keep your plan forever. Because of changes introduced in the 1996 federal budget, you're going to have to wind up your RRSP by December 31 of the year you turn 69. Wouldn't it be nice if you could somehow contribute to an RRSP even beyond age 69? Well, you can. One option is a spousal RRSP, which I'll talk about in Tip 72. Your other option is what I call the senior's over-contribution.

*P*avel turned age 69 in July 1999, and so he's going to have to wind up his RRSP by the end of 1999. But he has earned income for RRSP

*purposes in 1999 of $75,000. The result? Pavel is entitled to
$13,500 (18 percent of $75,000) of RRSP contribution room in
the year 2000. The problem, however, is that Pavel won't be able
to contribute to an RRSP in the year 2000 since his RRSP must
be wound up by the end of 1999. Does he lose the ability to
make an RRSP contribution for the year 2000? No!*

*Pavel is going to take advantage of his year 2000 contribution
room by making his year 2000 RRSP contribution in December
1999, before he winds up his RRSP forever. Provided that Pavel
has already maximized his RRSP contributions for 1999, making
an additional contribution of $13,500 in December will result in
an over-contribution to his RRSP, and will mean a penalty of
$115 for that month. Effective January 1, 2000, Pavel's over-
contribution problem disappears, because he's entitled to new
contribution room of $13,500 on that date (due to his 1999
earned income). The over-contribution made in December 1999
will provide Pavel with a $13,500 RRSP deduction in the year
2000, saving him $6,750 in taxes at a marginal tax rate of 50
percent. Even a tax accountant can see that $6,750 in tax savings
is greater than a $115 penalty!*

The key here is that you're going to need earned income for RRSP
purposes in the year you turn age 69 for this to work. With some
active tax planning, it may be possible to generate earned income for
yourself to allow use of this tactic. Your tax pro or financial advisor
can help.

TO MAKE A LONG STORY SHORT:

- You'll have to wind up your RRSP by December 31 of the year you turn 69.

- You may be able to take advantage of RRSP deductions beyond age 69
  through the senior's over-contribution, which involves making one last
  over-contribution to your RRSP just before winding up the plan at age 69.

- The tax savings from the future RRSP deduction will outweigh any penalties owing from the over-contribution.

Tim's Tip 68: Boost the value of your RRSP with tax-free rollovers.

If the name of the game is maximizing the contributions to your RRSP to build wealth for retirement, then you need to be aware of the opportunities to transfer potentially large sums to your RRSP, tax-free. These are called *tax-free rollovers*. I want to tell you about six rollover scenarios.

Transfers From One RRSP to the Next

I have a friend named Pat. He's always been the kind of guy who is never really satisfied with the return on his investments. So, Pat has jumped from one mutual fund RRSP account to the next at least five times in the last six years. Good thing for Pat that assets can be transferred tax-free among RRSP accounts. I, on the other hand, have changed RRSP accounts only once. I moved from an account with a reputable mutual fund company to a self-directed RRSP. A self-directed plan let me continue holding those mutual funds I owned, but I'm now able to hold many other kinds of investments as well. I like the flexibility. Whatever your reasons for changing, rest assured that the tax collector doesn't mind a move from one RRSP account to the next. Too bad Martin didn't know that. Here's his story.

Since Martin has not been thrilled with his RRSP's investment performance, he has decided to switch from one RRSP to another with different investment options. Last week he withdrew the full $30,000 sitting in his original RRSP and then wrote a cheque for $30,000 to his new RRSP carrier. In doing this, Martin made a mistake that cost him $10,000 in tax! You see, Martin only has $10,000 of RRSP contribution room *available. Because he made a $30,000 withdrawal, he has to report this amount as income this year. But he's only entitled to contribute $10,000 this year to an RRSP and claim a deduction for it. The remaining $20,000 will be exposed to tax this year. Yikes—bad move by Martin. He could have avoided any tax on the $30,000 by arranging for a direct transfer of his RRSP assets to the new account!*

Retiring Allowance Rollovers

It could be that you're entitled to receive a retiring allowance when you leave your current job. A retiring allowance could include any number of payments received by you, or your loved ones after your death, in recognition of your service. These payments might also include early retirement incentives or even damages received as a result of wrongful dismissal. At any rate, a retiring allowance can be rolled to your RRSP tax-free—up to certain limits.

The maximum that can be rolled into an RRSP tax-free is $2,000 for each year of service before 1996, plus an extra $1,500 for each year before 1989 in which you had no vested interest in any employer's contributions to a registered pension plan (RPP) or deferred profit sharing plan (DPSP). You'll be glad to know that this rollover does not have to be direct from your employer to your RRSP. That is, you'll be able to take the money into your hands personally and still roll those funds to an RRSP as long as you make that contribution within 60 days after the end of the year in which you received the payment. This rollover is made over and above your available contribution room.

Here's one last point: The 1998 federal budget improved things for those who transfer retiring allowances to RRSPs. This rollover often creates a sizeable RRSP deduction for the individual in the year the rollover is made. This used to create an Alternative Minimum Tax (AMT) problem in some cases. AMT is simply an amount of tax that

If you received a retiring allowance in 1994 or later years and rolled a portion of it to your RRSP, there's a good chance you may have run into the Alternative Minimum Tax (AMT) in the year of that rollover. But the 1998 federal budget has changed the AMT rules retroactive to 1994. So, if you still have any unused AMT credits outstanding from the past that arose from a retiring allowance rollover, you may be due for a cash refund from the tax collector. Make sure you receive it!

Revenue Canada will require you to pay, as a minimum, if you claim certain large deductions. This is no longer an issue. The feds have said that RRSP deductions will no longer be factored into the calculation of AMT.

RPP Assets to an RRSP

While most registered pension plans (RPPs) discourage or prohibit some transfers from the RPP to an RRSP, there are four situations where this can be done. Keep in mind that transfers from an RPP to an RRSP have to be made directly—you can't take these funds into your own hands first.

- **If you leave your job** for any reason, you may be entitled to take with you certain funds in the company pension plan that are earmarked for you. The amount you can take is generally called the *commuted value* of your pension. Before you get too excited about walking away with thousands of pension dollars at your disposal, be aware that the commuted value can generally be transferred to a locked-in RRSP only. You won't be able to make any old withdrawal from a locked-in plan. Locked-in RRSPs will restrict your withdrawals in a way that is consistent with the payments you would have received under the terms of your pension plan. The benefit of a locked-in plan is that, unlike your pension plan, you have complete control over your investments and could quite possibly generate a greater return on those assets than your pension plan would have offered you. This will spell greater income in retirement.

- **If you die** while still a member of your company pension plan, a tax-free transfer can be made to the RRSP or RPP of a surviving spouse.
- **If you separate or divorce**, and you have a written separation agreement or court order, a lump-sum amount can be transferred from your RPP to the RRSP or RPP of your spouse or ex-spouse.
- **If your pension plan has been amended** to retroactively reduce or remove the requirement for you to make contributions to your company's registered pension plan, you may be entitled to receive a return of your pre-1991 contributions plus accumulated interest. If you transfer this money directly to your RRSP, the transfer will be tax-free.

Inherited RRSP Assets

Your RRSP could cause you some grief as you try to come up with a way to avoid a tax hit on those assets when you die. In many cases, RRSP assets will be taxed on the deceased's final tax return, and whatever is left will pass to the heirs. There are two ways to transfer RRSP assets from the deceased's plan to another RRSP, RRIF, or annuity to defer tax a little longer. The first is to leave your plan assets to your spouse. The second is to transfer the plan's assets for the benefit of a dependent. Check out Chapter 9, Tip 94 for all the details.

Transfers Upon Marriage Breakdown

If you're planning to make an equalization payment to your spouse after separating or divorcing, you can use your RRSP assets to do it. You see, any payments transferred directly from your RRSP to your spouse's RRSP, RRIF, or RPP as a result of a marriage breakdown can be transferred tax-free. Before making a transfer, keep in mind that this rollover must follow a written separation agreement, or a decree, order or judgment by a competent tribunal. I dealt with tax issues around separation and divorce in Chapter 2.

U.S. IRA to an RRSP

You'd be surprised how often I'm asked whether or not it's possible to transfer assets to an RRSP from a U.S. Individual Retirement Account (IRA), which is effectively the U.S. version of an RRSP. The short answer is yes. Our tax law will allow a tax-free transfer to take place—and so I'm including this item in my list of tax-free rollovers. Here's the problem: You won't be able to avoid the long arm of the IRS on withdrawals from an IRA. You'll face tax at graduated U.S. tax rates, plus you'll face a 10-percent early withdrawal penalty if the withdrawal is made before age 59-and-a-half. The bottom line? Unless the U.S. tax hit is minimal, I usually advise that an IRA be kept intact, although each case deserves its own look. I'll deal with other U.S. tax issues in Chapter 7.

Tim's Tip 69: Ensure that your child files a tax return to maximize RRSP contribution room.

Seven years ago, when I told my cousin Erik that he should file a tax return, he gave me that "I-dunno-what-you're-talking-about-and-sounds-like-a-grown-up-kind-of-thing-to-do" sort of look. Erik was fifteen years old at the time. But he took my advice, and today he's reaping the benefits. If that special child in your life has earned any income at all, make sure he or she files a tax return. In fact, there's no requirement to file a return in most cases, unless the child's income exceeds the basic and supplementary personal tax credits totalling $6,956 ($6,707 in 1998), or if the child has capital gains to report, in which case Revenue Canada expects a return to be filed. But the benefits of filing a tax return when your child has earned income can't be ignored.

*W*hen Erik was 15 years old he started his own lawn-care service. It didn't make him rich, but it gave him some spending money and later helped to pay for his university *education. Even though his income each summer was well under $6,000, he filed tax returns anyway. The income he reported qualified as earned income and created RRSP contribution room. By the time Erik finished university, he had $5,000 worth of contribution room. This year, in his first year of full-time work after graduation, Erik is going to make that $5,000 contribution to his RRSP. This is going to save him over $2,000 in tax.*

Filing a tax return will benefit your child in two important ways. First, it's going to create valuable RRSP contribution room, which will save your child taxes down the road and provide a good head start in saving for retirement. Second, it will teach your child something about money and taxes if you keep them involved in the process.

TO MAKE A LONG STORY SHORT:

- There's no requirement to file a tax return unless income is over $6,956 or there are capital gains to report.

- Even if it's not required, helping your child file a tax return can be worthwhile because it will create valuable RRSP contribution room that will save your child tax down the road and provide a good head start in saving for retirement.

Tim's Tip 70: Claim your RRSP deduction in the right year.

Patience, my friend, patience. It's so tempting to make a contribution to an RRSP and claim the deduction on your tax return as soon as possible. But this doesn't always make sense. You see, you're not required to claim a deduction for your RRSP contribution in the year you make the contribution. Did you know that? In fact, you're able to claim that deduction in any future year. I'll admit, there are few

Action Step

If you're in your early sixties and you're concerned about the clawback of Old Age Security benefits, consider making contributions to your RRSP but saving the deduction for a future year when the clawback might be an issue.

things harder in life than forgoing a tax deduction when you know you could be claiming it today. The only thing harder is opening a bag of potato chips and eating just one. It takes willpower. Nevertheless, I'm going to suggest that in certain situations it makes a whole lot of sense to exercise some of that willpower and put off your RRSP deduction to a future year.

Picture this. You make a $5,000 contribution to your RRSP in February of 1999. The RRSP rules actually say that you can make your RRSP contribution for a particular year as late as 60 days following the end of that year (your 1998 contribution can be made as late as March 1, 1999). As a result, the $5,000 contribution you make in February 1999 will entitle you to a deduction in 1998, or any future year. If your marginal tax rate in 1998 is, say, 26 percent, then you'll save $1,300 ($5,000 x 26%) through the RRSP deduction. But suppose for a minute that your income in 1999 is expected to be significantly higher, pushing you into a 50 percent marginal tax bracket. By saving your RRSP deduction for just one year, you'll manage to increase your tax savings from that deduction. At a 50 percent marginal tax rate, your savings on a $5,000 contribution will be $2,500. Any financial advisor worth his or her salt will tell you that $2,500 in tax savings next year is better than $1,300 in savings today.

TO MAKE A LONG STORY SHORT:

- Your RRSP contributions will entitle you to a deduction on your tax return, but that deduction may be put off and claimed in any future year.

- Delaying the deduction may make sense when you expect to face a higher marginal tax rate in the next couple of years.

Tim's Tip 71: Contribute to your RRSP instead of paying down your mortgage.

Canadians love real estate. Canadians also love to pay down the mortgage on that real estate as quickly as possible. I can understand why. On a $100,000 mortgage amortized over 25 years with an interest rate of 8 percent, you're on course to pay over $131,500 in interest alone over 25 years. Scary, isn't it? But hold on a minute. When you've got to make a decision between paying down the mortgage or contributing to an RRSP, many Canadians make the wrong move. Your best bet, in almost every case, is to contribute to your RRSP. If you took the time to do the math, you'd agree with me.

Only in very rare circumstances does it actually make sense to pay down the mortgage first. If the following two conditions are *both* met, then by all means pay down the mortgage as your first priority:

- The interest rate on your mortgage is 3 percent higher than the rate of return of your RRSP, and
- You're committed to contributing two-thirds of your annual mortgage payments to your RRSP once the mortgage is paid off.

Meeting the first of these conditions is going to be unlikely, so your best option will generally be contributing to your RRSP first. But why not have your cake and eat it too? Here's how: Contribute to your RRSP each year, and use the tax savings to pay down the mortgage.

TO MAKE A LONG STORY SHORT:

- Except in very rare situations, you'll be better off making contributions to your RRSP than paying down the mortgage.

- Get the best of both worlds by contributing to your RRSP and then using the tax savings to pay down the mortgage.

Tim's Tip 72: Contribute to a spousal RRSP to equalize incomes in retirement.

Share and share alike. I think that the soul who first spoke these words was actually a Canadian looking to keep a lid on the family tax bill. I'm talking about one very effective strategy: splitting income with your spouse. You see, in an ideal situation, you and your spouse should have equal incomes during retirement. This keeps the total family tax bill at a minimum. The most practical tool for accomplishing this splitting of income is a spousal RRSP.

A spousal RRSP is simply an RRSP that you will contribute to, but that your spouse will make withdrawals from. You'll get a deduction for making the contribution, but your spouse, being the annuitant, will pay the tax on any withdrawals. How's that for moving income directly from one spouse to the next? Let me share with you a few facts and strategies surrounding spousal RRSPs.

Caution!

Keep in mind that you won't be entitled to additional RRSP contribution room to contribute to a spousal RRSP. That is, the total contributions to your own RRSP and to a spousal RRSP combined must be within your annual contribution limits. If you exceed your limit, you'll generally be able to withdraw the excess tax-free, but you'll face a penalty of 1 percent per month on the excess contribution until you withdraw it.

Avoiding Attribution on Withdrawals

Our tax law has been designed to avoid abuses of spousal RRSPs. To this end, any withdrawals your spouse makes from a spousal RRSP will actually be taxed in *your* hands if you made contributions to a spousal RRSP in the year of withdrawal or in the previous two years. For example, if your last contribution to a spousal RRSP was $5,000 in 1997, and your spouse withdraws $7,000 from a spousal plan in 1999, the first $5,000 of that withdrawal will be taxed in your hands since that's the amount of the withdrawal that can be attributed to contributions you made in the year of the withdrawal or the previous two years. To avoid this attribution of withdrawals, the withdrawals will have to wait until the third calendar year after you make your last contribution.

Contributing by December 31

You can effectively reduce the waiting period for withdrawals from a spousal RRSP to just two years—and still avoid attribution—by making spousal RRSP contributions by December 31 each year.

Dave has been contributing to a spousal RRSP for his wife Andrea. His last contribution was on December 31, 1997. Dave and Andrea gave birth to a child in 1999, and Andrea decided to stay home with the new baby for a while. Since Andrea's income will be quite low during this time, she has decided to withdraw $6,900 from the spousal RRSP in the year 2000. The $6,900 will be taxed in Andrea's hands, not Dave's, since Dave will not have made a contribution to the spousal RRSP in the year of the withdrawal (2000), or in the prior two years (1998 and 1999). The good news is that the funds inside the spousal RRSP were really tied up for just two years plus a day (December 31, 1997, to January 1, 2000). If Dave had made his last contribution to the spousal plan just one day later, in 1998, Andrea would have to wait a whole extra year before she could make withdrawals and avoid attribution of the income back to Dave. As an aside, since Andrea will have no other income in the year 2000, she won't face any tax on the $6,900 *withdrawal because this is less than her basic personal and supplementary credits of $6,956.*

Contributing Beyond Age 69

A spousal RRSP is a great tool for making contributions to an RRSP even when you pass age 69 and have wound up your own RRSP. You see, as long as your spouse is still 69 or under in the year, you'll be able to make a contribution to a spousal RRSP in the year, regardless of your own age. Of course, you'll need to have RRSP contribution room available before making any contributions.

Contributing With a Deceased's Assets

Here's a little-known tactic that could save your heirs a bundle of tax when you die. I'm referring to one final RRSP contribution that your executor is permitted to make. If you have RRSP contribution room available at the time of your death, your executor will be able to use your assets to make a contribution to a spousal RRSP. The deduction will be claimed on your final tax return. Your spouse will have to be age 69 or under in the year of your death to allow for this contribution. See Chapter 9, Tip 95 for more.

TO MAKE A LONG STORY SHORT:

- A spousal RRSP is a plan that you contribute to but your spouse makes withdrawals from.

- You're entitled to a deduction and your spouse will be taxed on any withdrawals, which accomplishes a perfect splitting of income.

- Watch out for attribution rules, which could tax some of the withdrawals in the hands of the contributor.

- A spousal plan can be used to make RRSP contributions beyond age 69, and to reduce taxes upon your death through a contribution by the executor.

Withdrawing From Your RRSP

You've worked hard to put money aside in your RRSP. At some point, those funds are going to be withdrawn from the plan. Most commonly, you'll withdraw them once you've decided to retire and you need a steady income from those investments. But there may be times in life when you decide that you need to make RRSP withdrawals sooner.

Before jumping at the chance to pull money out of your RRSP for reasons other than retirement, stop and think twice. You stand to give up plenty of growth in your RRSP by making withdrawals early. Want proof? Consider the cost of RRSP withdrawals shown in the graph. If you make a $5,000 withdrawal from your RRSP and you have 30 years to go before retirement, you'll give up $87,250 in retirement savings because of your withdrawal, assuming a 10 percent return on your money. A $20,000 withdrawal with 20 years to go before retirement will cost you $134,550!

If you still plan to make withdrawals from your RRSP, there are some tax-efficient ways to do this. Let's take a look at them.

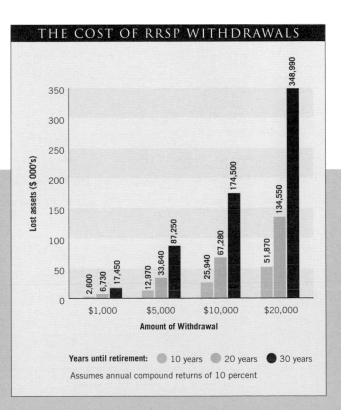

Tim's Tip 73: **Make RRSP withdrawals during periods of no or low income.**

There's no doubt that at certain times in your life you might find yourself strapped for cash. During these times, your RRSP can act as a source of income if need be. It could be that you're unemployed, on disability leave, or on maternity or paternity leave. Perhaps you're launching a new business and haven't started generating any income yet. In any event, these times of no or low income may allow you to make very tax-efficient withdrawals from your RRSP.

You see, every Canadian resident is entitled to the basic personal amount plus a supplementary tax credit, which combined will effectively shelter your first $6,956 ($6,707 in 1998) of income from any tax. Once your income is higher than this, the supplementary credit is clawed back by up to $500. The bottom line is that, if you had no other income, you'd be able to withdraw $6,956 from your RRSP and not pay a cent of tax on that income. Even if your income is over $6,956, you'll still enjoy Canada's lowest marginal tax rate, about 26 percent, on taxable income below $29,590.

You should realize that you're going to face withholding taxes when you make withdrawals from your RRSP. The withholding tax is 10 percent on withdrawals of $5,000 or less, 20 percent on withdrawals of $5,001 to $15,000, and 30 percent on withdrawals over $15,000. The percentages in Quebec are 21, 30, and 35 percent respectively. Think of these withholdings as installments on your taxes. In most cases these withholdings won't be enough to

Caution!

If you make withdrawals from your RRSP, the tax collector will not give back contribution room for you to make up that withdrawal later. That is, you'll lose that contribution room forever! This has to be considered a cost of making withdrawals over and above the tax you might pay on any withdrawals.

satisfy your full tax bill on the RRSP withdrawal, and you'll have to make up the difference when you file your tax return for the year of the withdrawal. In other cases, if your income is low enough, you may get back some of those withholdings as a refund when you file your return. If you want to keep these withholdings to a minimum, be sure to limit each withdrawal to $5,000 or less.

TO MAKE A LONG STORY SHORT:

- Withdrawing funds from your RRSP can be done tax-efficiently if your income is low, thanks to the basic personal and supplementary credits totalling $6,956 ($6,707 in 1998).

- Withdrawals will be subject to withholding taxes, which are simply installments toward your eventual tax bill.

Tim's Tip 74: Consider the impact of using RRSP assets to buy a home.

If you're thinking of buying a home but not sure where to find a down payment, your RRSP may be one option. In 1992 the Department of Finance introduced the Home Buyers' Plan (HBP), which was designed to help certain Canadians use RRSP money tax-free in order to buy a home.

Is this idea for everyone? Not really. The younger you are, the less sense the HBP makes. You see, if you take money out of your RRSP at a young age, even for a home purchase, you give up more growth inside your RRSP than someone who has, say, just 10 years to go before retirement. As a general rule, if you have 35 years or more to go before it's time to retire, then the HBP quite likely does not make sense on paper. Having said this, I'm not going to spoil the dreams of any young person with a heart intent on owning a home. So, do what your heart desires. But learn how the HBP works first!

Making Withdrawals

You'll be entitled to withdraw up to $20,000 from your RRSP tax-free for buying a home, as long as you haven't owned a home in the last four years. If you're married, then you and your spouse will each be entitled to a $20,000 withdrawal, provided neither of you has owned a home in the last four years and you're buying the new home jointly. Even if your spouse has owned a home in the last four years, you are entitled to make a withdrawal under the HBP, provided it was not your principal residence while you were married or living in a common law relationship.

The 1998 federal budget brought some good news. First, while it used to be that the tax collector would only let you use the HBP once in your lifetime, this rule changed in the 1998 federal budget. Once you've fully paid back your RRSP, you'll now be able to do it all over again with another home. Second, if you are disabled or support a disabled person, you may be eligible to make withdrawals under the HBP even if you have owned a home recently.

Once you've made a withdrawal under the HBP, you've got to close the purchase of a home by October 1 of the following year—called the *completion date*. So, if you make a withdrawal in 1999, your purchase will have to close by October 1, 2000. Can't manage to close the deal that quickly? The tax collector may be willing to provide an extension to that October 1 deadline, and you always have the option of putting the funds back into your RRSP by December 31 following the completion date—without a penalty. Keep in mind, too, that the rules require you to occupy your new home as your principal residence within 12 months after buying the place.

If you were hoping to buy that boat you've been dreaming of, and calling it your home under the HBP, you'll find yourself out of luck. The home must be located on solid ground in Canada, but other than this, most homes will qualify, including: detached and semi-detached homes, townhouses, condominiums, mobile homes, apartment units, and even a share in a cooperative housing corporation.

Making Repayments

If you make withdrawals under the HBP, you've got to pay that money back to your RRSP. You won't get a deduction for these repayments. At a minimum, the repayments must be made in equal annual installments over a 15-year period, and your first payment will have to be made in the second calendar year after the year of your withdrawal. If, for example, you withdrew $20,000 on July 31, 1999, you'd have to make your first repayment in the year 2001, and this repayment can be made within the usual RRSP deadlines for that year. That is, you could make your first repayment in the first 60 days of 2002, for the 2001 year. If you happen to miss a repayment, or repay less than you should, the deficient payment is added to your taxable income—just as any RRSP withdrawal would be.

Action Step

What if you've made a withdrawal under the Home Buyer's Plan but can't manage to close a home purchase before October 1 (the HBP completion date) of the year following your withdrawal? Not to worry. Simply recontribute those funds to your RRSP by December 31 of that year. The tax collector will let you do this without a penalty.

Don't be afraid to speed up your repayments to your RRSP. In fact, the sooner you repay those borrowed funds, the better. If you do accelerate your repayments, this will reduce the amount of each payment for the balance of the 15-year term.

Timing Your RRSP Contributions

When you're getting involved with the HBP, you've got to carefully plan out your RRSP contributions to ensure you'll be entitled to claim a deduction for them. Here's the deal: If you contribute to your RRSP and then withdraw those same funds within 90 days under the HBP, you won't be able to claim a deduction for that contribution. Any money that was already in your RRSP will be considered withdrawn first, before the new contribution is considered withdrawn. The bottom line is this: Always allow your contributions to sit for 91 days or more before withdrawing them under the HBP.

TO MAKE A LONG STORY SHORT:

- Under the Home Buyers' Plan (HBP), you may be eligible to make tax-free withdrawals from your RRSP in order to buy a home.

- The younger you are, the more it will cost you in RRSP growth to use the HBP.

- Money borrowed from your RRSP under the HBP must be paid back over 15 years.

- The rules are many and complex, so take the time to learn how the HBP works first.

Tim's Tip 75: Consider the impact of using RRSP money for full-time education for you or your spouse.

When I first read about this new program introduced in the 1998 federal budget, it seemed to me like a waste of effort on the part of the Department of Finance. Since that time, however, I've run into a number of Canadians who are going to taking advantage of this program, which becomes effective in 1999. I'm talking about using RRSP assets to finance full-time training or education for you or your spouse. This plan works much like the Home Buyers' Plan I talked about in the last tip, and complements the other education strategies I presented in Chapter 2.

Making Withdrawals

The feds have now made it possible for Canadian residents to withdraw money tax-free from RRSPs for full-time training or education. You'll be able to take up to $10,000 each year, over a four year period, to a maximum of $20,000 in total from your RRSP for education for you or your spouse. You'll be glad to know that "full-time" doesn't have to mean four years of schooling! It can simply mean a three-month enrollment in a qualifying educational program at an eligible institution. If you're disabled, even full-time isn't a requirement—part-time will also make you eligible for this plan.

Once you've made a withdrawal from your RRSP under this plan, you'll have to enroll in a qualifying program no later than January of the following calendar year. Sorry, but you won't be able to make any education withdrawals from your RRSP for your spouse if you still have a balance outstanding from withdrawals for yourself. However, your spouse can use his or her own plan to make withdrawals.

Action Step

Dropping Out

If you don't quite make it through your full-time program, you'll generally face tax on the amount of your RRSP withdrawals made under this plan. But don't panic. There are ways to avoid this tax hit. First, if you meet even **one** of three conditions, you'll manage to side-step the tax collector:

- You withdraw from the educational program more than two months after the year of your RRSP withdrawal.
- Less than 75 percent of your tuition costs are refundable when you withdraw from the educational program.
- You enroll in another qualifying program on a timely basis.

Making a withdrawal from your RRSP for education may be ideal if you're 40-plus and aren't quite sure what to do with the balance of your career, or if you have a real desire to build on your existing skills to increase your marketability. And if you received a retiring allowance from your former employer that was rolled into your RRSP, then any withdrawal you make won't hurt your RRSP as much— after all, you've just added a few thousand to your RRSP because of the retiring allowance.

Second, you can by-pass the ugly tax hit by repaying the amount withdrawn and filing an approved form with Revenue Canada. At the time of writing, the form wasn't available yet, but check with Revenue Canada (or visit their Web site at **www.rc.gc.ca**) since the form may now be available.

Making Repayments

You'll have to repay your RRSP withdrawals in equal installments over a 10-year period, and you—not your spouse—must be the annuitant of the RRSP. Your first payment back to your RRSP must be made no later than the first 60 days of the sixth year after your first withdrawal. So, if you make a withdrawal in 1999, your first payment will be due in the first 60 days of 2005. You may have to start your repayments sooner if, after your first withdrawal, you fail to qualify for the full-time education credit for three months in two consecutive years. In this case, you'll have to start your payments in the first 60 days of the year following the second of the two consecutive years.

Kind of confusing, isn't it? You might want to visit a tax pro for help if you're still not sure how the rules work. By the way, if you fail to make the proper repayments in any given year, you'll face tax on the deficient payments.

Timing Your RRSP Contributions

As with the Home Buyers' Plan, if you make a contribution to your RRSP and then withdraw those funds within 90 days under this plan, you won't be entitled to an RRSP deduction for the contributions. For more information, refer back to Tip 74 dealing with the Home Buyers' Plan.

TO MAKE A LONG STORY SHORT:

- The 1998 federal budget opened a door to make tax-free withdrawals from an RRSP for full-time training or education.

- You can withdraw up to $10,000 each year, over four years, to a maximum of $20,000 in total withdrawals.

- The plan is similar to the Home Buyers' Plan in many ways, and the rules can be complex. Take the time to understand the impact on your retirement savings before withdrawing RRSP money.

Tim's Tip 76: Take three steps to minimize the tax hit on RRSP withdrawals if you're planning to leave the country.

If you're thinking of leaving Canada, perhaps to live it up down south in your retirement, make sure that you leave your RRSP intact when you go. You see, regardless of where you move, you're likely to be better off in the long run by making RRSP withdrawals after you've given up Canadian residency, and not before.

M*ark and his wife Karen decided to move to the U.S. in 1998. They liked the thought of spending their retirement in the warmth of Arizona. Before leaving, they visited their tax advisor and took her advice before packing their bags. As a result, Mark and Karen decided to keep their RRSPs intact, so they simply informed the various mutual fund companies and financial institutions holding their investments that they would be non-residents of Canada in 1999. In addition, they sold all the assets inside their RRSPs and reinvested those proceeds just before leaving. Finally, they took great pains to make sure that they gave up Canadian residency properly. The result of all this? Mark and Karen will enjoy extremely tax-efficient withdrawals from their RRSPs.*

Did you catch the three steps taken by Mark and Karen? Let's look at them again.

Step 1: Leave the RRSP intact.

If you were to collapse your RRSP before leaving Canada, you'd face a significant tax hit because that withdrawal would be fully taxable in the year of your leaving. Mark and Karen avoided this by leaving their RRSPs intact until they had given up Canadian residency. If you wait until you're a resident of the U.S., or another country for that matter, the only tax you'll pay to Revenue Canada will be a 25-percent withholding tax on any withdrawals from your RRSP. Further, the 25-percent rate will generally be reduced to just 15 percent on *periodic* withdrawals, as opposed to *lump-sum* withdrawals from your plan—provided Canada has a tax treaty with your new country of residence.

By the way, to ensure that your withdrawals are considered *periodic* and eligible for the 15-percent withholding tax rate, you'll have to convert your RRSP to a RRIF first. This conversion can be done before or after you leave Canada. Once you're making withdrawals from your RRIF, be sure not to withdraw more than twice the minimum amount each year, otherwise the withdrawals will be considered lump-sum, and you'll face the higher 25-percent withholding tax rate.

Step 2: Step-up the cost base.

If you've taken up residency in the U.S., any withdrawals from your RRSP will be taxed by the U.S. (in addition to the Canadian withholding tax), but Uncle Sam won't tax the full amount of your withdrawals. Rather, you'll be entitled to withdraw from your plan, tax-free, the cost base (otherwise called the *book value*) of your RRSP investments as calculated on the day you took up residency in the U.S. So, if you can maximize that cost base, you'll be entitled to greater tax-free withdrawals in the U.S. Mark and Karen accomplished this by selling and repurchasing their RRSP assets—otherwise known as *stepping-up* the cost base of their RRSPs. You see, if you have investments in your RRSP worth $300,000 but you only paid

$100,000 for them, your cost base, or book value, is $100,000. If you sell those investments and reinvest the proceeds, your new cost base will be $300,000. This is a step-up in your cost base.

Keep in mind that you won't face a tax bill in Canada on the sales since it all takes place inside your RRSP where gains are sheltered from the Canadian tax collector. The only drawback is that you'll face some commissions on the sale of your plan assets, so consider this cost first.

Some are under the impression that simply moving RRSP assets from one financial institution or advisor to another will result in a step-up of the cost base of your investments. Sorry, it won't work. While your new RRSP carrier may not have a record of your true original cost base, you can bet the U.S. tax authorities will take the time to determine this figure if they decide to look into your RRSP withdrawals.

Caution!

Step 3: Give up residency properly.

Mark and Karen took great pains to make sure they gave up Canadian residency properly. And if you plan on taking up residency outside Canada, you should do the same. If Revenue Canada considers you to still be a resident of Canada, even after you've left the country, you'll face tax on your RRSP withdrawals at full Canadian tax rates, not the lower withholding rates.

Although no single factor will determine whether you're truly a non-resident, the tax collector will consider a number of things, and in particular:

- the permanence and purpose of your stay abroad (if you're gone for less than two years, you're presumed to be a resident of Canada the whole time unless you can demonstrate otherwise)
- your residential ties within Canada (your primary ties include your dwelling place, spouse and dependents, personal property, and social ties)

- your residential ties elsewhere (the courts have said that you must be a resident somewhere, and you can be resident in more than one country at the same time)
- the regularity and length of your visits to Canada.

To avoid an unpleasant tax hit on RRSP withdrawals once you're gone, be sure to follow all three steps outlined here. Why? Because in this game, it's not three strikes and you're out. Strike out on even one of these steps, and you could cost yourself significant tax dollars.

TO MAKE A LONG STORY SHORT:

- If you're planning to leave Canada, leave your RRSP intact and make withdrawals once you're gone. The only tax you'll face in Canada will be a maximum withholding tax of 25 percent, which could be reduced to just 15 percent.

- Be sure to follow these three steps to minimize the tax hit on your RRSP if you plan to leave the country: (1) Leave your RRSP intact; (2) Step-up the cost base of your plan assets; and (3) Give up residency properly.

Benefiting From RRIFs and Annuities

What would a discussion of retirement be without talking about registered retirement income funds (call 'em *riffs*) and annuities?

Tim's Tip 77: Roll your RRSP to a RRIF or annuity to defer tax well beyond age 69.

I've said it before: There's going to come a day when your RRSP just won't be around anymore. In fact, your RRSP will mature at the end of the year in which you turn 69. By that date, you'll have to wind up your RRSP and do something with the assets inside your plan. You'll have three options at that time:

- Make a lump-sum withdrawal from your RRSP.
- Buy an annuity with the proceeds of your RRSP.
- Transfer your RRSP assets to a RRIF.

You don't have to choose just one of these options. You can actually do all three without a problem. But which option is your best choice?

Make a Lump-Sum Withdrawal

Now here's an option for the high-flying, fast-living, senior. If you want to take your life savings, pay tax on the entire proceeds all in one year, then travel around the world for a year or two until your money runs out, you might like this option. But make no mistake, there is absolutely nothing tax-efficient about taking a lump-sum withdrawal from your RRSP when you wind up the plan. This option is, in my view, no option at all. Don't even think about it. You see, you can always make withdrawals at a later date from your RRIF if you want more cash—don't make the withdrawal at age 69 when your RRSP matures. Read on for better alternatives.

The average Canadian senior will have to grow his or her assets to about age 80 to avoid running out of money before running out of retirement. The reason? Canadians are living longer than ever, and if you start to draw down on your assets too soon, they may not last a lifetime. I'm not saying that you should avoid withdrawals; after all, this is not possible beyond age 69. But make sure that your assets are growing at a faster rate than your withdrawals annually—to about age 80.

Caution!

Buy an Annuity

The name of this game is deferring taxes. A lump-sum withdrawal won't do it, but an annuity can help. When you buy an annuity you are simply entering into a contract where you pay a sum of money to a company (usually a life insurance company) that agrees to pay to you a guaranteed sum of money each month for a period of time—usually your lifetime. Each annuity payment you receive will be fully taxed—but not until you receive the payment. There are two common types of annuities. The first is a *term-certain* annuity that will pay you a sum each month for a fixed period of years. The second is a *life* annuity that will pay you a sum each month for as long as you live. A life annuity can also be set up so that it's a *joint life* annuity that will make monthly payments to you and your spouse as long as one of you is alive. For additional cost, you can also add other features to your annuity, such as indexation to inflation, or a guaranteed term attached to a life annuity.

Annuities may be for you if you have no interest in investing your own money, and all you want is a guaranteed income for life. One of the drawbacks of an annuity is that once you and your spouse are gone, so is the annuity. That is, you shouldn't expect to leave your annuity to the kids, because they generally won't get anything. Another drawback to annuities is that the amount of your payments is determined by interest rates in effect at the time you buy the annuity. If rates are currently low, you might not end up with as high an income in retirement as you could achieve with a RRIF. Finally, if you choose the annuity option, don't wait until December 31 of the year you turn age 69 to make the purchase—after all, you'll be at the whim of current interest rates if you do this.

Roll to a RRIF

A RRIF is a great retirement plan. It works much like your RRSP. In fact, you can hold all the same investments in a RRIF that you could in your RRSP. However, there are two key differences between a RRIF and your RRSP. First, you can't make contributions to a RRIF. Second, you've got to make withdrawals from a RRIF each year. The amount of your withdrawals will depend on your age or the age of your spouse. A RRIF also works like your RRSP in that any assets in your plan will grow tax-free until they're withdrawn. If you want to transfer assets from one RRIF to the next, you'll be able to do this tax-free.

A RRIF is different from an annuity in that you control the investments that are made. If you're not comfortable with this task, the RRIF can still be a real hands-off option if you link up with a good financial advisor who can help with the investment decisions. Further, a RRIF can provide for a more flexible income in retirement because you can control the timing and the amount of your withdrawals, although you must make at least the minimum withdrawal each year. With an annuity, your annual income is basically fixed from the start. Another advantage of the RRIF is that it doesn't disappear upon your death or the death of your spouse. Your kids will actually receive the balance of your RRIF, albeit after taxes, once you're gone.

The key drawback to the RRIF is that, if you're not careful, you could make big enough withdrawals in the early years of the RRIF to leave you with very little income in your later years. Proper planning, however, should put this concern to rest.

In the end, you'll need to decide which of these three options is best for you. I believe that in most cases the RRIF is the way to go, but speak to a reputable financial advisor before making this final decision—you may have to live with your choice for a lifetime.

TO MAKE A LONG STORY SHORT:

- When your RRSP matures in December of the year you turn 69, you've got three choices for those assets: Make a lump-sum withdrawal; buy an annuity; or roll the assets to a RRIF.

- The annuity and RRIF options will allow you to defer tax, while the lump-sum option won't.

- In most cases, the RRIF option will be best, but speak to a reputable financial advisor about which is best for you before making a decision that you may have to live with for a lifetime.

Tim's Tip 78: Defer tax on your RRIF withdrawals as long as possible.

The longer you defer withdrawals from your RRIF, the longer you'll enjoy a tax deferral. There are two ways to minimize your RRIF withdrawals.

Base Withdrawals on the Younger Spouse

I remember reading one time about a 70-year-old man from Toronto who married a young woman aged 22. Someone had asked him: "Aren't you concerned about marrying a woman so much younger than you?" "Why should I be?" he said, "she's in great health." If I didn't know that they married for true love, I would suspect that maybe he had some tax planning in mind. You see, the required minimum withdrawals from your RRIF each year will equal the balance in your RRIF at the start of the year multiplied by a percentage based on your age, or the age of your spouse. If your spouse is younger, then the percentage that you've got to withdraw each year will be less if you use your spouse's age in the calculation. And the tax collector will let you to use the younger age.

Action Step

If you keep your annual RRIF withdrawals to the minimum amount, you'll avoid having taxes withheld by your financial institution. This will give you more money up front to meet your daily living needs. Keep in mind, the withdrawals are still taxable, so the fact that no withholding taxes are paid may mean you'll face a tax bill next April when you file your tax return, and you may be required to make installments to the tax collector quarterly.

When Ken set up his RRIF last year at age 69, he decided to base his RRIF withdrawals on the age of his spouse, Leslie, who was just 63 at the time. Ken had $100,000 in his RRIF at the beginning of this year, and because he was 69 at the start of the year, he *would have to withdraw 4.76 percent of his RRIF assets ($4,760) from his plan this year if he based those withdrawals on his own age. However, if he based the withdrawals on Leslie's age, he would only have to withdraw $3,700. As the couple gets older, the savings from using Leslie's age will become more pronounced.*

See the table on page 284 for minimum annual RRIF withdrawals based on your age or the age of your spouse.

Delay Your First Withdrawal

You'll be glad to know that you don't have to actually make any withdrawals from your RRIF in the year you set up the plan. For example, if you set up your RRIF in January 1999, you won't have to make any withdrawals until the year 2000. And when in the year 2000 do you suppose you'll have to make those withdrawals? Right—not until December 31! By leaving your assets to grow untouched in your RRIF as long as possible, you'll maximize the growth inside your plan and defer tax as well.

TO MAKE A LONG STORY SHORT:

- Defer tax as long as possible by minimizing how much you take out of your RRIF and by delaying those withdrawals until absolutely necessary.

- You can minimize your withdrawals by basing them on the age of the younger spouse, and you can delay your withdrawals until the end of the year following the year you set up the plan.

Understanding Registered Pension Plans

Registered pension plans (RPPs) are declining in popularity. More and more employers are letting employees fend for themselves in the world of retirement savings. Nevertheless, thousands of Canadians are still members of RPPs, or will become members, and there are strategies to consider here. But first, let's look at the two basic types of RPPs:

- With a **defined benefit plan**, you can expect to receive pension benefits based on a formula—often a percentage of your last few years' salary. Your employer bears some risk in this type of plan since a promise is being made to you that a certain level of benefits will be paid out when you retire.
- With a **defined contribution plan** (also called a *money purchase* plan), both you and your employer may make contributions, but there's no guarantee about how much will be sitting there for you at retirement. The contributions will be paid to you, plus accumulated growth on those assets, but no promises are made beyond that.

If you're a member of a defined contribution pension plan, be sure to keep tabs on the level of your benefits accruing inside the plan. Under this type of plan, you bear the risk that there might not be enough money for you at retirement. If it looks like the pension may fall short of what you need to live comfortably in retirement, then start an investment program today designed to make up the shortfall!

Caution!

If you're a member of an RPP, you've no doubt noticed that the tax collector is not going to let you contribute as much to your RRSP as your neighbour who is not a member of a pension plan. Enter: the *pension adjustment* (PA). Your PA is an amount that, in a nutshell, equals the total of your contributions plus your employer's contributions to an RPP each year. The amount of your RRSP contribution room will be reduced by the amount of this PA each year. This keeps all Canadians on a level playing field when saving for retirement. That is, in theory, pension plan members will not have an advantage over those saving for retirement through an RRSP alone.

Tim's Tip 79: **Consider opting out of your company pension plan if you have the choice.**

I know this sounds radical, but if you have a choice of taking part in the pension plan or not, you should give serious thought to opting out. Let me explain. One thing that can really hurt your retirement savings is to move from one employer with a pension plan to another without a plan. You see, if you stop your membership in a company pension plan, the chances are very high that you will not walk away from that pension plan with all the money that you and your employer contributed to that plan for you. This is particularly true if you've only been in the plan a short time—say three years or less.

Now, let me ask you this. What is the probability that you'll change employers between today and the time you retire? There's a darn high probability of that, I would say. In fact, it's not unusual today to find employees who have worked for five or more employers by age 45. If you take part in a pension plan and move to another employer who may or may not have a pension plan, my bet is that you'll walk away with much less than you figured you would.

Thanks to changes introduced in the 1997 federal budget, you may be entitled to a *pension adjustment reversal* that effectively gives you back some of that lost RRSP contribution room that arose from the pension adjustment over the years while you were in the plan. But this is a far cry from actually giving to you all the cash that was earmarked in the RPP for you. You'll still have to find the cash somewhere to make a contribution to use up that room.

Consider this also: If you leave a company pension plan and move to an employer without a plan, you could lose the ability to contribute to any kind of retirement plan for a full year. For example, if you were a member of an RPP in 1999 and $13,500 of contributions were made to that plan on your behalf in 1999, then you'd have a pension adjustment reported on your 1999 T4 slip that will prevent you from making contributions to your RRSP in the

Did You Know?

According to Statistics Canada, in 1991, seniors made up 10.3 percent of the population in Toronto, 11.4 percent in Montreal, and 12.8 percent in Vancouver. The population of those who are elderly ranges from 3 percent in the Northwest Territories to 15 percent in Saskatchewan.

following year—year 2000. If you were to leave your employer on January 1, 2000, and join another employer without a pension plan, you would be in a tough spot. You would not be able to make contributions to an RPP since you're no longer a member of one, nor could you make RRSP contributions because of your PA from 1999. Talk about a rip-off—a full year without contributions to a tax-deferred retirement savings plan.

The bottom line is this: An RRSP is portable, meaning that you can change employers and not worry about losing a beat in your retirement savings. The same cannot be said for RPPs in every situation. You have to weigh this fact against the benefits of a pension plan, which could include a guaranteed income in retirement (under a defined benefit plan). On the other hand, if you're quite sure you'll be with your employer for a significant period of time, then a company pension plan can make sense.

TO MAKE A LONG STORY SHORT:

- When you leave a company pension plan you could very likely be short-changed on the benefits you take with you, particularly when you haven't been a member of the pension plan for long.

- When you leave a pension plan and don't join another, you could lose the ability to use a tax-deferred retirement savings plan for a full year.

- An RRSP is much more portable than a pension plan, but each situation should be evaluated separately.

Tim's Tip 80: **Look into an individual pension plan (IPP) to avoid a big tax hit when leaving your company pension plan.**

This tip may not apply to everyone, but it's great when it works—as it did in Greer's case. She came to my office very recently to talk about her pension options.

reer is a teacher and has chosen to take an early retirement. The RPP that she's a member of sent her a statement explaining her options. Option 1: She can take a pension starting the month she leaves the school board. Since she's only 54, this pension is significantly reduced compared to the amount she would receive if she retired at age 65. Option 2: She can take her pension starting at age 65. Option 3: She can take the value of her pension benefits in one lump-sum amount (called her commuted value) and transfer most of this commuted value to a locked-in RRSP, with the balance being taxable in her hands. What's her best bet?

The Most Common Option

Greer wanted to take the commuted value of her pension—option 3. I don't blame her. It's a popular option. You see, in Greer's case, this commuted value amounts to $450,000. If she's able to invest this money properly, she could provide herself with a better retirement income than the RPP was promising her. Her biggest concern is that, of the $450,000, just $350,000 can be transferred to a locked-in RRSP for her. Under our tax law, there will always be a limit to how much can be rolled tax-free from your RPP to a locked-in RRSP. The remaining $100,000 in Greer's case will face tax in her hands. That's no small tax bill.

The IPP Solution

When I asked Greer what she planned to do after leaving the school board, she told me that she wants to start a business working with children with learning disabilities. "Terrific," I said. I suggested to Greer that it might make sense for her to become the shareholder and employee of a corporation set up to provide these services. The corporation could then sponsor a pension plan specifically for Greer—called an individual pension plan (IPP). An IPP is really a type of RPP. With an IPP set up, it will be possible in Greer's case to transfer the full $450,000 commuted value from her school board pension to her new company pension plan. She'll manage to defer tax on the $100,000 she otherwise would have paid tax on. She was thrilled.

An IPP is not the type of stunt to try at home. You'll need a tax pro experienced in IPPs to set this idea in motion. The idea may not work for everyone. For example, the RPP that you're leaving has to allow for transfers to the new IPP, and you should really be operating an active business to legitimize the setting up of your corporation and the IPP. If all your ducks are in a row, however, this idea could make sense.

Caution!

TO MAKE A LONG STORY SHORT:

- You might have two or three options available when you leave a pension plan. It's quite common to take the commuted value of the plan when this is an option.

- Consider setting up an IPP if you will be running a business. This may allow a tax-free transfer of your commuted value to the new plan.

- Speak to a tax pro experienced in IPPs to set this plan in motion.

Getting into the Game

With careful planning, you can look forward to a golden future. And the sooner you start your plan in motion, the brighter your financial picture will be. Turn now to the Tax Planning Tip Sheet at the front of the book and review the strategies that you read about in Chapter 6. Check *Yes* or *Not Sure* for each strategy that you think might apply to you. When you're finished this book, take your Tip Sheet to a tax professional for more information or help in implementing the strategies.

AMERICAN LEAGUE RULES: UNITED STATES CONNECTIONS

In the United States you might get away with murder, but never tax evasion. Just ask Al Capone.

7

Stepping up to the plate when it comes to dealing with the U.S. tax system is going to take a keen eye. And, like Canadian tax law, the U.S. tax system can throw you a wicked knuckle ball when you least expect it. With some helpful tips from this chapter, and a little planning and preparation, you'll have the tools needed to beat the tax collector in the U.S. This chapter will speak to Canadians who invest in the U.S., as well as snowbirds, part time U.S. residents, and others with U.S. connections.

Reporting Your U.S. Income

Tim's Tip 81: Claim a foreign tax credit when you've paid withholding taxes to Uncle Sam.

The fact is, certain types of income received from U.S. sources are subject to taxes in the U.S. If you live in Canada, these taxes usually take the form of withholding taxes of 5 to 30 percent, payable to the Internal Revenue Service (IRS). For the most part, Canadian residents won't find any advantage to earning U.S. source income from a tax point of view. Here's why: You'll have to report the full amount of your U.S. income on your Canadian tax return since Canadian residents are taxed in Canada on worldwide income.

> **Did You Know?**
>
> On March 31, 1931, gangster Al Capone was convicted of tax evasion in the U.S. for side-stepping $251,748.93 in taxes. He was never convicted of murder. Just goes to show—you might get away with murder, but don't mess with the tax collector!

But the story's not over. You'll be entitled to claim a foreign tax credit on Schedule 1 of your Canadian tax return for any U.S. or other foreign taxes paid. This credit prevents a double-tax problem where you're paying tax on the same income in more than one country. Seems fair, doesn't it?

Here's the bottom line: You'll end up paying tax at Canadian tax rates, but you'll send a portion of the tax to the IRS (the withholding tax) and the rest to Revenue Canada. A variety of income types give rise to a foreign tax credit. Let's take a look at the most common sources.

- **Interest Income**

Interest income earned on bonds or other debt instruments will attract a 10-percent withholding tax that will be collected by the company that pays the interest. The major exception to this rule is interest earned on deposits in U.S. banks. This interest is generally tax-free if paid to a non-resident. If your U.S. bank has been withholding tax at source, give them a completed Certificate of Foreign Status (which they should be able to provide) to avoid those withholdings.

- **Dividends**

The withholding rate applied to dividends is currently 15 percent under the Canada-U.S. tax treaty.

If you're a U.S. citizen living in Canada, you'll be treated differently for U.S. tax purposes than Canadian citizens are. All U.S. citizens, regardless of where they live, must file a full-blown tax return in the U.S. And this means you'll have to report your worldwide income to Uncle Sam. As a result, you won't be subject to withholding taxes in the U.S. If you're a U.S. citizen who has been neglecting to file in the U.S., be warned that you could face civil and criminal penalties.

Caution!

- **Pension Payments**

Periodic payments from a U.S. source pension will be subject to withholding taxes at 15 percent. If the payment is in the form of a lump sum, it will attract a withholding tax of 30 percent, which approximates the regular U.S. tax rate.

- **Capital Gains**

There's good news for those of you investing in U.S. securities. A sale of U.S. stocks and bonds that generates a capital gain will not normally be taxed in the U.S. as long as you're a resident of Canada—the tax treaty will protect you. The exception is the rare circumstance where you own a U.S. real property holding corporation. This is a corporation whose majority of assets are U.S. real estate. The sale of these shares will be treated the same way as the sale of U.S. real estate by an individual—and I'll talk more about real estate in a minute.

• Social Security

The rules around social security have flip-flopped twice in the last two years. It used to be that a 25.5-percent withholding tax applied to U.S. social security payments made to Canadian residents. Not so anymore. Here's how the current rules work: The Canadian-resident recipient reports the income in Canada only. The U.S. no longer withholds any tax. These new rules were made retroactive to 1996. By the way, the rules work the same for Canada Pension Plan (CPP) recipients resident in the U.S. That is, tax will be paid in the U.S. alone, and not in Canada.

• Other Payments

Alimony and maintenance are exempt from withholding tax in the U.S. And if you happen to earn employment income in the U.S., that income will not be subject to withholding or other taxes in the U.S. as long as the income amounts to $10,000 (U.S.) or less in the year. Even if the income is over $10,000 (U.S.), it will still be tax-free in the U.S. if you were present in the U.S. for less than 184 days, and if you were paid by a Canadian-resident employer who did not have a permanent establishment in the U.S. in the year.

Did You Know?

Provided you've been resident in Canada for at least 40 years after you reached the age of 18, you'll be entitled to full Old Age Security (OAS) benefits at age 65, even if you leave Canada. If you were resident in Canada for less than 20 years after you reached 18, and you leave Canada, your OAS benefits will cease after six months.

TO MAKE A LONG STORY SHORT:

- Certain types of income from the U.S. will be subject to withholding taxes down south.

- As a Canadian resident you'll be entitled to a foreign tax credit in Canada for U.S. or other foreign taxes you pay.

- Be sure to claim the tax credit to ensure you're not double-taxed on the same income in different countries. The calculation is done on Schedule 1 of your tax return.

Profiting From U.S. Real Estate

Last summer, Carolyn and I spent a week visiting her brother and his family in Alabama. We spent a good part of the week at the family's cottage (they call them lake houses down south), not far from Birmingham. It was beautiful. While we were there, we met some fellow Canadians at the lake. Turns out they own a lake house and rent it out most of the year. I had a good talk with them about the tax rules affecting their U.S. property.

Tim's Tip 82: Use the net rental income method on your U.S. rental property in most cases.

The U.S. will normally impose a 30-percent withholding tax on your gross rental revenue. You can avoid this by filing Form 4224 with the individual collecting and remitting the tax (the person renting the property from you), and electing to use the net rental income method.

*L*ucy and Silvio own a rental property in Alabama, and they rented it to Nadia for six months at $1,000 per month. Unless Nadia is given Form 4224, she is obliged to withhold 30 percent of the rent ($300 each month) and remit it to the IRS. If the election is made and the form is filed, then Lucy and Silvio will escape the 30-percent withholding tax, but they will be obliged to file a U.S. tax return each year to report the actual income and expenses from the rental property. Turns out that Lucy and Silvio's tax bill is much lower under this method—the net rental

Action Step

income method—than remitting a full 30 percent of the gross rents.

Under the net rental income method, you'll deduct from income all the property taxes, interest, maintenance, insurance, and other costs associated with the property—including depreciation, which is mandatory in the U.S.

Before deciding on the net rental income method, keep these points in mind:

Be sure to work through the tax calculations to determine whether you'll be better off using the net rental income method for paying tax on your rental income in the U.S., or whether simply paying the 30-percent withholding tax on gross rents is better. The decision is not the same for everyone. Get the help of a tax pro if you can't do the calculations yourself, because this decision could save you a bundle each year.

- Not all expenses will be deductible under this method. Generally, you'll need to allocate your expenses between the personal-use portion and the rental portion based on days the property was rented.
- When a property is used personally for less than 15 days each year or 10 percent of the time available (whichever is greater), you won't need to allocate expenses as personal-use.
- When a property is rented out for less than 15 days each year, there's no need to report any rental income and no expenses are deductible.
- When you elect to use the net rental income method, the election is generally irrevocable.

TO MAKE A LONG STORY SHORT:

- When you own a rental property in the U.S., there are two ways of paying tax on the rents you earn: a withholding tax, or the net rental income method of reporting.

- The net rental income method will generally provide the greatest tax savings.

Tim's Tip 83: Take two steps to minimize the tax hit on the sale of your U.S. real estate.

Let's hope that the U.S. real estate you bought turns out to be a good investment. And if it does, this could mean some tax to pay to the IRS later when you sell the property at a profit. You can minimize your tax hit in a couple of ways.

Minimize Withholding Tax

Normally, the sale of your U.S. real estate is going to attract a 10-percent withholding tax that is remitted by the buyer or the buyer's agent to the IRS. The tax is calculated as 10 percent of the actual sale price of the property, and not the gain on the sale. Keep in mind, this withholding tax doesn't remove your obligation to file a U.S. tax return to report the sale of your property. No sir. You'll have to report that sale—normally on Form 1040NR if you're a Canadian citizen and resident—and you may have to hand over more tax to the IRS. The 10-percent withholding tax is simply treated as an installment on the taxes owing. If you sell the property for little or no profit, then you might actually recover some or all of that 10-percent tax withheld.

Action Step

If you want to avoid the 10-percent withholding tax that is normally due when a Canadian citizen and resident sells U.S. real estate, sell the property to an individual who plans to occupy the property as a principal residence, and keep the selling price below $300,000 (U.S.). In this case, the IRS will waive the requirement for the buyer to withhold that 10 percent.

You can apply to the IRS for a withholding certificate based on your expectation that the U.S. tax owed will be less than 10 percent of the sale price. This certificate will tell the buyer how much money to withhold, if any. But remember, this exception applies only to the withholding tax. The gain on the sale will still attract tax, and you will still need to file a tax return reporting the gain or loss to the U.S. government.

Minimize Your Taxable Gain

Calculating your gain or loss on the sale of your U.S. property is not rocket science, but you'll want to do it right to minimize the tax bill you could face. In a nutshell, here's the formula to calculate your gain or loss:

	Net proceeds on sale
Minus	Cost base
Equals	Gain or loss on sale

Seems simple enough, right? Well, hold on. You need to make some adjustments to these figures to make sure you're not paying too much tax. Consider this: The net proceeds are calculated by taking the selling price minus all selling expenses—including commissions, fees, and similar expenses (most of these appear on your closing statement). If you forget these additional costs, you could be paying too much tax.

As for your cost base, be sure to take the original cost and add the cost of any major improvements—also called capital improvements. If the property is a rental, then these capital improvements would not have been deductible; rather, they increase your cost base when selling the property. And if your property was a rental, then you've got to deduct from the cost base the amount of any depreciation on the property—whether you previously claimed that depreciation or not! This is going to increase your capital gain. If you owned the property solely for personal use, then no depreciation need be taken and your cost base is not adjusted.

Make sure you visit a tax pro if you owned your U.S. property before September 27, 1980, and it has been exclusively for personal use. You see, special rules exist for Canadian residents in this boat. Under the Canada-U.S. tax treaty, only the gain since January 1, 1985 might be taxed. To take advantage of this provision, you'll need a valuation of the property at January 1, 1985.

Make sense so far? Once the gain has been determined, you can now deduct all the accumulated rental losses that you've been claiming over the years, if any.

Grace owns a home in Florida, which she rents out half of the year. She has owned the house for three years and has had rental losses averaging $3,000 (U.S.) each year. The house originally cost $100,000 (U.S.) and Grace has spent $25,000 (U.S.) over the years renovating the house. All the required tax returns have been filed over the three years. This year, Grace sold the house for $150,000 (U.S.) to a person who intends to use the house as his principal residence. What do you suppose Grace's gain on the sale is, if her real estate commissions were $6,000 (U.S.), and depreciation on the home was $13,000 (U.S.) over the three years? Time to crunch a few numbers. Here is Grace's gain:

Net proceeds on sale ($150,000 – $6,000)	$ 144,000
Cost base ($100,000 + $25,000 – $13,000)	($ 112,000)
Gain on sale	$ 32,000
Net rental losses from prior years (3 years x $3,000)	($ 9,000)
Net gain on sale	$ 23,000

Don't forget that any gain or loss on the sale of your U.S. property will also have to be reported on your Canadian tax return if you are resident in Canada. Don't worry about paying tax on the same gains in both Canada and the U.S.—the foreign tax credit I talked about earlier will protect you from this.

TO MAKE A LONG STORY SHORT:

- When you sell your U.S. real estate, you'll be subject to a 10-percent withholding tax that the buyer will have to remit to the IRS.

- Minimize this tax by selling to someone planning to use the property as a principal residence, or by applying to the U.S. for a withholding certificate.

- Minimize your taxable gain on the sale by making appropriate adjustments to your sale proceeds and your cost base.

Cutting Your Gambling Losses

Tax is definitely a game I can help you to win. As for roulette, blackjack, craps, the ponies, and the rest—you're on your own I'm afraid. There's not much I can do to help you win in games of chance! But if you walk away from the casino or race track poorer than when you arrived, there may be some consolation.

Tim's Tip 84: Register at a casino or hotel to track gambling losses for tax savings.

Recent changes to the Canada-U.S. tax treaty will now treat Canadian residents in the same way as U.S. citizens and residents with regard to gambling. Specifically, Canadian residents can now deduct gambling losses from gambling winnings in the same year.

As in the past, gambling and lottery winnings will be subject to a 30-percent withholding tax at the time of winning, although

If you buy that lotto ticket and strike it rich, you'll be glad to know that your lottery winnings are tax-free in Canada. Not so in the U.S.—the IRS will be right by your side waiting to collect some of those winnings. By the way, the expected value of lottery winnings is, on average, six cents for every dollar spent in a lifetime on tickets.

winnings from blackjack, baccarat, craps, roulette and the Big-6 wheel are exempt from tax. If you're hoping to carry your losses back to previous years, or ahead to future years, don't get your hopes up. Winnings and losses cannot be carried back and forth and offset against other years. If you've received winnings that have had tax withheld and you can substantiate losses, you should consider filing a tax return—Form 1040NR—to claim some of these losses back. Keep in mind, you cannot claim a refund for tax withheld on gambling winnings prior to 1996. Also, if you've received tax-exempt winnings or you have no substantiated losses, don't bother filing a 1040NR tax return—you're not going to get any tax back.

The easiest way to provide the IRS with the information required to substantiate gambling losses is to register at one of the hotels or casinos and establish an account. As money is withdrawn from the account, a record is produced showing all your cash withdrawals. In the past, this has been accepted by the IRS as proof of gambling losses.

When filing your return, include the withholding slip the casino gave you, showing your winnings and the amount withheld plus the official record indicating your withdrawals from the casino account. This return should be filed by the regular deadline for Form 1040NR, which is June 15.

TO MAKE A LONG STORY SHORT:

- Canadian residents can now claim U.S. gambling losses to offset winnings.

- Register at a casino or hotel and establish an account to substantiate your gambling losses.

- File a tax return, Form 1040NR, to claim your losses and recover any withholding tax.

Staying Canadian

If you're planning to spend time in the U.S. each year, there are some things you should keep in mind to avoid the long arm of Uncle Sam.

Tim's Tip 85: Understand the implications of becoming a resident of the U.S.

Becoming a resident of the U.S. for tax purposes can add a whole world of complexity to your tax affairs. If you inadvertently become a resident south of the border, you'll be required to file a U.S. tax return and pay U.S. tax on your worldwide income.

The IRS will consider you a U.S. resident for tax purposes if you hold a green card or if you meet the substantial presence test. How does it work? If the following formula adds up to 183 days or more, then you've met the substantial presence test and you'll be a U.S. resident.

Don't assume, just because you're considered a resident of Canada for Canadian tax purposes, that the IRS will agree with you. You might also be considered a U.S. resident for U.S. tax purposes! Being a resident of both Canada and the U.S. at the same time will do nothing but complicate your tax affairs.

Caution!

THE SUBSTANTIAL PRESENCE TEST

Add	The total days you are present in the U.S. in the current year.
	(It must be at least 31 days or you will not be caught by this test.)
Plus	One-third of the days you were present in the U.S. in the prior year.
Plus	One-sixth of the days you were present in the U.S. in the second prior year.

If the total of these is 183 days or more, then you have met the substantial presence test.

As a rule of thumb, if you were physically present in the U.S. for 122 days (four months) a year over the last three years, you'll meet this test and be deemed a U.S. resident.

How Do You Spell Relief?

If you meet the substantial presence test, there is still one avenue of relief that could allow you to escape having to file a full-blown tax return in the U.S. If you truly have a closer connection to Canada than the U.S., despite meeting the dreaded substantial presence test, then you can file a Closer Connection Statement with the IRS, Form 8840, telling the IRS about this closer connection. Filing this form will get you out of the obligation to report your worldwide income to Uncle Sam. To claim a closer connection to Canada, you must be present in the U.S. fewer than 183 days in the current year and file Form 8840 by June 15 of the following year (that is, file by June 15, 1999, for the 1998 year).

TO MAKE A LONG STORY SHORT:

• Avoid becoming a U.S. resident for tax purposes if you hope to keep your tax affairs from becoming a complex quagmire.

- If you spend, on average, more than 122 days each year in the U.S., you might meet the substantial presence test, which will deem you to be a resident of the U.S.

- If you meet the substantial presence test and are deemed to be a resident of the U.S., filing Form 8840 could solve your problem.

Considering U.S. Estate Taxes

Tim's Tip 86: Determine whether you're a candidate for U.S. estate taxes.

While Canada does not levy estate taxes upon death, the U.S. does. And if you're a Canadian citizen living in Canada, but you own U.S. property, you could be hit with a U.S. estate tax bill upon your death. The kinds of U.S. properties that I'm talking about include: U.S. real estate; shares of U.S. public or private corporations; debt obligations issued by U.S. residents; personal property in the U.S.; and more. The tax bill you can expect is based on the fair market value of those U.S. assets on the date of your death.

By the way, I should mention that, even if you're considered a resident of Canada for Canadian tax purposes, you might still be considered domiciled in the United States. I know it may sound confusing, but domicile in the U.S. is something different than

If you don't calculate carefully, you might just count too many days of presence in the U.S., which could cause you to meet the substantial presence test. In your calculations, be sure to exclude any days in which you were in the U.S. as a student, teacher or trainee, professional athlete temporarily in the U.S. to compete in a charitable event, or diplomat with full-time diplomatic or consular status. If these exceptions apply to you, they also automatically apply to your immediate family.

Caution!

residency in either Canada or the U.S. And if you're considered to be domiciled in the U.S., you'll be liable for U.S. estate tax on all your assets—not simply on those U.S. assets that I talked about in the preceding paragraph. In most cases, a little planning will let you avoid being considered domiciled in the U.S., and you'll have nothing to worry about. I won't go into the definition of U.S. domicile here, but you should check with your tax pro if you're spending lots of time in the U.S., just to make sure you won't be caught.

Once you recognize that you're a candidate for a U.S. estate tax bill, you should consider a number of planning strategies to minimize these taxes. See Tip 101 in Chapter 9 for all the details.

TO MAKE A LONG STORY SHORT:

- You could be liable to pay U.S. estate tax if you own U.S. assets or are considered domiciled in the U.S.

- If you think you're a candidate for U.S. estate taxes, refer to Tip 101 in Chapter 9 for details on how to minimize this tax bill.

Getting into the Game

You could be well on your way to tax savings on both sides of the border. Turn now to the Tax Planning Tip Sheet at the front of the book and review the strategies introduced in Chapter 7. Check *Yes* or *Not Sure* if you think a tip might apply to you. When you've finished this book, take your Tip Sheet to a tax pro if you want more information or help in implementing your plan.

A LEAGUE OF THEIR OWN: QUEBEC TAX ISSUES

If a man does not keep pace with his companions, perhaps it is because he hears a different drummer.

8

I have much respect for the province of Quebec because it has managed to do what others haven't. Quebec has developed a tax system that, in some ways, makes more sense than the federal system. At the same time, having a tax system that's different from the federal system brings new challenges. Namely, if you hope to win the tax game in Quebec, you've got to play by two sets of rules. This chapter is for those of you who are residents of Quebec.

Walking to a Different Drummer

Let's look at issues affecting taxpayers in Quebec, and some tax strategies to make you a winner. In particular, we'll focus on key differences between the federal and Quebec tax systems, and zero in on recent changes in Quebec.

Tim's Tip 87: Understand the significant changes resulting from the 1997 Quebec budget.

On March 25, 1997, the Quebec budget announced sweeping changes to the Quebec tax system that will impact your tax return in 1998 and beyond. There are two key changes to talk about: new tax rates, and Quebec's new simplified tax filing system.

New Tax Rates

Starting in 1998, Quebec moves to a new three-bracket tax rate system, replacing the old five-rate system from 1997 and earlier years.

QUEBEC TAX RATES: 1998 AND BEYOND	
Taxable Income	**Marginal Tax Rate**
$0 – $24,999	20 percent
$25,000 – $49,999	23 percent
$50,000 and over	26 percent

In creating these new brackets, the budget also eliminates the 5-percent and 10-percent surtaxes, and the 2-percent income tax reduction for low- and middle-income taxpayers. The budget also increases the non-refundable tax credit rate from 20 percent to 23 percent.

How are these changes going to affect you? According to the government, the changes will decrease the tax burden by 15 percent per year for households with income under $50,000. Taxes will be reduced by 3 percent for households with income greater than $50,000.

The Simplified System

The second major change this legislation introduced is the simplified alternative tax system. I think we'd all agree that a simpler system is better. This simplified system is an optional way to file your tax return. It replaces a number of individual deductions with a single lump sum tax deduction of $2,350 per person. This $2,350 amount is converted to a credit at the new 23-percent rate to ultimately produce a $541 reduction in taxes. If you choose the simplified system, you'll be entitled to this credit, but you'll lose the ability to claim a number of expenses, including moving expenses, medical expenses, support payments, employment expenses, union or professional dues, investment expenses, the dividend tax credit, labour-sponsored fund credits, tuition fees, and others.

But there's more. If you and your spouse both opt for the simplified system, the two of you can choose to file a joint Quebec tax return. This could mean half the paperwork. Finally, the new simplified system will also allow spouses to transfer to each other any non-refundable tax credits that are not replaced by the lump-sum credit.

Claude has been worrying about his 1998 Quebec tax return. He's not sure whether he should file under the general tax filing system or use the simplified filing system. In a nutshell, he'll be better off under the simplified system if his lump-sum credit is greater than the total of the replaced deductions. But he shouldn't worry about trying to decide whether to choose the general filing system or the new simplified system. If he chooses the general system and the simplified system would have been better for him, the government will assess his tax return under the simplified system to give him a bigger tax break.

Revenue Quebec is trying to make it easy for you to choose between the general or simplified tax systems by providing a work chart to help you determine which system is best, and by telling you which system is better for you based on your previous year's tax return. If you're still not sure whether to file your tax return under the general or simplified system, just use the general system. Revenue Quebec will assess you under the simplified system if it is to your advantage.

TO MAKE A LONG STORY SHORT:

• The 1997 Quebec budget brought big changes to the province's tax system, including changes to tax rate brackets and the introduction of a new simplified tax filing system.

• The simplified system will replace a number of deductions with a single lump-sum tax credit.

Tim's Tip 88: Understand the differences between federal and Quebec taxes, and plan accordingly.

Let's take a look at the more significant differences between the federal and Quebec tax systems. If you don't understand these differences, your tax planning might work in one jurisdiction and not the other. Keep in mind, I'm not able to cover all the differences here, so you'd be wise to visit a tax professional before putting into place any fun and fancy tax strategies.

• **Refundable Child Care Tax Credit**
  Instead of a deduction for child care expenses, Quebec offers a refundable tax credit. The credit is reduced as your income rises. The credit equals a certain percentage of your child care expenses, to a maximum of $5,000 in child care expenses. For people in the lowest income bracket, a 75-percent credit is available, but this credit is reduced to 26 percent as income rises. As of 1998, the refundable portion of eligible child care expenses will be based on net family income above $26,000.

• Charitable Givings

Quebec changed its rules related to charitable giving in its 1998 budget by more closely harmonizing those rules with the federal rules. Beginning in 1998, the ceiling for charitable donations claimed in a given year will be 75 percent of net income, up from the former 20 percent. This limit is increased to 100 percent in the year of death and the year before death. The limit for donations to the Crown has been reduced from 100 percent of net income to 75 percent. Quebec has still not followed the federal lead regarding gifts of securities; that is, there is no reduction in the capital gains rate offered by Quebec for gifts of certain publicly traded securities. Special rules also apply in Quebec for donations of works of art to recipients other than museums or governments.

• Tuition Fees

In Quebec, tuition fees will generate a 23-percent non-refundable tax credit. Unlike the federal law, any excess or undeducted tuition fees cannot be transferred to a spouse or parent but will be pooled and carried forward to offset future taxes. To compensate those who support students, the province introduced an enhanced non-refundable credit for dependents. This credit is equal to $380 per semester if the dependent is a full-time student at a post-secondary institution.

• Moving Allowances

In the 1997 Quebec budget, the province announced that if your employer requires you to move and gives you a moving allowance, you can exclude from income

Beginning in 1998, be sure to claim a non-refundable tax credit for interest paid on student loans. Quebec has adopted the federal rules that provide tax relief for these loans. In Quebec, the credit is equal to 23 percent of the loan interest paid. And if you choose not to claim a credit in a particular year for such interest paid, you'll be able to claim that credit in any future year. You'll have to file a general tax return, rather than a simplified return, to claim this credit.

the portion of this allowance that equals two weeks of your salary at the new location. Quebec has also adopted the federal rules introduced in the 1998 federal budget regarding reimbursements for losses on the sale of a home, fair market value guarantees, and interest subsidies. See Chapter 3, Tip 23c and d.

• Personal Tax Credit

Do you live by yourself? If so, the province offers a non-refundable tax credit. You've got to live alone or with dependent children, in your own self-contained home, for the entire calendar year. The credit is reduced by 15 percent for family incomes over $26,000, and is totally eliminated for incomes at or above $33,000. For 1998, this credit will be a maximum of $242.

• Health Services Fund Contribution

This contribution (call it a tax if you want) is payable on all income other than employment income, Old Age Security, alimony and the 25-percent gross-up amount added to any Canadian dividends you receive. The income that is specifically included is business income, investment income, pension income, and capital gains. The maximum contribution is $1,000, and once paid it is eligible for a 23-percent non-refundable tax credit.

• Union, Professional, and Association Dues

Effective for 1997 and later years, union and professional dues are no longer allowed as a deduction for Quebec tax purposes. You'll now be eligible for a 23-percent tax credit on these fees.

• Seniors' Credits

If you're over 65, you're allowed a non-refundable tax credit worth up to $506 in 1998. This credit is reduced by 15 percent of any family income over $26,000, and disappears by the time family income reaches $33,000. A credit for retirement income is also available on up to $1,000 of eligible income. The maximum credit is $230, and it's affected by the same reduction rules. Finally, a $550 refundable credit may be available to individuals living with the elderly.

• **Medical Expenses**

You won't be happy with changes in the medical expense rules introduced in 1997. Beginning in 1997, you won't be entitled to claim any medical expenses unless they exceed 3 percent of your *family* income. The floor used to be 3 percent of your *individual* income or $1,614, whichever was less. As a result of this change, many Quebec residents won't be able to claim the expenses anymore. For those who can claim medical expenses, costs for training courses related to the care of disabled dependents may now be claimed, thanks to the 1998 Quebec budget.

Here's some advice for those of you with incomes over $50,000. If you have incurred professional or association dues and you report self-employment income on your tax return, be sure to claim those dues as a deduction against your business income rather than as a tax credit. The credit only offers tax relief equalling 23 percent of the dues. But if your income is over $50,000, the tax savings will amount to 26 percent provincially if the dues are claimed as a deduction against business income.

• **Disabled Persons' Credit**

If you're disabled, the province will give you a credit worth up to $506 in tax savings in 1998. The credit can be transferred from a dependent child to a parent. The Quebec legislation leans heavily on federal law to define who is disabled.

• **Legal Fees and Marriage Breakdown**

In Quebec, you can deduct legal fees paid in a court application to increase or decrease your alimony or maintenance. The federal rules

Don't bother claiming capital cost allowance (CCA) in Quebec on your home if you have a home office. Why? Because, as with the federal government, Revenue Quebec may disallow use of your principal residence exemption on the portion of your home used in the business. This could mean a tax bill if you sell your home at a profit later!

allow a deduction only for legal fees to enforce a court-ordered payment of maintenance or alimony. The Quebec and federal governments agree on one thing here: Neither will allow a deduction for the legal fees to establish a right to receive payments.

• Safety Deposit Box Fees

Not that this deduction was going to make you rich anyway, but you should realize that fees for safety deposit boxes are no longer deductible in Quebec, beginning in 1998.

• Home Office

I touched on this issue in Chapter 4, Tip 40. The unfortunate fact is that Quebec has decided to limit home office expenses to just 50 percent of eligible expenses that are otherwise deductible. I'm talking about mortgage interest, property taxes, utilities, insurance, and similar expenses.

• Registered Home Ownership Savings Plans

In 1996, the province announced that it is doing away with Registered Home Ownership Savings Plans (RHOSPs) by the year 2000. Be sure to use your RHOSP funds for a qualifying purpose before the end of 1999.

*J*eanette contributed to an RHOSP a few years ago and currently has $3,000 in the plan. If she doesn't use those funds for an approved purpose by the end of 1999, she is going to face tax on the full amount in the plan. Since she is not planning to *buy a new home just yet, she decided to withdraw those funds to buy some new furniture and appliances she has wanted. These are qualifying purchases, so she'll avoid the tax hit due to occur in 1999. Jeanette could also have used the funds for renovations on her existing home.*

If you don't make that withdrawal, Quebec will tax you on the funds in the plan. Here's the game plan: Withdraw your RHOSP funds and use them to buy a new home, make qualifying renovations, or buy that new furniture or appliance you've been admiring—and do this before the end of 1999!

- **Adoption Expenses**

If you adopt a child, either locally or from overseas, you may be entitled to claim a refundable tax credit for the costs incurred in the adoption process. The credit is 20 percent for up to $10,000 worth of expenses, to a maximum credit of $2,000 per child. The eligible costs include legal fees, travel costs, agency fees, and other costs.

- **Other Differences**

You should be aware that there are differences between federal and Quebec tax rules in the following areas as well: family allowances for children; political contributions; the overseas employment tax deduction; artists' deductions; and deductibility of private health services plan contributions for the self-employed.

TO MAKE A LONG STORY SHORT:

- The federal and Quebec tax systems are different in many areas.

- Be sure to understand these differences so that your income tax planning works both federally and in Quebec.

Investing in Quebec

Tim's Tip 89: Take advantage of special investment incentives offered only to residents of Quebec.

It's time to take a look at tax incentives that only residents of Quebec can enjoy. These incentives were designed to encourage investment in economically important areas in Quebec. If you're not living in Quebec, sorry—just read 'em and weep.

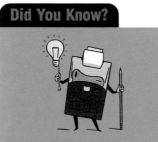

Did You Know?

Regardless of where you live in Canada, any unused capital losses that arose prior to 1986 can be applied to offset any other type of income—not just capital gains—up to $2,000 annually. The reason? Tax laws change over time, and our tax law used to allow capital losses to be used in this way. Pre-1986 capital losses have been grandfathered.

Quebec Stock Savings Plans

A Quebec Stock Savings Plan (QSSP), or Régime d'épargne action (REA), is an incentive introduced by the province back in 1979 to encourage investment in the stock or debentures of publicly traded growth corporations operating mainly in Quebec. If you buy these shares as part of a public issue, you'll be entitled to a deduction against Quebec tax of 50 percent, 75 percent or 100 percent of the cost of the investment, depending on the size of the company. This deduction is further limited to a maximum 10 percent of your net income for the year. Special rules apply to employees and regional venture capital QSSPs.

Quebec Business Investment Companies

A Quebec Business Investment Company (QBIC), or Société de placements dans l'entreprise québécoise (SPEQ), is the private-company equivalent of the QSSP. Basically, a QBIC is a private investment company incorporated in Quebec with the sole purpose of buying new shares in eligible private companies as a way to provide financing to those companies. The deduction available is slightly different than for QSSPs. You'll receive your share of a 150-percent deduction of the QBIC's eligible investments in the year the QBIC makes that investment, which might not be this year. This deduction will be limited to 30 percent of your net income. Again, special rules apply to employees and a regional QBIC.

Co-operative Investment Plans

Co-operative investment plans (CIPs), or Régimes d'investissement coopératif (RIC), were started with the intention of providing Quebec co-operatives with funds to expand. The deductions available are similar to the QSSP. Investments in a CIP can provide a deduction as high as 150 percent in some situations.

QSSP Investment Funds

In an attempt to provide the diversification advantage of mutual funds while still providing capital to small business, the Quebec government has allowed the creation of QSSP Investment Funds (QIFs). These funds invest in QSSP shares. The advantage to this approach is that you can claim the deduction in the year you invest in the QIF; plus you'll manage to reduce your risks since QIFs offer great diversification.

Action Step

If you're running into a problem with a clawback of certain tax credits or Quebec government benefits because your income exceeds the applicable thresholds, or if you face tax on withdrawals from your registered retirement savings plan (RRSP), consider investing in a QSSP, QBIC, CIP, QSSP Investment Fund (QIF), or flow-through shares that will provide you with a tax deduction. The deduction will bring your income down, and will help to minimize the impact of the clawback of your credits or benefits.

Exploration Expenses

Special rules exist for shares of companies doing oil and gas or mining exploration in Quebec. For example, certain companies in this sector have issued *flow-through* shares; for these shares, the company renounces its right to deduct certain expenses so that those deductions "flow through" to the shareholder. Here's the good news: Quebec will let you deduct 125 percent of the exploration costs renounced and passed along to you. For companies doing surface mining or drilling for oil and gas after May 9, 1996, this deduction is increased to 175 percent. Flow-through shares in the resource sector may also entitle you to a capital gains exemption on their eventual sale.

TO MAKE A LONG STORY SHORT:

- Consider investing in one of a number investments that offer attractive tax incentives to residents of Quebec.

- These include: QSSPs, QBICs, CIPs, QIFs, and flow-through shares.

Getting into the Game

Turn now to the Tax Planning Tip Sheet at the front of the book and review the strategies you've read about in Chapter 8. For each one, ask yourself, "Does this apply to me?" Armed with the *Yes* and *Not Sure* answers, visit a tax professional for more information on each strategy, or for help implementing the ideas. *Bonne chance*.

BOTTOM OF THE NINTH: PLANNING FOR YOUR ESTATE

Live your life, play the game, then tip your hat to the crowd.

9

Brace yourself: This chapter is about both death *and* taxes. You might be feeling tempted to pass by these next few pages. In fact, when I first wrote this chapter, I handed it to my neighbour George for his opinion. He claimed that he didn't have time to read it—he was going to the dentist. "George, what about next week? Can you read it by then?" I asked. "Uh, I don't see how, Tim. I'm hoping for a root canal," he said.

Hmm. I guess a root canal is decidedly more appealing than thinking about death any day of the week.

The only problem, of course, is that neglecting that day when you won't be here anymore is tantamount to handing a blank cheque to the tax collector. And make no mistake, estate planning is not simply for those who are in a later stage of life. Let's face it, even the best pitchers can be taken out of the game early. Whether you're thirty years old or eighty years young, you need to plan for your tax bill upon death.

Knowing What to Expect

Tim's Tip 90: Understand the deemed disposition of your assets upon death.

It's no secret that, when you die, the tax collector usually follows the undertaker to your door. In fact, did you know that, upon your death, you are deemed to have sold everything you own at fair market value? It's true. And if you own any assets that have appreciated in value, you could face a tax bill on death that might just be large enough to wipe out the entire federal debt, give or take. And while it would certainly be generous of you to think of your nation that way, my guess is that if you've got to choose between the tax collector and your loved ones, you'd rather leave your remaining assets to family, friends, or charity.

What this means, of course, is that you're going to have to plan for your taxes upon death—today! Once you're gone, so are the opportunities to minimize the tax collector's share of your estate. The lesson is simple: Calculate what you expect your tax bill to look like upon death, then use the strategies in this chapter to bring that tax liability down. If you're not sure how to crunch the numbers, visit a tax professional who can help you with the calculations.

TO MAKE A LONG STORY SHORT:

- Upon death you're deemed to have sold everything you own, which could result in a whopping tax bill.

- Once you're gone, so are the opportunities to minimize this tax hit.

- Calculate your tax bill expected upon death, and then use the ideas in this chapter to reduce the tax bite. Visit a tax pro to help with the calculations, if necessary.

Giving It Away Today

Tim's Tip 91: **Give assets away during your lifetime for tax and probate savings upon your death.**

One sure-fire way to avoid income tax and probate fees when you die, is to die broke! Don't get me wrong, I'm not suggesting that you should spend the last few years of your life living on the streets

While it's true that your death will cause a deemed disposition, or sale, of all that you own, there are two other common situations that can give rise to this same deemed disposition at fair market value. The first is where you give an asset away to someone other than your spouse. The second is where you give up Canadian residency. The problem with a deemed disposition is that, since you're not actually selling anything, there are no sale proceeds with which to pay the tax bill. Proper planning can help to minimize the tax burden on a deemed disposition.

Caution!

and sleeping on a park bench just to beat the tax collector. You might, however, consider giving away some of your assets during your lifetime. A side benefit to this idea is that you'll be able to see your children or other heirs enjoy that inheritance while you're still around.

Make sure you don't cause a deemed disposition of your assets without realizing it! Canadians are notorious for doing this. For example, you may change your mutual fund account from "Jane Doe" to "Jane Doe and Sally Doe, joint with right of survivorship." Sure, this is going to avoid probate fees on your death—which is why people do this. The problem? Jane has just given away one half of her investments to Sally. This results in a deemed disposition of one half of those investments, and a potential tax bill! Don't create a tax hit for the sake of saving probate fees!

Caution!

If you're going to take me up on this idea, just be aware that our tax law could create a tax bill for you in the year you give an asset away. You see, when you give something away, you're deemed to have sold it at its fair market value at the time you make the gift. If the asset has gone up in value, you might just trigger a taxable capital gain when giving it away.

There are a couple of ways to minimize any tax bill that might arise. First, give away assets that won't create a taxable gain. I'm referring primarily to cash or your principal residence. However, if you're going to give away the home, be sure to have a written agreement with your heirs that will give you the right to use the home during your lifetime (you'd hate to be kicked out if relations with your heirs took a turn for the worse). Second, if you're giving away assets that will lead to a tax bill, consider giving those assets away slowly, over a number of years, so that you don't trigger a huge tax bill in a single year. Otherwise, you could be pushed into a higher marginal tax bracket.

TO MAKE A LONG STORY SHORT:

- The tax collector can't tax you on assets you don't own at the time of your death.

- Consider giving assets away today to minimize taxes and probate fees upon death, but beware of the *deemed disposition* at fair market value that could lead to a tax bill when you make the gift.

Tim's Tip 92: **Consider an estate freeze to minimize your tax bill on death.**

Maybe you've heard of this thing called an estate freeze. It's a common technique used to freeze the value of certain assets today and to pass any future growth in value to your kids or other heirs.

The Benefits

Here are some of the key benefits of an estate freeze:

- By freezing the value of certain assets today, you'll be able to establish, fairly accurately, what your tax liability is going to be upon death. This will allow you to plan for payment of those taxes.
- By passing the future growth in the asset's value to the next generation, you'll manage to defer income tax on that growth until a much later time. In fact, taxes may not be due until your heirs die, or until they sell the assets, whichever comes first.
- A freeze might allow you to take advantage of the *enhanced capital gains exemption* if you own shares of a qualified small business

When you complete an estate freeze, you are effectively transferring ownership of the frozen assets to your kids or other heirs. You can imagine the problem with this. Your kids or other heirs may want to do something with those assets that you disapprove of. When you complete the freeze, make sure that you maintain control over the assets if you're concerned about the control issue. This can be done by, for example, providing yourself with more voting shares than your heirs in the corporation used to complete the freeze. If you use a trust for the freeze, name yourself as trustee.

Caution!

corporation or qualified farm property. This exemption is available to all Canadian residents and can shelter up to $500,000 of capital gains from tax—see Chapter 5, Tip 50 for more.

- There's no need to give up control over the frozen assets during your lifetime.

The Methods

How do you complete an estate freeze? I'd put you to sleep for sure if I tried to detail the many steps to completing a freeze. Let me just say that there are two very common methods of freezing an estate. The first is through use of a corporation. By transferring your growing assets to a company and taking back, in return, preferred shares in that company that are frozen in value, you'll manage a successful estate freeze. Common shares in the company, which may appreciate in value over time, can be issued to your children, or anyone else. The second method is through use of a trust—called an *inter vivos* trust. The idea is that you'd transfer certain assets to a trust today for the benefit of your children, or anyone you'd like.

In either case, you can bet you'll need the help of a tax pro to look after the nitty gritty details, because you may trigger a taxable event when placing your assets in the corporation or trust, although there are generally ways to avoid this in the case of the corporation.

TO MAKE A LONG STORY SHORT:

- By completing an estate freeze you'll manage to pass the future growth of the frozen assets to your heirs or others of your choice.

- This will, among other things, freeze your tax bill upon death, enabling you to estimate and plan for those taxes ahead of time.

- A corporation or trust are most commonly used to freeze an estate.

Giving It Away at Death

Tim's Tip 93: **Leave it to your spouse to defer the tax hit longer.**

Remember, when you die you will be deemed to have sold your assets at fair market value. This could give rise to a tax bill. The common exception to this rule is when you leave assets to your spouse. You see, when you leave something to your spouse, the ugly *deemed disposition* that takes place will no longer take place at fair market value. Rather, you will be deemed to have sold those assets at your original cost. The result? No tax to pay! In this case, you'll manage to defer the tax bill until the death of the surviving spouse.

Leaving assets to your spouse on your death will avoid a tax hit. Leaving assets to your kids or other heirs will generally give rise to tax if the assets have appreciated in value since you bought them, or on your RRSP or registered retirement income fund (RRIF). So, if you're going to leave anything to your kids or other heirs, leave them the assets that won't be subject to much tax, if any. There are four assets in this category: cash, life insurance benefits, a principal residence, and investments that have not appreciated in value very much.

Bill passed away last year. His assets consisted of a home, RRSPs of $400,000, non-registered investments worth $100,000 for which he had paid $60,000, and cash of $100,000. Bill left everything to Lois, his wife, with the exception of the cash of $100,000 and some life insurance proceeds of $100,000. How much tax do you suppose was triggered by Bill's death? The answer is zero. Nil. He managed to escape tax on any assets that had appreciated in value by leaving those assets to Lois. Since he wanted to leave something to his kids, he left them those assets that weren't subject to income tax at the time of his death.

Do you follow what happened in Bill's situation? Bill left his wife any assets that might have given rise to a tax hit upon his death. This included his registered retirement savings plans (RRSPs) and non-registered investments. He also left the home to Lois, not because it would have otherwise been subject to tax (since his principal residence exemption will work, even on death, to shelter any profits from tax), but because Lois still needed the home to live in.

Here's a final point worth noting. If you wish, you can transfer your assets to a spousal trust upon your death. This will have the same tax-free effect as if you had left the assets directly to your spouse. With a spousal trust, all the income earned on the assets placed in the trust will accrue to your spouse while he or she is still alive. No one other than your surviving spouse can access the assets (the capital of the trust) while that spouse is still alive. There may be many reasons to set up a spousal trust rather than leaving the assets directly to your spouse. I'll talk about one of the key reasons in Tip 96.

TO MAKE A LONG STORY SHORT:

- Leaving assets to your spouse or a spousal trust upon death will allow you to avoid the effect of a deemed "sale" at fair market value of those assets when you die.

- If you're going to leave assets to the kids upon your death, leave them with those assets that will be subject to little tax, if any: cash, life insurance benefits, a principal residence, or assets that have not appreciated much in value.

Tim's Tip 94: Minimize the tax on your RRSP or RRIF assets upon death by naming the right beneficiaries.

A common question pondered by many Canadians is this: "How can I avoid tax on my RRSP or RRIF assets when I die?" The answer isn't always easy. Your first line of defence is always to name your spouse as the beneficiary of your plan. Beyond this, the opportunities to avoid tax become slim, but if you have certain dependents, there may be other opportunities.

Your Spouse as Beneficiary

If you name your spouse as the beneficiary of your RRSP or RRIF, then your plan assets will transfer directly to your spouse's plan upon your death on a tax-free basis. If your surviving spouse is age 69 or younger in the year of your death, those assets can be transferred to his or her RRSP, otherwise they'll be transferred to your spouse's RRIF. Your spouse generally has 60 days following the year of your death to make the deposit to his or her own plan.

Your Dependents as Beneficiaries

If you're not able to leave your RRSP or RRIF assets to a spouse, chances are good that you're going to leave the assets to your kids or grandchildren. In the vast majority of cases, this is going to mean a tax bill. Typically, you'll face tax on these plan assets on your final tax return; then the balance is distributed to the children or grandchildren. But like most rules in tax, there are always exceptions. In this case, there are two:

I've met many Canadians who have been divorced and are re-married, and who have decided to leave their RRSP or RRIF to the kids rather than the new spouse. If you plan to leave your new spouse anything on your death, leave all or a portion of those RRSP or RRIF assets—it's generally the only way to avoid tax on those assets. Leave the kids with other assets—even a principal residence (with instructions that the house is to be occupied by your new spouse until his or her death). Leaving the kids with the full RRSP or RRIF will create a tax bill that could wipe out half of those assets—a high price to pay.

- **Infirm Dependents.** You'll manage to avoid the tax collector if you leave your RRSP or RRIF assets to a child or grandchild, of any age, who was financially dependent on you at the time of your death due to a physical or mental infirmity. Your dependent will be eligible to transfer your plan assets tax-free to his or her own RRSP, RRIF, or annuity.

- **Minor Dependents.** If a minor child was financially dependent on you at the time of your death, the child will be eligible to buy an annuity to age 18 using your RRSP or RRIF assets. This won't defer tax for very long in most cases, but it beats paying tax on the plan assets in one year. If the minor is infirm, then the rules for infirm dependents apply.

It's always best to name the appropriate person as beneficiary of your RRSP or RRIF on the plan application form itself. However, naming the appropriate person in your will accomplishes the same thing.

TO MAKE A LONG STORY SHORT:

- You'll always manage to avoid tax on your RRSP or RRIF assets upon death by naming your spouse as the beneficiary of your plan.

- You may also manage to defer tax on your plan assets by transferring your RRSP or RRIF to a person financially dependent on you at the time of your death.

Tim's Tip 95: Instruct your executor to make a final contribution to your RRSP after your death.

Believe it or not, the tax collector won't mind one bit if the executor of your estate makes RRSP contributions on your behalf once you're gone. But keep some things in mind here:

After your death, no contributions can be made to your own RRSP. Rather, contributions will have to be made to a spousal RRSP on your behalf. You'll receive the deduction, but your surviving spouse will pay the tax on any withdrawals.

Your spouse must be under age 69 on December 31 of the year you die in order for a contribution to be made to a spousal RRSP; otherwise no contribution can be made.

You must have RRSP contribution room available at the time of your death to enable your executor to make a spousal RRSP contribution on your behalf.

Any contribution to a spousal RRSP after your death will provide a deduction on your final tax return. This can help to minimize the taxes that would otherwise arise on your death.

The tax savings that will be passed to your heirs from an RRSP contribution after your death will range from 26 percent to 54 percent of the contribution, depending on your province and the level of income reported on your final tax return.

TO MAKE A LONG STORY SHORT:

- The executor of your estate may be able to make final RRSP contributions on your behalf after you're gone.

- The contributions must be made to a spousal RRSP, within your contribution limits.

- A deduction may be claimed on your final tax return for these contributions.

Did You Know?

The final tax return for a deceased taxpayer is due six months after the date of death, or April 30 of the year following the year of death, whichever is later. If, for example, you died on November 30, 1999, your executor would have until May 30, 2000, to file your final tax return. By the way, your executor may file up to four separate tax returns for you, depending on the type of income you earned in your last year.

Tim's Tip 96: Save your heirs tax by setting up a testamentary trust in your will.

A testamentary trust is a terrific tool for splitting income. It works this way: A trust would be created upon your death through instructions in your will. All or a portion of your assets would be transferred to the trust upon your death, and your intended heirs would be the beneficiaries of the trust.

Any investment income earned on the inheritance each year may now be taxed in the trust, rather than in the hands of your beneficiaries. You see, the trust is considered to be a separate person for tax purposes, and will be taxed at the same graduated tax rates as any individual. Rather than adding any investment income directly to the beneficiary's income where it will be taxed at his or her marginal tax rate—very likely between 41 and 54 percent—simply split income with the trust by having the trust pay tax on the income instead, at graduated rates.

R ic died last year and left assets directly to his wife Shirley, now living in Kelowna, B.C. Ric's assets generate $60,000 annually in investment income for Shirley. Since Shirley already has income of $60,000 annually from other sources, she now has $120,000 of income to report on her tax return each year. The tax bill to Shirley is going to total $50,300 in 1998. Ric could have done things differently. He could have set up a testamentary trust for Shirley through his will upon his death, and Shirley would be enjoying the benefits of splitting income with the trust. In this case, the trust would now be paying tax on the $60,000 earned on the inheritance each year, while Shirley would continue to pay tax on her other income. But the combined total tax bill between Shirley and the trust would be just $38,870—a full $11,430 less than without the trust! By the way, that's $11,430 in tax savings each year. Now that's something worth writing home about!

The reason for the tax savings with the testamentary trust is simple: Both Shirley and the trust are entitled to low marginal tax rates on the first $29,590 of income. By having both Shirley and the trust paying tax, the number of dollars taxed in the lowest tax bracket is multiplied. Your tax savings may not be as high as in the example I've given here, but savings of up to about $11,000 (maximum) each year are possible. The actual amount will depend on your income and province of residence.

Here are some last thoughts: You may want to set up a separate trust for each beneficiary, to maximize the number of dollars that can be taxed in the lowest bracket. The trusts would provide that income may accumulate in the trusts, and that tax-free capital distributions could be made to beneficiaries.

TO MAKE A LONG STORY SHORT:

- A testamentary trust provides an opportunity for your heirs to split income with the trust, maximizing the number of dollars that will be taxed in the lowest tax bracket.

- Setting up a testamentary trust must be done in your will.

- The tax savings can be up to about $11,000 (maximum) annually, depending on your income level and your province of residence.

When setting up a testamentary trust, the option exists to have the income in the trust taxed in the hands of the beneficiary in any given year. This is done by *paying* the income to the beneficiary, or by making it *payable to* the beneficiary. And this may be a good idea if, for example, the beneficiary has little or no other income and will enjoy the first $6,956 ($6,707 in 1998) of income tax-free due to the basic and supplementary personal credits.

Tim's Tip 97: **Give to charity and save a bundle. But do it properly!**

Let's face it, one of the joys of giving to charity is seeing your donations put to good use, so you may want to consider giving to charity during your lifetime. And if you want to avoid probate fees, giving to charity today is going to help, since you'll no longer own those assets on the date of your death. Having said this, making a donation upon your death could go a long way toward reducing any tax bill you might face at that time. Regardless of whether you plan to make your donations during your lifetime, after your death, or a bit of both, why not give in a manner that's going to save the most tax? There are three out-of-the-ordinary methods of giving to charity that I want to talk about.

Donating Securities

The tax collector changed the rules around charitable giving in the 1997 federal budget to make things easier for charities, and the new rules could help you save more tax than ever on certain donations. The rules say that you'll be entitled to claim donations totalling up to 75 percent of your net income annually. This increases to 100 percent in the year of your death. And if your donations exceed this amount in the year of death, the excess can be carried back and claimed in the year before your death—up to 100 percent of your income in that year as well.

The new rules also favour donating mutual funds, stocks, bonds, and other securities, rather than cash.

Bernadette owned shares in XYZ Corporation on the date of her death. XYZ is traded on the Toronto Stock Exchange, and the shares were worth $25,000 on the date she died, but she had paid just $10,000 for the shares a couple of years earlier. These shares were deemed to have been disposed of upon Bernadette's death, which would have triggered a $15,000 capital *gain and a tax bill of $5,625 if she had not left the shares to charity. Bernadette, however, left instructions in her will for her executor to donate these shares to her favourite charity after her death. The result is that the $15,000 gain is only 37.5-percent taxable! That's right, just $5,625 ($15,000 x 37.5%) of the gain is subject to tax. Normally, three-quarters of the gain would have been taxable under the usual capital gains rules. The result? The tax owing on this $15,000 gain will now be just $2,813—half of what it would have been. To top it off, a donation credit will be provided based on the $25,000 fair market value of the shares. This credit will be claimed on Bernadette's final tax return and will amount to $10,875 in tax savings (varying slightly by province and income level).*

You'll notice that Bernadette paid $2,813 in taxes on her capital gain, but received a donation credit of $10,875 to more than offset these taxes. The net benefit to Bernadette's estate is $8,062 ($10,875 minus $2,813).

So here's the game plan: Instead of cash, consider leaving securities that have appreciated in value to your favourite charity. This can be done by leaving instructions in your will for your executor to donate specific securities to a charity of your choice. Your heirs will thank you, since the tax savings could be significant.

By the way, the preferential 37.5-percent taxable rate for donated securities only applies until the end of the year 2001. Call this an experiment of the federal government if you'd like. Chances are, however, that this new rule will be extended beyond 2001, so I wouldn't hesitate to leave securities to your favourite charity in your will. And you'll be able to take advantage of these new rules during your lifetime as well. That is, donations of mutual funds and securities listed on a prescribed stock exchange during your lifetime will also result in greater tax benefits than they did before the 1997 federal budget.

Establishing a Charitable Remainder Trust

With a charitable remainder trust (CRT), you can donate certain investments to a trust during your lifetime. Your favourite charity is named as the capital beneficiary of the trust so that, upon your death, or upon the death of a surviving spouse, the investments pass to the charity. During your lifetime, you're entitled to all income generated by the investments in the trust. You get tax relief right away for the investments you have transferred to the trust. The value of the donation credit is determined by an actuarial calculation based on your age. The older you are, the greater the tax credit when setting up a CRT.

Caution!

There are two things to remember if you're going to set up a charitable remainder trust. First, the trust will be irrevocable—once it's set up, there's no turning back! Second, transferring investments to a charitable remainder trust could trigger a taxable capital gain if those investments have appreciated in value. The donation credit received from the gift, however, will soften the blow of any taxable gain.

Giving Life Insurance

There are generally three ways to help your favourite charity with life insurance: (1) make the charity the beneficiary of your policy; (2) transfer ownership of a policy to the charity and make the charity the beneficiary; or (3) make your estate the beneficiary and leave instructions in your will for a donation to be made to charity.

In the first scenario, guess how much tax relief you'll get. Zero. Your charity still benefits, but no tax credits are available, since you never actually possess the money that ends up in the charity's coffers.

In scenario two, transferring ownership of a policy will provide you with a donation credit for any cash value that exists at the time of transfer, plus a credit for any premiums paid by you after that date. Sorry, you won't receive a credit for the death benefit when it's paid to the charity upon your death. There may be a tax cost on any cash surrender value that exceeds the cost base of the policy in this scenario, but the donation credit should outweigh this.

Scenario three is my favourite. When your estate is the beneficiary of the policy and then donates the proceeds to charity, a donation credit can be claimed on your final tax return. And in the year of your death this spells major tax relief since, in that year and the preceding year, you're entitled to claim donations of up to 100 percent of your income. One drawback is that, unlike scenarios one and two, you'll face probate fees, but the tax savings from the donation will be even greater than these fees.

TO MAKE A LONG STORY SHORT:

- Giving to charity during your lifetime or upon death can provide significant tax savings. Making donations during your lifetime will also save probate fees.

- Consider donating securities instead of cash.

- Consider a charitable remainder trust or life insurance as tax-efficient ways to help your favourite charity.

Tim's Tip 98: Suggest an offshore inheritance trust to non-resident family members.

Okay, I admit, this idea can be sensitive to implement. But the tax savings can be so significant, I've just got to share the idea with you. Picture this: You have a relative who lives in another country and for Canadian tax purposes is definitely a non-resident of Canada. This relative of yours also plans on leaving an inheritance to you. You're now in a prime circumstance to save tax by using an offshore trust.

To set up an offshore inheritance trust, you'll need to approach the non-resident individual to explain the strategy. That individual will then have to ensure that his or her will provides for the testamentary trust to be set up in the offshore jurisdiction upon death. Once the non-resident dies— it's too late to set this up! Be sure to get professional advice on which jurisdiction is best for the trust.

Here's how it works: Rather than leaving assets directly to you upon death, your relative should consider leaving them in a trust, with you as beneficiary. That trust, however, should be resident in a low or no-tax jurisdiction—not in Canada. Any income earned in the trust annually will not be taxed in the trust if there are no income taxes where the trust resides. The benefit is obvious: The funds in the trust can accumulate tax-free— much like they would in your RRSP. But this arrangement is better than any RRSP. Here's why: The funds in the trust can be paid out to you as tax-free distributions of capital (not income) from the trust. You won't face a cent of tax on those distributions! And there's absolutely nothing illegal about it.

TO MAKE A LONG STORY SHORT:

- If you're expecting a non-resident relative to leave you an inheritance, arrange for the inheritance to be placed in an offshore trust with you as beneficiary.

- Arrangements must be made before your relative dies.

- Tax-free distributions of capital can be made from the trust, making it more attractive than an RRSP.

Providing Tax-Free Death Benefits

Tim's Tip 99: **Negotiate a $10,000 death benefit with your employer.**

You may not realize this, but you can make arrangements today for your employer to pay a full $10,000 to your heirs upon your death as a death benefit. A death benefit is simply an amount paid, after your death, in recognition of your service to your employer.

In actual fact, death benefits are taxable, but the first $10,000 paid out is exempt from tax. The surviving spouse of the deceased employee is the one who gets the exemption but, to the extent the spouse receives less than $10,000 in death benefits, any remaining recipients can split the balance of the exemption.

So, next time you're reviewing your salary with your employer, or you start a new position, negotiate for a death benefit. Think of this as $10,000 of life insurance with no premiums to pay.

TO MAKE A LONG STORY SHORT:

- Your employer can pay a $10,000 death benefit to your spouse or other beneficiaries on a tax-free basis.

- At your next salary review or new position, negotiate to have such a payment made. It's like life insurance without any premiums.

Tim's Tip 100: **Use life insurance to soften the blow of a tax bill at the time of your death.**

Sometimes, avoiding a tax hit on death is impossible. In this event, life insurance may be your answer if you're hoping to leave a little more behind.

The Role of Life Insurance

The deemed disposition that I talked about in Tip 90 can leave your estate with a large enough tax bill to wipe out half the assets you were hoping to leave to your heirs. Consider also the result when the second spouse in a family dies and leaves any remaining RRSP or RRIF assets to the kids: Virtually half the assets of the plan will disappear when the tax collector comes knocking.

Further, some assets can create a hefty tax bill upon your death without providing the cash for those taxes to be paid. For example, private company shares that have appreciated in value, or a vacation property, can both give rise to taxes, and yet it can be difficult to sell either of these in order to provide the necessary cash to pay the taxes owing.

This is where life insurance can be your friend. If you're able to estimate today your taxes upon death, you may be able to buy enough life insurance to cover the taxes owing. Remember our talk on estate freezes (Tip 92)? A freeze can help you to establish your tax bill ahead of time, which is going to make it easier for you to buy the appropriate amount of insurance.

Action Step

When buying life insurance to cover your taxes owing on death, consider joint, second-to-die insurance. This is a policy that will pay out benefits upon the death of the second spouse. This insurance is easier to get since only one spouse needs to be insurable, and the premiums are generally cheaper since two events have to take place before the insurance proceeds are paid: both you and your spouse must die. This type of policy makes sense because you won't generally need the insurance until the second spouse has died. After all, there will be little tax to pay on the death of the first spouse if most assets are left to the surviving spouse.

Paying for the Insurance

Obviously your age and health will be important considerations in deciding whether this idea is for you. Life insurance may not be an option if you're in poor health or you're elderly (generally, over age 80). But even where the premiums are high, these may still cost you less than the tax bill at the time of your death. Hey, why not approach your kids or other heirs to see if they are able and willing to help cover the cost of these premiums? After all, they're the ones who stand to benefit from a reduced tax burden when you die.

People usually get a good laugh out of me suggesting that the kids pay for the life insurance. But let me tell you how to sell it to them. Your kids should think of these premiums as an investment that will lead to tax-free investment returns down the road. Suppose, for example, it's going to cost $8,000 each year in premiums for $400,000 of insurance on your life. If you've got four kids, that's $2,000 each per year. If you live for another 20 years, that's a total investment by each child of $40,000 ($2,000 times 20 years) at which time each child would receive $100,000 ($400,000 for four children). That works out to an annual return of 8.8 percent for each child—tax-free! Of course, the sooner you die, the higher the return for your beneficiaries. Not to scare you, but you might want to watch the brakes on your car!

TO MAKE A LONG STORY SHORT:

- Sometimes it's impossible to avoid a tax bill on death. If you want to minimize the impact of this, life insurance may be your best bet.

- Life insurance will be particularly important when you expect a tax bill on death with little cash available to pay those taxes.

- Consider asking your heirs to pick up the tab for the insurance; after all, they're the ones who will ultimately benefit.

Planning for U.S. Estate Taxes

Tim's Tip 101: Forecast your U.S. estate tax and apply eight strategies to minimize the tax bill.

Prior to changes introduced in 1995 to the Canada-U.S. tax treaty, Canadians who owned U.S. assets were subject to U.S. estate taxes on the value of those assets as figured on the date of death. A meagre $60,000 deduction from the value of those assets was provided when making the estate tax calculation. The U.S. estate tax was levied in addition to the taxes paid in Canada, if any, upon death. The result? Double taxation.

Did You Know?

According to the *Guinness Book of World Records*, the largest personal tax levy ever reported was $336 million on the estate of Howard Hughes. Kind of makes your quarterly installments seem a little more bearable—doesn't it?

The New Rules

Today, you could still face a tax bill, but you'll now find greater relief. Which assets are subject to U.S. estate tax? Anything considered a *U.S. situs* property, including:

- real estate (a vacation property, rental property, private home, or business property)
- shares of a U.S. corporation (public and private companies)
- debt obligations issued by U.S. residents (individuals or government)
- personal property located in the U.S. (cars, boats, jewellery, furnishings, club memberships, and more).

The tax is levied on the fair market value of these assets on the date of your death, and the tax rate for U.S. estate taxes ranges from 18 to 55 percent of your U.S. assets, with most people facing a tax bill between 25 and 35 percent.

Now for the tax breaks offered: Canadian citizens residing outside of the U.S. who have estates of $1.2 million (U.S.) or less will only be subject to U.S. estate taxes on certain U.S. property. For the most part, this property will include real estate, business assets when a permanent establishment is maintained in the U.S., and resource properties. But that's not all. Canadians will be entitled to a unified credit of $192,800. This credit can be used to offset, dollar for dollar, the U.S. estate tax bill otherwise owing. In actual fact, Canadians won't generally receive the full credit of $192,800 since it's prorated based on the percentage of total assets located in the United States.

L ynda owned a condominium in Colorado worth $275,000 (U.S.) on the date of her death. Her total assets upon death were valued at $1,000,000 (U.S.). Lynda's U.S. estate taxes were calculated to be $79,300 (U.S.) before the unified credit. The unified credit that she was able to claim was $53,020, calculated as follows: $192,800 x $275,000/$1,000,000. Lynda's total estate tax bill was $26,280 (U.S.) ($79,300 minus $53,020).

The unified credit is reduced when only a portion of your assets are located in the U.S., and this will be the case for most Canadians. You'll be glad to know that an additional marital property credit of up to $192,800 is available if you leave your U.S. assets to your spouse upon your death. Further, you won't have to worry about the double-taxation problem anymore since any U.S. estate taxes paid will be eligible for a foreign tax credit in Canada (that is, the U.S. estate taxes paid can be used to reduce your Canadian tax bill in the year of death). You should note that the rules for a U.S. citizen who happens to be living in Canada are slightly different, but if you're in this boat you'll be eligible for similar tax relief.

Minimizing U.S. Estate Taxes

Try these eight ideas on for size to minimize the impact of U.S. estate taxes:

- Keep your U.S. assets below $1.2 million to avoid estate tax on all but your U.S. real estate and a couple of other uncommon U.S. assets.
- Consider holding your U.S. assets inside a Canadian corporation.
- Give property to your spouse and children over time, since each person is entitled to his or her own unified credit.
- Buy life insurance to cover any U.S. estate tax liability.
- Restructure your debt so that non-recourse loans are secured by your U.S. assets, since this debt will reduce the value of your taxable estate.
- Move your U.S. assets back to Canada.
- Leave your U.S. property to a qualified domestic trust (QDOT). This type of trust does not eliminate U.S. estate tax, but can defer it until the death of the second spouse.
- Rent instead of own. You're not going to pay estate tax on assets you don't own, so consider renting a place in your favourite location down south rather than buying.

TO MAKE A LONG STORY SHORT:

- U.S. estate taxes will apply to any *U.S. situs* property you own on the date of your death.

- Recent changes in the Canada-U.S. tax treaty make this estate tax blow easier to take, but you still need to plan.

- Apply one or more of the eight most common strategies to minimize U.S. estate tax.

Getting into the Game

Maybe you can't take it with you, but you can certainly have a say in where it goes after you're gone. Start now by turning to the Tax Planning Tip Sheet at the front of the book and reviewing the tips for Chapter 9. Ask yourself, "Does this tip apply to me?" Your *Yes* and *Not Sure* answers could lead to big tax savings for your estate—and that's good news for you, your heirs, and your favourite charitable causes.

Glossary of Abbreviations

ABIL	allowable business investment loss
ACB	adjusted cost base
CCA	capital cost allowance
CCPC	Canadian-controlled private corporation
CDN	Canadian Dealing Network
CESG	Canada Education Savings Grant
CICA	The Canadian Institute of Chartered Accountants
CIP	cooperative investment plan (Quebec)
CNIL	cumulative net investment loss
CPP	Canada Pension Plan
DPSP	deferred profit sharing plan
EHT	Employer Health Tax (Ontario)
EI	Employment Insurance
GAAR	general anti-avoidance rule
GIC	guaranteed investment certificate
GST	Goods and Services Tax
HBP	Home Buyers' Plan
HST	Harmonized Sales Tax
IPP	individual pension plan
IRA	Individual Retirement Account
LSVCC	labour-sponsored venture capital corporation
OAS	Old Age Security
PA	Pension Adjustment
QBIC	Quebec Business Investment Company
QDOT	qualified domestic trust
QIF	QSSP Investment Funds
QPP	Quebec Pension Plan
QSBC	qualified small business corporation
QSSP	Quebec Stock Savings Plan
QST	Quebec Sales Tax
REA	Régime d'épargne action
REIT	real estate investment trust
RESP	Registered Education Savings Plan
RHOSP	Registered Home Ownership Savings Plan
RPP	registered pension plan
RRIF	registered retirement income fund
RRSP	registered retirement savings plan
SAR	stock appreciation right
SIN	Social Insurance Number
SPEQ	Société de placements dans l'entreprise québécoise

Marginal Tax Rates for 1998

These tables will help you determine your 1998 marginal tax rate. When it comes to tax planning, this is probably the most important number for you to understand. It will help you to calculate both your tax savings from a deduction and your after-tax investment returns. It will also tell you how much tax you will pay on your last dollar of income. You'll notice that Canadian dividends are taxed at a lower rate, thanks to the dividend tax credit. Foreign dividends, on the other hand, are taxed at the same rates as regular income.

G lenda lives in Newfoundland and had taxable income of $45,000 in 1998. She made a $10,000 RRSP contribution in 1998. Since her marginal tax rate is 44.3 percent (see the Newfoundland table), the deduction for her RRSP contribution saved her $4,430 in taxes in 1998 ($10,000 times 44.3 percent). Glenda had also sold some stocks at a $1,000 profit in 1998, and she reported that capital gain on her tax return. At her level of income, capitals gains attract tax at a marginal rate of 33.3 percent, so she paid $333 in tax on that gain. Finally, Glenda holds some interest-bearing investments that generated an 8-percent rate of return in 1998. Her after-tax rate of return was 4.46 percent, calculated as 8 percent times (1 minus her marginal tax rate of 44.3 percent). Expressed another way, that would be $8 \times (1 - 0.443) = 4.46$.

BRITISH COLUMBIA

Marginal Tax Rates (%)

Taxable Income			Interest and Regular Income	Capital Gains	Canadian Dividends
$ —	to	$6,707	—	—	—
6,708	to	6,956	25.9	19.4	7.0
6,957	to	19,456	26.4	19.8	7.6
19,457	to	29,590	25.9	19.4	7.0
29,591	to	46,515	39.5	29.6	24.1
46,516	to	54,830	40.7	30.5	24.8
54,831	to	59,180	44.6	33.5	27.2
59,181	to	62,193	49.8	37.3	33.6
62,194	to	78,222	50.4	37.8	34.0
78,223	and	over	54.2	40.6	36.6

ALBERTA

Marginal Tax Rates (%)

Taxable Income			Interest and Regular Income	Capital Gains	Canadian Dividends
$ —	to	$6,707	—	—	—
6,708	to	6,956	17.3	12.9	4.7
6,957	to	9,825	17.6	13.2	5.1
9,826	to	16,875	29.8	22.4	9.3
16,876	to	19,456	25.7	19.3	7.9
19,457	to	29,590	25.2	18.9	7.3
29,591	to	45,059	38.3	28.8	23.7
45,060	to	46,515	39.3	29.5	24.2
46,516	to	59,180	40.4	30.3	24.9
59,181	to	62,193	45.0	33.8	30.7
62,194	and	over	45.6	34.2	31.1

SASKATCHEWAN

Marginal Tax Rates (%)

Taxable Income			Interest and Regular Income	Capital Gains	Canadian Dividends
$ —	to	$6,707	—	—	—
6,708	to	6,956	17.3	13.0	4.7
6,957	to	7,337	17.6	13.2	5.1
7,338	to	10,000	28.1	21.1	10.0
10,001	to	14,000	33.1	24.8	16.3
14,001	to	19,456	28.1	21.1	10.0
19,457	to	19,725	27.6	20.7	9.4
19,726	to	29,590	28.6	21.5	9.9
29,591	to	39,638	42.6	32.0	27.4
39,639	to	46,515	44.8	33.6	28.9
46,516	to	59,180	46.0	34.5	29.6
59,181	to	62,193	51.0	38.3	35.9
62,194	and	over	51.6	38.7	36.3

MANITOBA

Marginal Tax Rates (%)

Taxable Income			Interest and Regular Income	Capital Gains	Canadian Dividends
$ —	to	$6,707	—	—	—
6,708	to	6,956	17.3	13.0	4.7
6,957	to	7,968	17.6	13.2	5.1
7,969	to	19,456	30.4	22.8	12.6
19,457	to	21,500	29.9	22.5	12.0
21,501	to	29,590	27.9	21.0	9.5
29,591	to	30,000	41.7	31.2	26.6
30,001	to	46,515	43.7	32.7	29.2
46,516	to	59,180	44.8	33.6	29.9
59,181	to	62,193	49.5	37.2	35.8
62,194	and	over	50.1	37.6	36.1

ONTARIO

Marginal Tax Rates (%)

Taxable Income			Interest and Regular Income	Capital Gains	Canadian Dividends
$ —	to	$6,707	—	—	—
6,708	to	6,956	17.3	13.0	4.7
6,957	to	8,875	17.6	13.2	5.1
8,876	to	11,040	32.4	24.3	9.4
11,041	to	19,456	25.0	18.8	7.2
19,457	to	29,590	24.5	18.4	6.6
29,591	to	46,515	37.5	28.1	22.8
46,516	to	50,968	38.7	29.0	23.6
50,969	to	59,180	40.9	30.7	24.9
59,181	to	61,174	45.6	34.2	30.8
61,175	to	62,193	49.7	37.3	33.6
62,194	and	over	50.3	37.7	34.0

QUEBEC

Marginal Tax Rates (%)

Taxable Income			Interest and Regular Income	Capital Gains	Canadian Dividends
$ —	to	$6,707	—	—	—
6,708	to	6,785	14.5	10.8	3.9
6,786	to	6,956	34.5	25.9	17.9
6,957	to	19,456	34.8	26.1	18.2
19,457	to	25,000	34.5	25.9	17.9
25,001	to	29,590	37.5	28.1	21.6
29,591	to	46,515	45.2	33.9	31.2
46,516	to	50,000	46.3	34.8	31.9
50,001	to	59,180	49.4	37.0	35.7
59,181	to	62,193	52.0	39.0	39.0
62,194	and	over	52.6	39.5	39.4

NEW BRUNSWICK

Marginal Tax Rates (%)

Taxable Income			Interest and Regular Income	Capital Gains	Canadian Dividends
$ —	to	$6,707	—	—	—
6,708	to	6,956	27.6	20.7	7.4
6,957	to	19,456	28.2	21.1	8.1
19,457	to	29,590	27.6	20.7	7.5
29,591	to	46,515	42.3	31.7	25.7
46,516	to	59,180	43.4	32.6	26.4
59,181	to	62,193	48.4	36.3	32.7
62,194	to	95,404	49.0	36.8	33.1
95,405	and	over	50.4	37.8	34.1

NOVA SCOTIA

Marginal Tax Rates (%)

Taxable Income			Interest and Regular Income	Capital Gains	Canadian Dividends
$ —	to	$6,707	—	—	—
6,708	to	6,956	17.3	13.0	4.7
6,957	to	9,719	17.6	13.2	5.1
9,720	to	15,000	27.6	20.7	8.0
15,001	to	19,456	32.6	24.4	14.2
19,457	to	21,000	32.0	24.0	13.5
21,001	to	29,590	27.0	20.3	7.3
29,591	to	46,515	41.3	31.0	25.2
46,516	to	59,180	42.5	31.9	25.9
59,181	to	62,193	47.4	35.6	32.0
62,194	to	79,059	48.0	36.0	32.4
79,060	and	over	49.7	37.3	33.5

PRINCE EDWARD ISLAND

Marginal Tax Rates (%)

Taxable Income			Interest and Regular Income	Capital Gains	Canadian Dividends
$ —	to	$6,707	—	—	—
6,708	to	6,956	27.4	20.5	7.4
6,957	to	19,456	27.9	20.9	8.1
19,457	to	29,590	27.4	20.5	7.4
29,591	to	46,515	41.9	31.4	25.5
46,516	to	48,077	43.0	32.3	26.2
48,078	to	59,180	44.6	33.4	27.2
59,181	to	62,193	49.7	37.3	33.6
62,194	and	over	50.3	37.7	34.0

NEWFOUNDLAND

Marginal Tax Rates (%)

Taxable Income			Interest and Regular Income	Capital Gains	Canadian Dividends
$ —	to	$6,707	—	—	—
6,708	to	6,956	29.0	21.7	7.8
6,957	to	19,456	29.6	22.2	8.5
19,457	to	29,590	29.0	21.7	7.8
29,591	to	46,515	44.3	33.3	27.0
46,516	to	58,500	45.5	34.1	27.7
58,501	to	59,180	47.3	35.5	28.8
59,181	to	62,193	52.8	39.6	35.6
62,194	and	over	53.3	40.0	36.0

NORTHWEST TERRITORIES

Marginal Tax Rates (%)

Taxable Income			Interest and Regular Income	Capital Gains	Canadian Dividends
$ —	to	$6,707	—	—	—
6,708	to	6,956	23.7	17.8	5.2
6,957	to	12,000	24.2	18.1	5.8
12,001	to	19,456	24.4	18.3	6.1
19,457	to	29,590	23.9	17.9	5.5
29,591	to	46,515	37.1	27.8	21.9
46,516	to	48,000	38.3	28.7	22.7
48,001	to	59,180	38.5	28.9	23.0
59,181	to	62,193	43.0	32.3	28.6
62,194	to	66,000	43.6	32.7	29.0
66,001	and	over	44.4	33.3	30.0

YUKON

Marginal Tax Rates (%)

Taxable Income			Interest and Regular Income	Capital Gains	Canadian Dividends
$ —	to	$6,707	—	—	—
6,708	to	6,956	25.8	19.3	6.9
6,957	to	19,456	26.3	19.7	7.6
19,457	to	29,590	25.8	19.3	6.9
29,591	to	46,515	39.4	29.5	24.0
46,516	to	59,180	40.6	30.4	24.7
59,181	to	60,470	45.2	33.9	30.6
60,471	to	62,193	46.0	34.5	31.0
62,194	and	over	46.6	34.9	31.4

Federal Personal Tax Rates for 1998

Your total tax bill is made up of both federal and provincial taxes. The following table shows the federal component only. For the provincial personal tax rates, see page 279. Your federal tax rate is applied to the taxable income figure on line 260 of your tax return.

FEDERAL PERSONAL TAX RATES FOR 1998	
Taxable Income	**Tax Payable**
$ — to $29,590	17 percent of income
$29,591 to $59,180	$5,030 plus 26 percent on income over $29,590
$59,181 and over	$12,724 plus 29 percent on income over $59,180

NOTES:

1. A surtax of 3 percent of basic federal tax is added after taking into account personal tax credits (see the Personal Tax Credits table on page 281) and dividend tax credits. If your taxable income is less than $46,515, this surtax is reduced by 50 percent for 1998. As your taxable income rises above $46,515, the surtax reduction is clawed back until it is eliminated at taxable income of $62,192.

2. An additional surtax of 5 percent of basic federal tax will apply if your basic federal tax exceeds $12,000 after tax credits and before the 3-percent surtax.

Provincial Personal Tax Rates for 1998

Check the following table for the income taxes levied by your province. Except in Quebec, the provincial tax is simply calculated as a percentage of the basic federal tax. Certain provinces also levy flat or surtaxes, as detailed in the notes below.

Province	Tax Rate as a Percentage of Basic Federal Tax
British Columbia	50.50
Alberta	44.00
Saskatchewan	49.00
Manitoba	51.00
Ontario	42.75
Quebec	see note 6
New Brunswick	61.00
Nova Scotia	57.50
Prince Edward Island	59.50
Newfoundland	69.00
Northwest Territories	45.00
Yukon	50.00
Non-resident	52.00

PROVINCIAL PERSONAL TAX RATES FOR 1998

NOTES:

1. British Columbia imposes a surtax of 30 percent to B.C. tax over $5,300. An additional surtax of 26.05 percent applies to B.C. tax over $8,660.

2. Alberta levies a surtax of 8 percent of basic Alberta tax over $3,500 and a flat tax of 0.5 percent of Alberta taxable income.

3. Saskatchewan imposes a flat tax of 2 percent of net income plus a surtax of 15 percent on Saskatchewan tax (including the flat tax) in excess of $4,000. Further, a Debt Reduction Surtax of 10 percent will apply to basic Saskatchewan tax plus the flat tax. The Debt Reduction Surtax is eliminated or reduced for those with lower incomes. This reduction can amount to $150 per taxpayer and up to $300 per dual-income household.

4. Manitoba levies a flat tax of 2 percent of net income and a surtax of 2 percent of net income over $30,000.

5. Ontario imposes a surtax—called the Fair Share Health Care Levy—of 20 percent of Ontario tax exceeding $4,057.50 plus an additional levy of 30 percent of Ontario tax exceeding $5,217.50.

6. Quebec Personal Tax Rates for 1998:

Taxable Income	Tax Payable
Nil to $25,000	20% of income
$25,001 to $50,000	$ 5,000 + 23% over $25,000
$50,001 and over	$10,000 + 26% over $50,000

Residents of Quebec receive a reduction of their federal taxes equal to 16.5% of Basic Federal Tax. Taxpayers have the right to file under the simplified system or the general system.

7. New Brunswick levies a surtax of 8 percent of New Brunswick tax over $13,500.

8. Nova Scotia levies a surtax of 10 percent of Nova Scotia tax over $10,000.

9. Prince Edward Island levies a surtax of 10 percent of basic P.E.I. tax over $5,200.

10. Newfoundland levies a surtax of 10 percent of basic Newfoundland tax over $7,900.

11. Yukon levies a surtax of 5 percent of Yukon tax over $6,000.

Personal Tax Credits for 1998

Personal tax credits are applied to reduce your tax bill, dollar for dollar, each year. The credits listed here are non-refundable credits, meaning that they can be used to bring your tax bill to nil, but are not refundable for cash if they happen to exceed your tax liability.

The combined federal and provincial values reflect the basic federal tax, low-rate federal surtax, and provincial tax, but do not reflect the high income federal surtax, the supplementary personal tax credit, or any provincial surtaxes or flat taxes.

PERSONAL TAX CREDITS FOR 1998 COMBINED FEDERAL AND PROVINCIAL VALUES

Jurisdiction	Basic Personal Amount	Married or Equivalent[1,2]	Dependent Credits[1]	Age Amount for over 65[3]	Disability Tax Credit[3,4]
Federal	$1,098	$915	$400	$592	$720
British Columbia	1,685	1,405	614	909	1,105
Alberta	1,614	1,345	588	870	1,058
Saskatchewan	1,669	1,391	608	900	1,094
Manitoba	1,691	1,409	616	912	1,109
Ontario	1,600	1,334	583	863	1,049
Quebec (note 5)	1,989	1,898	1,357	506	506
New Brunswick	1,801	1,501	656	971	1,181
Nova Scotia	1,762	1,469	642	950	1,156
P.E.I.	1,784	1,487	650	962	1,170
Newfoundland	1,889	1,574	688	1,018	1,238
Northwest Territories	1,625	1,354	592	876	1,066
Yukon	1,680	1,400	612	906	1,102

NOTES:

1. This credit is reduced for a dependent's income over $538 for the married/equivalent-to-spouse credit, and over $4,103 for the dependent's credit.

2. To qualify for the equivalent-to-spouse credit, eligible dependents are those under age 18 living with and related to the taxpayer, or the taxpayer's parents/grandparents, or other persons who are related to the taxpayer and are infirm.

3. These credits may be transferred to a spouse. The credits available for transfer are reduced by the amount resulting from the application of the credit reduction rate to the transferor's net income in excess of $6,456. The age amount will be clawed back for seniors with incomes over $25,921 and will disappear completely at an income of $49,134.

4. These credits may be transferred to a supporting parent or grandparent. The credit is reduced when the transferor's income exceeds $6,456.

5. The federal figures do not reflect the federal tax abatement available to residents of Quebec. The amounts shown are the 1998 credit values and credit percentages for the simplified Quebec provincial income tax system and are adjusted as follows:

   - The equivalent-to-spouse credit is nil, but a single parent may claim a credit of $275. The amount is reduced by 6 percent of earnings in excess of $26,000.

   - The person-living-alone credit is $242.

   - The credit for the first dependent child is $598.

   - The credit for the second and subsequent dependent children is $552.

   - The credit for other dependents is $518 (or $1,357 if disabled).

   - A refundable credit for adoption expenses was introduced in the 1994 Quebec budget, equal to 20 percent of eligible adoption expenses to a maximum credit of $2,000.

   - All other credits and some deductions were replaced by the addition of $541 of personal credit per spouse, including but not limited to QPP/RRSP/tuition/medical/dividends and dues.

Minimum Annual RRIF Withdrawals

Minimum annual withdrawals from a registered retirement income fund (RRIF) are based on the value of the assets inside the RRIF on January 1 each year. Simply find the appropriate percentage in the table below and multiply it by the value in the RRIF on January 1. RRIFs established before 1993 are generally *qualifying RRIFs* and annuitants should use the right-hand column, below.

The appropriate age for this calculation is your age at the start of January 1 each year. If you are under age 65, the formula to calculate your minimum withdrawal percentage is 1 *divided by* (90 *minus* your age).

MINIMUM ANNUAL RRIF WITHDRAWALS (%)

Age	General	Pre-1993 Qualifying RRIFs
65	4.00	4.00
66	4.17	4.17
67	4.35	4.35
68	4.55	4.55
69	4.76	4.76
70	5.00	5.00
71	7.38	5.26
72	7.48	5.56
73	7.59	5.88
74	7.71	6.25
75	7.85	6.67
76	7.99	7.14
77	8.15	7.69
78	8.33	8.33
79	8.53	8.53
80	8.75	8.75
81	8.99	8.99
82	9.27	9.27
83	9.58	9.58
84	9.93	9.93
85	10.33	10.33
86	10.79	10.79
87	11.33	11.33
88	11.96	11.96
89	12.71	12.71
90	13.62	13.62
91	14.73	14.73
92	16.12	16.12
93	17.92	17.92
94 or older	20.00	20.00

Index

We make financial advisors look good. Very good.

Tim Cestnick is not only the author of this book, he is the president of our firm, The WaterStreet Group Inc. We are Canada's leading tax resource to financial advisors from coast to coast. We provide tax education and consulting, and we make advisors look good—very good, in fact. You see, when clients turn to a financial advisor for tax or estate planning help, *advisors turn to us.*

So let us act on your behalf—no matter where across this country you happen to be. After all, no one understands tax and estate planning issues like we do. And no one is better at creative solutions than we are.

- Client seminars
- Advisor education and training
- Email tax information service
- Newsletters
- Professional writing

- Personal and corporate tax planning
- Corporate reorganizations
- Individual Pension Plans
- Estate planning
- Revenue Canada representation

We're the best kept secret on the street.

The WaterStreet Group Inc.

420 North Service Road East, Suite 200, Oakville, ON L6H 5R2
Phone: [416] 410 4410   Fax: [416] 410 4411   Web: www.waterstreet.ca